THE MYSTICAL THEOLOGY
OF
SAINT BERNARD

CISTERCIAN STUDIES SERIES: NUMBER ONE HUNDRED AND TWENTY

THE MYSTICAL THEOLOGY
OF
SAINT BERNARD

by
Etienne Gilson

Translated by
A.H.C. Downes

Cistercian Publications
Kalamazoo
1990

FIRST PUBLISHED FEBRUARY 1940
BY SHEED AND WARD
LONDON AND NEW YORK

REPRINTED WITH PERMISSION BY
CISTERCIAN PUBLICATIONS INC.
KALAMAZOO, MICHIGAN
1990

*The work of Cistercian Publications is made possible in part
through support from Western Michigan University to
The Institute of Cistercian Studies.*

The editors are grateful to
Editoriale Jaca Book, Milan, for their
permission to translate and publish Jean Leclercq's
introduction, originally published and copyrighted
by them as 'Étienne Gilson, san Bernardo et
la stora della spiritualità'.

Printed in the United States of America

To
MY PUBLISHER AND FRIEND
M. J. VRIN
TO WHOSE UNWEARYING GENEROSITY THIS
COLLECTION OWES ITS EXISTENCE
THIS TWENTIETH VOLUME
IS DEDICATED

E. G.

PREFACE

AFTER a repeated study of the principal mystical writings of St. Bernard it seemed to me that I had sufficiently made out the great ruling lines of his doctrine to enable me to dedicate to him an entire course at the Collège de France in 1933. Invited in the same year by the University College of Wales (Aberystwith) to give five lectures on some question connected with the history of medieval ideas, I essayed to sum up for this new public what is perhaps the most neglected aspect of the Cistercian mysticism, that, namely, which, for want of a better name, we may call its "systematics". In fulfilment of a promise then made, I now publish these lectures, somewhat expanded in substance; happy thus to testify my gratitude to the Welsh University which invited me, and to a faithful public, whom neither the natural difficulties of the subject, nor the timidity of a professor in a language not his own, could ever effectively discourage.

The subject is clearly delimited in the very title of this work. It is concerned neither with the life of St. Bernard, nor with his theology at large, nor even integrally with his mysticism; but with that part only of his theology on which his mysticism rests. Even St. Bernard's own personal mystical experiences, attractive as their study would be, are here touched upon only incidentally and for the sake of the theological speculations which interpret them. This limitation is due to my desire to draw out apart, so as to set it in a clear light, the one really important conclusion that emerges from these studies. "The mysticism of

St. Bernard," writes M. Pourrat, "is not set out in any systematic form . . . it has moreover no scientific character; it is essentially practical." That I believe to be entirely misconceived. If the highly simplified diagram of his doctrine here proposed can be accepted, in spite of all its skeleton-like emaciation, as correct, we shall still be able to say that St. Bernard was in no wise a metaphysician, but he must remain in our eyes a theologian whose speculative vigour and power of synthesis puts him among the greatest. That his mystical theology is essentially the science of a way of life is not to be doubted, but I hope to show that it is nevertheless a science, and that its structure could hardly be more rigorously synthetic than it is. To see this, however, we shall need a certain patience until its main lines have been brought to light. That done, all will become clear. When the author's principles are known, his language understood, his treatises, even his sermons, speak with all the severe precision and exact technique of the most densely-packed pages of St. Anselm or St. Thomas Aquinas. No one is likely to forget the soul of the mystic; but I think, on the other hand, that we shall come to know it better for the future, the less we forget the thought of the theologian.

CONTENTS

Atqui Deum et hominem, quia propriis exstant ac distant et voluntatibus et substantiis, longe aliter in se alterutrum manere sentimus, id est, non substantiis confusos, sed voluntatibus consentaneos. Et haec unio ipsis communio voluntatum, et consensus in caritate. Felix unio, si experiaris; nulla, si comparaveris.

S. BERNARD, *In Cant. Cant.*, LXXI, 10.

Introduction

Étienne Gilson, St Bernard, and the History of Spirituality
by
Jean Leclercq

The Mystical Theology of St Bernard was published in its first edition in 1934. Even if it does not speak the last word on the abbot of Clairvaux (and who could be so presumptuous as to say that?), it remains the finest book ever written on the subject. To be sure, it does not clarify everything that puzzles us. Since that time have appeared many works of singular achievement which focus on particular aspects of the life and work of Saint Bernard. But none of them has been able to match the penetration, the pure power of synthesis, or the craft of Gilson. Indeed, the literary quality of the work, as much as its doctrinal content, have guaranteed its success, or should I say instead, its influence.

The book's existence was borne on the wings of a double movement: the author's own evolution and that of medieval studies during the years in which he wrote. Medieval scholarship itself knew the strong stamp of his personality and his work. In my autumn years, I accept the invitation to remember this teacher and friend. Let me go back to that period when I was his disciple, at a time when his own pre-eminence in the field was approaching its high point. This is important for we cannot evaluate the book unless we locate it properly in its context.

The late Gilson can, in fact, be said to have brought to the notice of university scholars of our century, not only medieval theology in general, but that of Saint Bernard in particular. One might have considered this field the preserve of ecclesiastics. Some thus distinguished themselves, but their labors did not succeed in escaping the confines of a very restricted area. In the year 1927, Charles Homer Haskins could publish his now famous classic, *The Renaissance of the Twelfth Century*[1] and not devote one single chapter to theology. Yet, not many years later, Gilson began to bring to the attention of medievalists the value these medieval theologians contained, if one would only undertake to read them.

The task I have in mind is not a biography of Gilson: that work has already been undertaken by Gilson's own Pontifical Institute of Medieval Studies at Toronto. The book is a full one because of the careful attention given it. My task here is, instead, to highlight great moments of Gilson's discovery of the Medieval Age, and these I will fill out with some personal reminiscences.

The author was born in Burgundy in 1884. At the outbreak of the First World War, he had already finished his thesis on Descartes, a two volume work published in 1913.[2] While preparing these tomes on the founder of modern philosophy, Gilson himself admitted later that he could not understand Descartes's thought without knowing the sources available to Descartes and the use he made of them. Descartes, interestingly enough, is the one who turned Gilson toward the scholastics. Military service interrupted his studies. Returning to work, he followed up the earlier volumes with his *Études de philosphie médiévale*, in 1921, and with *Philosophie du moyen âge* and the first redaction of *Thomisme* (*The Christian Philosophy of St Thomas Aquinas*) in 1922. These three works were an immediate success and they

1. Where I translate a book title or article reference, either the original is in English or there is a standard English translation.

2. *Index scolastico-cartésien* (Paris: Alcan, 1913); *La liberté chez Descartes et la théologie,* (Paris: Alcan, 1913). Later there would appear: *Études sur le rôle de la pensée médiévale dans la formation du système cartésien* (Paris: Vrin, 1930).

are still in print. As for the last work, he never managed to
stop rewriting it, and it became forever bulkier, until people
joked with him about his interminable *Thomismes.*

Just as Descartes had led him to Saint Thomas, so also
Thomas alerted him to the imperative of knowing his
(Thomas's) contemporaries and sources. Accordingly, he
produced studies such as *The Philosophy of St Bonaventure* and
The Christian Philosophy of St Augustine. While trying to tame
these two giants, Gilson clarified for himself enduring and
essential questions, and this enabled him to organize and
master a formidable body of information. He became a
professor at the *Collège de France.* Each year, he would select
for his teaching matter a new author or subject. This habit
resulted in a regular and unbroken series of studies on Saint
Anselm, Saint Bernard, Abelard, Dante, Petrarch and Duns
Scotus, as well as a history of the concepts in The *City of God.*
One day he caught himself declaring what was only all
too obvious: 'The thirteenth century could not have
happened without the twelfth.' And so the zeal to achieve an
overall grasp of the scholastic period led him inevitably to
uncover the riches of doctrinal content in the authors who
preceded it.

Gilson had a way of disconcerting his colleagues by the
simplicity and ease with which he handled abstract questions.
I was a student at Rome at the time when both he and
Jacques Maritain received what was for each of them their
first doctorates *honoris causa* from the Angelicum. I
remember that the *aula magna,* just recently added to the
university, was filled to capacity. On the next day, in the
principal hall of the *Cancelleria* palace, Gilson gave a public
conference on being and essence. One of our professors was
hard at work on the same problem, but he was employing a
diction which could only be styled convoluted. This professor
rose to his feet in indignation and promptly exited the hall in
protest of the insouciance Gilson displayed in reducing to

clarity what was heretofore the private sacred ground of misty
complexity. In another publication, I have had the
opportunity of noting down my memories of Maritain.[3] And
since his name has been mentioned, this is perhaps the place
to couple these two masters and friends who shared the same
gift of neutralizing the obscurity in philosopnical problems.
One day, in response to one of our questions, Gilson
exclaimed, 'I will not consent to becoming a member of the
French Academy as long as Maritain is not there.'

Back in the thirties, such *periti* as Pierre Mandonnet and
Dom André Wilmart labored over the indexing, the editing
and the critical analysis of the texts of Saint Thomas and
many other writers. Gilson, meanwhile, as the philosopher,
remained uninterested in mere scholarly documentation.
His it was to breathe new life into these ancients. We have in
the prophet Ezekiel: '*Prophecy! Make these dry bones live.*' A
group of disciples and followers—among them, Marie-
Dominique Chenu, Marie-Magdeleine Davy, Marie-Thérèse
d'Alverny and others—gathered around him. He did not
hesitate to put them in their place if he thought it justified. I
can still remember the early courses which were later to
become *Dante the Philosopher*. There was one occasion when
he quite literally tore to pieces a grandiose work of
Mandonnet called *Dante le théologien*. This particular piece
had included a study on the symbolism of numbers. Gilson
coolly let out that he had recalculated the numbers and had
found that the author's math was wrong. He delivered his
opinion forcefully but with tact, thus insuring that
Mandonnet's piece was not accepted.

After one of his lectures at the *Collège de France*, we would
go to what was called the 'shop', the philosophical bookstore

3. 'Maritain e Merton come li ho conosciuti', in AA.VV.,
Contemplazione e ricerca nella società secolarizzata (Milan: Massimo, 1984)
pp. 17–29.

of Joseph Vrin which was not far away at the *Place de la Sorbonne*. There friends would gather to 'chat'. I had taken a course at Sant'Anselmo in Rome from Anselm Stoltz. As part of the course, Stoltz had taken a position opposed to Gilson's interpretation of the ontological argument of Saint Anselm. While some thought that the argument was nothing but an exercise in dialectic to prove the existence of God, my former professor held that the whole thought process of the argument moved on the level of spiritual experience. Gilson took up a middle position which accepted something from both of these and he did it by suggesting a new and creative use of the term *gnosis*. Shorn of its problematic and all too precise meanings from the past, it could claim a clean new meaning well suited to present needs. Needless to say, though Gilson convinced me, I lost none of my esteem for my Roman *maître*. On the question of Averroism or the notion of Christian Philosophy—a problem much debated at the time—, Gilson applied a unique combination of brilliance and common sense. His clarity set him apart from the learned specialists who always managed to come up with more tags and explications than he. Would he not one day write that it is no good having a note pad instead of a heart?

A little later, beginning at the end of the forties, he initiated a discussion on the phrase *regio dissimilitudinis*, specifically on its sources, whether Plotinian, Augustinian, or other. Then, while attending the divine office with some Augustinians on their patronal feast, he noticed the two-word phrase in one of the responsories—a text which would have been sung every year from the Middle Ages on. Need anyone look anywhere else?

The striking thing about Gilson, even more than the penetrating force of his intellect, was his power of synthesis. He did not feel bound to come down on the side of one author or system rather than another. His mind ranged freely. Descartes and the scholastics, Saint Bonaventure and

Saint Thomas, Saint Bernard and Abelard—these pairs were
held in a balance of equal esteem. By way of demonstration,
he said to me one day, 'I have given my son three names of
medieval saints: Bernard, Francis, and Dominic.' In the
collections and series which he edited and in his *Archives
d'histoire doctrinale et littéraire du moyen âge.*, he accepted books
and articles which dealt with numerous texts and periods.
His was the art of encouragement and stimulus. How many
times, in our conversations, did he goad me to publish a text
or to write up an article which he would then publish.

His humanism, which he kept intact throughout all his
historical research, found full expression in the studies he
crafted on music and the plastic arts, on problems in
psychology and on the current social and political scene. All
the facets of his broad culture were played with full
resonance in the volumes of *Études d'art et de philosophie.* With
books of widespread circulation and appeal, he contrived to
help Joseph Vrin finance the more esoteric and occasionally
numerous tomes which appeared in Vrin's philosophical
catalogue. As a mark of special gratitude, Gilson dedicated to
Vrin his own *Mystical Theology of St Bernard.*

The young Gilson was not spared difficulties either. When
he got Vrin to publish my thesis, *Jean de Paris et l'ecclésiologie du
XIII siècle* (its publication was delayed because of the War), he
consoled me over the typographical errors that remained in
the book even after the proofs were corrected by telling me
that when his *Thomisme* was ready for printing, a poorly
appointed printery was all there was to be found, one hardly
suited for the kind of literary enterprise he hoped to carry
out. Even so, the errors did not keep people from reading
the book.

Let me use this forum to recall another kind of meeting
with him—a meeting which was to prove decisive in shaping
the course of my work from the forties on. At that time, I was
working away in the manuscript department of the

Bibliothèque Nationale at Paris. The overwhelming number of
unedited manuscripts forced on me an anguished choice:
whether to spend my energy on the scholastics of the
thirteenth and fourteenth centuries and on the ecclesiology
of the fifteenth, or, something just as attractive, to study the
monasticism of the eleventh and twelfth centuries. On a day
of particular frustration and confusion, I telephoned Gilson.
'Come and see me', was his answer. For an entire afternoon
he regaled me with problems confronting the whole of
monastic culture. At the end, his efforts had their effect. He
convinced me that there was an ample number of
researchers already at work on the scholastics. Why doesn't
somebody concentrate on the monks of old? Soon I was hard
at work on *John of Fécamp*, then *Peter of Celle*. These he
included in his series *Études d'histoire de la spiritualité*. A little
later, when I sent him *The Love of Learning and the Desire for
God*, I could assure him this book could never have been
written without him. Richard William Hunt remarked to me
one day in the Bodleian Library at Oxford: 'We shall never
know all that we owe Gilson.' It is only right, therefore, that
his disciples who survive him pay this debt of gratitude.

Some thought him difficult. I never considered him such.
To me he was always congenial, a connoisseur of every kind
of good thing. He was numbered with honor among the
Chevaliers du Taste-Vin who met in the wine cellar of Cîteaux
at Dijon. In his acceptance speech at the French Academy,
he discoursed with good-natured irony on the impossibility
of governing a people, his own, who had a different cheese to
go with every kind of wine. During the war years, threatened
with the skimpy parisian rations, he had me bring him
cheeses from my home region, whose formula, according to
tradition, went back to the monks of Marolles.

He was devout. One of the first stories I ever heard about
him came from a priest who used to vacation in the village of
Vermenton. At the daily morning Mass, one lone parishioner

remained and then got up and left the church as soon as his thanksgiving was completed. When the priest asked around in the village, they told him it was Gilson.

Later on and more than once, he recounted to me his emotional experience during the Great War, when one of his comrades fell beside him on the battlefield and asked him to hear his confession. He refused, but the dying man began anyway and Sergeant Gilson could only pray for him. In the sixties, when he invited me to spend some time at the Institute of Medieval Studies at Toronto, I got to know some of his friends and acquaintances in the city. They held him in veneration. One of them said to me: 'We think of him as a saint.'

His own faith and his refined sense of human nature were manifest in his pursuit of scholarship as well as holiness. This came to be abundantly obvious when he inaugurated the chair of the history of spirituality at the *Institut Catholique* at Paris. Our mutual friend André Combes was there, and he roused Gilson's enthusiasm for Thèrése of Lisieux. Indeed, this medievalist was sensitive to any and all who were witnesses, in any period, to an intense participation in the mystery of Christ. The address he developed on that occasion, which was to initiate a new series of publications, was more than an instruction on method; it was a plan of life.

ANALYSIS AND SYNTHESIS

Before Gilson, Saint Bernard was a figure to be admired but not to be taken seriously by theologians. A devotional author and nothing more was the accepted opinion. And then along came a famous university professor, and a layman at that, who uncovered the doctrine and applied the label 'theology' to the title of the book he wrote about him. To call these moves anything but revolutionary would be an understatement. In the opening lines of his preface, Gilson made his intentions crystal clear: he intended to examine the system of the teaching of St Bernard on a very particular point—specifically, the theology on which he based his mysticism. This is the central core from which all the rest emanates. Slowly but surely it dawned on us that here with Saint Bernard, we are in the presence of what can only be described as dogmatic theology. Right from the start, Gilson did not hesitate to oppose Père Pourrat, even though he was the author of the standard manual on the history of spirituality which had gone through many printings and been translated into diverse languages, and even though Pourrat brought to bear on his opinions the immense prestige of the most famous seminary in France, St Sulpice. Pourrat, like everyone else, not only ignored but denied the synthesis and theological strength in the teaching of Saint Bernard, seeing in him only a practical spiritual guide.

Gilson had the ability to read texts with a freshness and in a manner at once artless and ingenuous, as if he were the first one to read them and as if nothing had ever been written on them before him. Saint Bernard emerged in his eyes as a 'theologian whose capacity for synthesis and whose speculative power put him in the company of the greatest.'[4] The person who delivered himself of this statement had also penned various works on Saint Augustine, Saint Thomas, Saint Bonaventure and Descartes. With an unimpeachable authority, he courageously broke with an entire tradition of interpretation on twelfth century mysticism. This is his enduring contribution. Like all great pioneers, he discovered a field of exploration heretofore unknown and not even suspected. All that was to follow looks back for its origin to his initiative. With an approving nod, he presided over this whole endeavor, offering encouragement and courtesy to researchers. He trusted them and did not interfere or start

4. See below, p 2.

debates. Almost twenty years later, as preparations were being made for the Congress at Dijon in 1953 to honor the Eighth Centenary of St Bernard's death, I invited him to officiate or at least to participate. Without false modesty, he declined, saying that he was content to follow the proceedings *from afar* so as not to disturb his summer retreat at Vermenton. When the acts of the congress appeared, we adopted a title inspired by his work: *Saint Bernard théologien.* In the opening address I felt duty bound to give him due recognition.[5] And the index of names bears me out, since his name appears as one of those most frequently cited.

Gilson put in bold relief not only the 'brilliant speculative power of St Bernard'[6], whose writings 'flowed with the precision and technical security of the densest pages of St Anselm and St Thomas'[7], but also Saint Bernard's 'method'.[8] Saint Bernard's obvious attention to clarity and consistency goes clean against Haskins' opinion that the Cistercian mysticism had a rather obscure foundation.[9] The historian in Gilson set about to establish a chronology by which he could locate Saint Bernard in the evolution of the 'problem of love' in the twelfth century. This phrase formed part of a title of a book which had important repercussions in that period.[10] I speak of Pierre Rousselot, the young Jesuit of great promise who was cut down in the Great War along with many other scholars and writers with a bright future. Gilson took up the torch from these fallen. On the foundation of a precise chronology, he was able to show the exact relation between

5. 'Introduction. S. Bernard et la théologie monastique du XII siècle', in *S. Bernard théologien. Actes du Congrès de Dijon. 15–19 septembre 1953, Analecta Sacri Ordinis Cisterciensis* 9 (1953) p 8.

6. See below, p 34.

7. See below, p 2.

8. See below, p 38.

9. See below, p 5.

10. P. Rousselot, *Pour l'histoire du probleme de l'amour au moyen âge* (Münster-in-Westfalen: Aschendorff, 1908).

Saint Bernard and the other proponents of the mystical
theology of the twelfth century. Among these, William of
Saint Thierry had already inspired several doctrinal studies.
André Wilmart unravelled the mystery of the dating of some
of William's works by a careful analysis of the manuscripts.
But it was Gilson who led the way in a theological
examination of William's doctrine.

Gilson described the man Saint Bernard this way: a man of
skeletal thinness, a pale face, his red fair put a flame on his
cheeks as if to reveal the hidden ardor of his soul.[11] His
interior life was a history of careful development. At thirty-
five years of age, the time of the publication of his first
treatises, he had reached his full maturity. Gilson always felt
this conclusion confirmed, for he could recognize no further
evolution in the Abbot of Clairvaux. He had been formed
against a backdrop of strong cultural, ecclesial and monastic
elements, and from these he could not be separated. Gilson
was able to identify immediately Saint Bernard's tie to the
humanistic past. It was Cicero who influenced his concept of
friendship. The dating of Saint Bernard's own reading of the
De Amicitia has now been able to be precisely fixed,[12] but first,
the fact that Saint Bernard read it had to be established. A
whole concept of love arose out of this. It enriched Saint
Bernard and the entire Cistercian school, and this shed light
as well on the romances of Chrétiens de Troyes. Even the
'passionate drama of Heloise and Abelard can be seen in a
more positive mode; in fact, it emerges as a rich source of

11. E. Gilson, 'La mystique de la grâce dans la Queste du Saint-Graal',
in *Les idées et les lettres* (Paris: Paris, 1932) pp 83–84.
12. R. Gelsomino, 'S. Bernardo di Chiaravalle e il De amicitia di
Cicerone', in *Analecta monastica*, 5, Studia Anselmiana, 43 (Rome:
Pontificium Institutum S. Anselmi—Herder, 1958) pp. 80–186. See also
'Cicerone precursore di Ovidio', in *I monaci e l'amore nella Francia del XII
secolo* (Rome: Jovence, 1984).

ideas, more than is usually supposed'.[13] Gilson would soon
devote one of his most forceful and moving studies to the
story of these two.

At the same time, he provided some clues for those who
wanted to go further (sometimes too far) along this line than
he had. His hunch as to the influence of Origen has been
proven right, for it is undeniable. He also raised the issue of
Gregory of Nyssa and Maximus the Confessor. Without
knowing it, he started a trend of suspecting Greek Eastern
influence everywhere, especially among the Cistercians of
the twelfth century. This direction is being readjusted
today.[14] In the same fashion, what he wrote on the *regio
dissimilitudinis* gave rise to a long series of studies, some of
great value, like that of Pierre Courcelle. Certainly, the
formula derives from Plato, is found in Saint Augustine and,
as was noted above, figures in the liturgical office of Saint
Augustine's feast. There is little doubt that the Bishop of
Hippo read it, but Gilson, who wanted his own son educated
in a Benedictine school, and wanted to prove to the
Benedictines that he knew their rule, found the formula in
Saint Bernard. Saint Bernard led him to Saint Benedict and
Saint Benedict to Cassian. Proceeding step by step, he arrived
in this way at the fountainhead of a tradition not only of
literary dependence, but one that has been lived and
experienced down to this day. Gilson always balked at facile
over-simplifications, such as that perpetrated by George
Gordon Coulton in English-language circles. Moreover he
penned some marvelous phrases which, in French, have
passed into the category of aphorisms to describe the

13. See *below*, p 15.

14. The most recent contribution to this question is by G. Madec, 'A
propos des sources de Guillaume de Saint-Thierry', in *Revue des études
augustiniennes* 24 (1978) pp 302–309.

reconciliation between renunciation and the cultivation of the beautiful.[15]

The passage from charity to ecstasy is traced out by Saint Bernard in his treatise 'On the Love of God'. Contrary to commonplace formulas of not very great weight, Bernard stresses the importance, even the value, of the body as the base for a decidedly positive and altogether admirable anthropology.[16] All this is quite easy to see if one holds steadfastly to Bernard's 'technical language'. This is why Gilson paid such attention to terms even to the point of being rigorous. What a delightful surprise to find a mystic bear up under close philological scrutiny of the kind usually applied only to secular authors. Here too, Gilson was the first to make such an investigation. The book remains wonderfully clear, solidly crafted, and easy to follow. Many important and tantalizing themes get presented either in the text or in the notes, but without burdening the reader. Everything is so well digested and organized that what we end up having is a book of extraordinary literary grace. Yet Gilson is aware of the literary traps; he is not controlled but rather is in control of his own art and his own style. The book closes with some striking pages on mystical union. Once someone has read the book, one is ready to take up Saint Bernard. There, one shall find many arresting but seemingly

15. The phrase that has become the most celebrated is the one in which Gilson says of the Cistercians: 'They have renounced everything save the art of good writing'. To speak of the literary stature of the Cistercians was another 'first' for Gilson. Since his time, there have been several studies on this question, for example , D. Sabersky-Bascho, *Studien zur Paronomasie bei Bernhard von Clairvaux* (Fribourg/ Switzerland: Universitätverlag, 1979).

16. I have cited several texts in 'The Love of Beauty as a Means and an Expression of the Love of Truth', in *Mittellateinisches Jarhbuch* 16 (1981) pp. 62–72.

disparate ideas, but one will also learn to suspect, yes, even to trust, that everything has been ordered in a cohesive synthesis.

LATER RICHES

Gilson concluded his book by scaling the heights of 'pure love'. But along the way, he had encountered some problems which, from the viewpoint of the main flow of his book, were marginal. Nevertheless, having glimpsed or intuited their importance, he collected them in a series of appendices. In later years, he and others would plow these furrows deeper. His was the genius to raise issues. For example, the two-page study on *curiositas* pointed out the relevance of this concept. Its whole history was then catalogued and the nuances which the different stages of tradition had wrought on it were distinguished.[17]

Then we have the *excursus* entitled *Abelard* which actually deals more with Heloise who is vindicated in it, if she really needed to be. All Gilson wished to say on the subject of these two can be found in this second appendix. When he came to entitle his book on the couple, *Heloise and Abelard*,[18] he was to give the significant first place to her. One could even ask if we would have the moving correspondence between the two were she not a partner on an equal footing with the Master, and perhaps even his superior. The unfortunate Berengar of Tours thought himself obliged to attack Bernard in order to defend Abelard. But he has received only ridicule for his pains. Gilson affirms this without mercy in his third

17. This is what I have tried to do in the essay "Curiositas" et le retour á Dieu chez S. Bernard', in *Bivium. Homenaje a Manuel Diaz y Diaz* (Madrid: Gredos, 1983) pp. 133–141.

18. Régine Pernoud has followed suit in *Héloïse et Abélard* (Paris: Michel, 1970).

appendix. Several recent studies concur with the basic
argument of his verdict.[19]

But the two most valuable appendices are those on courtly
love and William of Saint Thierry. We have already
mentioned how Gilson's few pages have opened up a whole
new field of research, particularly in the United States. Let
me say in passing that nowhere has his influence been so
widespread as in countries of English as well as French
culture. Before going to found the Institute of Medieval
Studies at Toronto, he travelled to America to give
conferences. In Great Britain at Aberdeen, he delivered the
Gifford Lectures which later appeared in print as *The Spirit of
Mediaeval Philosophy*. The theology of Saint Bernard was first
presented at the University College of Wales. Then, with
Toronto as his frequent home base, he would go to speak in a
variety of places, always returning to consult with and to
listen to a whole new generation of scholars of the
generation after Haskins. He derived satisfaction in taking a
lively interest in the writers he himself had sponsored. He
was proud to be a member of the French Canadian Academy.
In Québec, as well as in the States, his influence has been
wide. Today, for example, William of Saint Thierry is
probably the most studied author of the twelfth century. This
'Williamology', if I may use the expression, is nowhere as
active or at as high a level as in the New World. When the
Pope granted the 'Pontifical' title to the Institute at Toronto,
he gave recognition to the good services Gilson had
rendered to the cause of Catholic culture in this large and
important part of the world.

Gilson took seriously the whole question of courtly love,
especially when Albert Pauphilet's *La Queste du Saint Graal*

19. I have given a bibliography in *Monks and Love in Twelfth-century
France: Psycho-historical Essays* (Oxford, Clarendon Press, 1979).

appeared.[20] For a specialist in philosophy and theology like
Gilson, an associate and friend of Martin Grabmann and
Clemens Baeumker, to be at the same time capable of writing
with real competence on the question of courtly love was and
is a rarity. In all esoteric fields of study such as this, there
abound experts who are either unknown or undervalued. It
took someone of the stature of Gilson to be able to intuit that
Saint Bernard could not be understood unless we took into
consideration his whole social and cultural environment.
Gilson was very modern in his ability to understand the
literature in which a whole culture expressed itself.

With his usual faultless logic, Gilson had no trouble
discerning that, by reason of its own proper nature, courtly
love cannot for all the world be taken for mystical love. At the
time, considerable and sometimes impressive scholarship was
brought to bear on the pros and cons of this problem. Now
that everyone has had a say, it seems that once again, the
good sense of Gilson had enabled him to see the situation
with clarity. Between the two ways of loving there stands an
essential difference; on this view Gilson took up a radical
position. This did not mean that he excluded entirely the
proposition that there was some kind of relation and mutual
influence between these two kinds of literature and authors.
They have sought, and indeed they in some way are obliged,
to use the same language. Bernard's diction tends to be
biblical. But when both sides come to formulate or analyze
the states of the soul, they tend to use the language of human
love. And Bernard and William are much more profound
than their secular contemporaries. Thus it is no surprise that
in the generation after Bernard, the language of the soul and
the language of courtly love grew closer together. Bernard,
for his part, had taken from the romances several themes

20. 'La mystique de la grâce dans la Queste du Saint-Graal', in *Les
idées et les lettres* (Paris: Vrin, 1932) pp. 59–91.

which, for all that, were common to all love writings. Did
Bernard, directly or indirectly, inspire the Grail legend? The
discussion continues. Each wave of the debate throws up a
new opinion. Gilson had the good sense to try to liberate the
whole field from premature answers. Here one could wish
for a satisfying synthesis. But before that can appear, there is
much painstaking work to be done in comparing texts,
themes, and concepts of love—love-sickness, languishment
and love-death, as well as of marriage in every one of the
poets and romance writers, the trouvères and the
troubadours, the philosophers, theologians, mystics'
historians, canonists and so on.[21]

Yet someone had to make a beginning, and this Gilson did.
During these last ten years, we have watched a heated
controversy boil up over the authenticity of the
correspondence between Heloise and Abelard. Should we
ascribe this masterpiece to an anonymous forger of the
thirteenth century? A formidable array of scholarship has
been mobilized to sustain or refute this hypothesis. The
consensus of opinion favors authenticity. Gilson put together
a combination of intuition and erudition for his argument:
'It's just too beautiful not to be true.' He consulted and
concurred with Dom André Wilmart, the noted expert on
textual criticism, whom he named a 'brilliant and beloved
Benedictine' without actually giving out his identity.[22] But no
one was in any doubt as to whom Gilson referred. Critical
analysis and good interpretative sense joined forces to give a
sound verdict. It would be like adding verses to a psalm by

---

21. In my *For an Interdisciplinary Study of Love and Marriage in the
Twelfth Century*, (University of West Virginia Press) I have proposed a
program of research projects. See also my *Monks on Marriage. A Twelfth
Century View* (New York: Seabury, 1982).

22. Étienne Gilson, *Heloise and Abelard* (Ann Arbor, University of
Michigan Press, 1960).

employing appropriate images so that no seam in the literary fabric could be noticed.

Throughout his *Mystical Theology of St Bernard*, Gilson never concedes anything on this one point: what might be termed Saint Bernard's radicalism, that unconditional and limitless generosity of his love for God. Bernard summoned to it or banished from it any and all other literature on theories of love, depending on the case at hand. *L'amour fou* is what the love of God is—the same love which was manifest in the Incarnation, and which is ceaselessly poured by the Holy Spirit into the hearts of men and women who welcome it. This is Bernard's love which he wanted to be formed in his own readers. It is a love at once active and committed, as Gilson's noted contemporary, Emmanuel Mounier, would say. To have the greatest number of lay persons possible in key position of high competence in the society, there to give witness to Christ and his Church—this was Gilson's aim. He spelled this out in an article in *La vie intellectuelle*. This is the finest testimony he left to those of us who so rejoiced in his teaching and in his lavishly bestowed friendship. Gilson has written eloquently on the *schola caritatis*. Yet in his own person as well as in his work, he forged a synthesis of learning and love.

Translated by
Francis Kline ocso
Abbey of Gethsemani
6 November 1989.

THE MYSTICAL THEOLOGY
OF ST. BERNARD

CHAPTER I

REGULA LXXIII

IN the year 1112 the youthful Bernard, accompanied by
four of his brothers and about twenty-five of his friends,
entered the Abbey of Cîteaux. These unlooked-for recruits
brought new life to a monastic reform in danger of perish-
ing of inanition. The essential facts are too well known to
need repetition;[1] but we are concerned, on the other hand,
to know what it was that these young men looked for at
Cîteaux, and what they were to find on entering. Apart
from this the existence of the Cistercian asceticism and
mysticism is hardly to be explained.

For its very existence sets us a problem. Historians speak
currently to-day of the "Renaissance" of the twelfth century.
The expression can be easily justified, but the remarkable
thing is that this renaissance, in the minds of those who use
the term, would seem to be projected in clear relief on the
sombre background of the Cistercian mysticism. "This
century, the very century of St. Bernard and his mule, was
in many respects an age of fresh and vigorous life. The
epoch of the Crusades, of the rise of towns, and of the
earliest bureaucratic states of the West, it saw the culmination of Romanesque art and the beginnings of Gothic; the
emergence of the vernacular literatures; the revival of
the Latin classics and of Latin poetry and Roman law; the

recovery of Greek science, with its Arabic additions, and
of much Greek philosophy; and the origin of the first
European universities. The twelfth century left its signature
on higher education, on the scholastic philosophy, on
European systems of law, on architecture and sculpture,
on the liturgical drama, on Latin and vernacular poetry.
The theme is too broad for a single volume or a single
writer." [2]

All that is very true, and truer than the eminent historian
supposes. St. Bernard, and this mule from which he so
obstinately averted his eyes, are no mere foil to this renaissance but an integral part of it. Possibly they are even its
most striking expression, for St. Bernard is the very opposite
of the uncouth monk; he knows very well what he blasphemes,
he simply finds it inadequate. The mystical literature of the
twelfth century harmoniously completes the profane and
crowns it, and was soon to reform it to its own image. For
anyone not content with these parallel sections of history,
each excavated by an historian who cares nothing for the
section adjoining, the flowering of courtly poetry and courtly
romance, all this amorous literature in the French tongue,
is preceded and accompanied by an abundance of theological
speculation on love; it runs in an uninterrupted succession
of works from one end of the century to the other, and over
into those that follow. For us, however, concerned as we
are with the twelfth alone, let it suffice to say that three
groups of theologians would seem to have initiated and
conducted the movement. Even here we have no absolute
beginning; but the twelfth century marks, in this matter as
in so many others, a fresh starting-point, a stirring of new
life, whose fruitfulness we may still appreciate. The Carthusian school, of which Guigo I appears to have been the
originator; the Benedictine and Cistercian school, founded
by William of Saint-Thierry and St. Bernard; the school of

the Victorines, with Hugh and Richard of Saint-Victor, all took up the problem of love with a jealous predilection. Each of these doctors, or his disciples, would take up a position on the question and solve it, not pretending to create all his materials out of nothing, but simply adapting them to his own mode of thought and feeling. We may find a place among these for certain isolated figures such as Abelard, intruders as they may seem at first sight; but their aberrations sometimes acted like a ferment and proved fruitful even in the very reactions they provoked. Can we yet attempt a chronological table of all these authors and works? The time, it seems, is not yet ripe, especially since the dates of many are not to be certainly fixed save within large limits—say of a decade more or less. But the patient researches of Dom Wilmart, who has done so much to disentangle this involved literary skein, will help us at any rate to set up a few landmarks; and around these, in sufficient approximation, we may group the rest. A table of this kind, in spite of all its uncertainties, even its inexactitudes, will at least suffice to suggest the importance and continuity of the effort put forth during the whole of the twelfth century to elucidate the problem of love. We confine ourselves to the authors of chief importance in the Carthusian, Benedictine, and Cistercian schools, and to their most representative works.

Approximate dates	Author	Works
1115	GUIGO I the Carthusian	*Meditationes*, Migne, *Pat. Lat.*, CLIII, 590 *et seq.*
1121 (somewhat earlier)	P. ABELARD	*Introductio ad theologiam*, P.L., CLXXVIII, 979–1114.
1119/35	WILLIAM OF SAINT-THIERRY	*De contemplando Deo*, P.L., CLXXXIV, 365–380. *De natura et dignitate amoris*, P.L., CLXXXIV, 379–408. *Meditativae orationes*, edit. M.M. Davy, Paris, J. Vrin, 1934.

Approximate dates	Author	Works
1125	SAINT BERNARD	*Epistola de caritate ad Carthusianos,* (forms the last part of the *De dilig. Deo,* cap. XII–XV), P.L., CLXXXIII, 995–1000.
1125/26		*De gradibus humilitatis et superbiae,* P.L., CLXXXII, 941–972.
1127/35		*De diligendo Deo,* cap. I–XI; P.L., CLXXXII, 973–995.
1135/38		*In Cant. Canticorum,* sermones I–XXIV; P.L., CLXXXIII, 785–899.
1136/40	P. ABELARD	*In Epist. ad Romanos,* P.L., CLXXVIII, 783–978.
1138/53	SAINT BERNARD	*In Cant. Canticorum,* sermones XXV–LXXXVI; P.L., CLXXXIII, 899–1198.
1138	WILLIAM OF SAINT-THIERRY	*In Epist. ad Romanos,* P.L., CLXXX, 547–694.
1141/42	AELRED OF RIEVAULX	*Speculum caritatis,* P.L., CXCV, 503–620.
1144	WILLIAM OF SAINT-THIERRY	*Speculum fidei,—Aenigma fidei,* P.L., CLXXX, 365–440.
1145		*Epistola aurea ad Fratres de Monte Dei,* lib. I–II; P.L., CLXXXIV, 307–354.
1145/50	GUIGO II, the Carthusian	*Scala claustralium,* P.L., CLXXXIV, 475–484.
1154/67	GILBERT OF HOLLAND	*In Cant. Canticorum,* sermones I–XLI; P.L., CLXXXIV, 11–252 (Sermon XLI, which contains the funeral oration for Aelred of Rievaulx, belongs therefore to 1167).
1160/70	GUIGO II, the Carthusian	*Meditationes* (ed. M. M. Davy, *La vie spirituelle,* 1934).
1163/64	AELRED OF RIEVAULX	*De oneribus,* P.L., CXCV, 361–500.
1164/65		*De spirituali amicitia,* P.L., CXCV, 659–702.
1166		*De anima* (ined.).
1167/72	GILBERT OF HOLLAND	*In Cant. Canticorum,* sermones XLI to the end.
1187/89	ADAM THE CARTHUSIAN	*De quadripertito exercitio cellae,* P.L., CLIII, 799–884.
1190	ANONYMOUS	*Meditationes piissimae de cognitione humanae conditionis,* P.L., CLXXXIV, 485–508.

Two men dominate all this history: St. Bernard of Clairvaux and William of Saint-Thierry. We shall have to consider them together, and that, indeed, is not the least of the difficulties of this study. For at one and the same time they are very different and not to be kept apart. The one, that is Bernard, is incontestably the greater as regards sanctity and doctrinal depth, but the other, William, yields to him in no way—excels him indeed at times—in the power he shows in elaborating the common doctrinal synthesis. The problem is further complicated by their mutual relations in time. Everything would be much simpler if we could consider Bernard as the master and William as the disciple. William indeed would have us believe it, and it is true that he was so; but has then the disciple nothing to teach his master? Consider the dates. Bernard was born in 1090, William towards 1085, possibly even as early as 1080, and he was thus the elder by five years at the least. Bernard died in 1153, William towards 1148—before the man whose life he had begun to write. We see then that they were almost exactly contemporary, and William is not to be regarded as a young man coming to St. Bernard as to a master who is to teach him everything, and receiving a doctrinal synthesis already complete. Nor is this all. William was not from the first a Cistercian. Educated at Reims, in the Benedictine monastery of Saint-Nicaise, he took the monastic habit there, was elected Abbot of the monastery of Saint-Thierry in 1119; and it was only in 1135 that he laid down his office to enter the Cistercian monastery of Signy. Undoubtedly in 1135 the doctrine of St. Bernard was fully formed, but then so also was that of William. [3] Even while we recognize that as early as 1125 the personal influence of Bernard was spreading well beyond the limits of the growing Order, it is but just to note that the ascetic and theological formation of William is not directly due to him. When, and to the extent to which, these two lives became entwined, in which direction went

the influence? We do not know. Even if we admit that
Bernard gave almost everything, did he then receive
nothing? Again, we do not know. However it be, William
undoubtedly maintains a very distinct individuality of his
own; his work counts, and if it had altogether perished that
of Bernard would not suffice to replace it.

Behind these two masters certain secondary figures are
visible in the background. Aelred of Rievaulx, although
belonging to a later generation, still directly depends upon
St. Bernard. Living wholly within the twelfth century, he
is not divided from the latter by any considerable interval;
and although various doctrinal influences interposed between
them, accentuated, no doubt, by their individual differences,
he remains nevertheless a qualified interpreter of the master
whose presence in his writings may be constantly felt.
Others might be cited, such as Gilbert of Holland and Isaac
de l'Etoile, but these three names may serve to designate
the three founders and principal interpreters of what we may
fairly call the Cistercian school, taking this in itself and apart
from the wide and deep diffusion of its influence into the
Carthusian school, for example, and generally speaking
beyond the limits of the Cistercian Order. What then had
these men in common, and how, in so far at least as it exists,
is their unity to be explained?

We cannot forbear to note in the first place a similarity
of intellectual formation and tastes which in men of so
diverse an origin is very remarkable. Apart from Isaac, in
whom we recognize the evident marks of a lively interest
in dialectics and metaphysics, none of them seem to have
been touched by the philosophical movement of their day.
If, perforce, we must classify them, we may put them into
the ranks of the anti-dialecticians. St. Bernard was to attack
Abelard and Gilbert de la Porrée, and it was William of
Saint-Thierry who urged him on. Aelred was to live

tranquilly outside the controversies of the schools, and Isaac, save in a few remarkable sermons, cultivates psychology rather than metaphysics. We may say in a general way that their secular culture is mainly literary. Here it remains distinct even from the school of Chartres, inasmuch as Plato is now held in no more honour than Aristotle; both are treated as sophists whose reasoning is condemned in advance to issue in error because they lacked the light of faith. On the other hand, all the foregoing representatives of the Cistercian school take pains with their writing. They are stylists. Brought up in the school of Cicero and St. Augustine, they have renounced everything save the art of good writing. St. Bernard, indeed, achieved a highly personal Latin style, adorned but not overcharged with Biblical citations, harmonious, and of a deeply intimate sonority—*Doctor mellifluus*—at once faithful to the classical tradition and rejoicing in the liberty of a living tongue: His periods are firmly articulated, often pointedly antithetical, and when the right moment comes he likes to condense his thought into brief formulae of striking force. For the rest, he slips but rarely into declamation, descends occasionally to puns, and such is his facility in the matter of alliteration that it appears in places where those who find it laborious would prefer its omission. For him it was no labour, he need not even seek it; the only thing we may occasionally regret is that he took no pains to eliminate it. That is all that still hangs about him from the profound hesitation of his early years—whether to become a man of letters or to become a saint? Bernard found ways to remain a man of letters and to become a saint into the bargain.

This imposing series of works will doubtless have but slender interest for certain historians for whom the style of thought and feeling of an epoch is no part of its history. It is none the less indicative of a deep and continuous current

for which we should certainly fail to find any analogy in
the eleventh century and which was perceptibly to affect the
direction of the thirteenth. It is one of the quite indispensable
features in the landscape of the twelfth, and it is incorporated
into the totality of the picture in virtue of traits whose importance will escape nobody—at any rate when they have
once been perceived. For all those who know it admit that
the twelfth century was, in its own way, an age of humanism.
It was much more so, assuredly, than is usually supposed.
Classical Latin scholarship was then cultivated more or less
everywhere and by no means only at Chartres. No doubt
in this connection we are quite right in thinking of Chartres
—but how many other schools of literary activity have disappeared and left no trace behind! Of the very modest
school of Saint-Vorles, for example, we should know next
to nothing did we not know that medieval Latin literature
is in its debt for St. Bernard. And that is a point which is
not without its importance even for the study of Cistercian
mysticism, for in renouncing the world to enter at Cîteaux,
St. Bernard renounced this Latin culture along with the
rest—too late no doubt, in a sense, since he was already
possessed of it. Later on he was to recommend his novices
to leave their bodies behind at the monastery gates, and
bring nothing inside but their minds. He had done the thing
himself; but then, how much else had entered the monastery
along with his mind! Doubtless he had insisted on forbidding
entrance to Ovid, but Horace gained a footing there, Persius
and Juvenal provided some shafts for the use of the contemner
of the world; and above all an unexpected guest slipped
quietly in, insinuating himself by unforeseen ways into the
very heart of mystical theology: Cicero.

The influence of Cicero on the courtly conception of love
in the twelfth century has been insufficiently appreciated by
historians of French literature. His doctrine of disinterested

friendship, springing from love of virtue, centred wholly on virtue, source of all moral worth and nobility, finding all its reward in itself, was certainly not unknown to the poets of that day. Of course it cannot be considered as one of the sources of Cistercian mysticism as such, for obviously there is nothing mystical about it; nevertheless, if we would put the Cistercian theology of love into its proper place in the picture of the twelfth century, we shall certainly have to make its acquaintance. In virtue of what they have in common, these kindred movements, some of which are manifest strangers to the spirit of Christianity, ought apparently to be referred to non-Christian sources; and one such source presents itself at the outset as possible, even probable, and that is precisely this twelfth-century humanism. Might it not have had its influence on St. Bernard as well as on the poets of courtly love?

It is certainly not immediately easy to see what Antiquity could have to teach Christians concerning the nature of love. The men of the twelfth century read only Latin; in Latin literature Ovid was the sole theorist of love available; and we know that his ideas would hardly prove of much service to those who sought to build up a doctrine of love which should be, even if not mystical, at any rate acceptable to Christians. We shall see indeed that Ovid's invasion of the literary schools provoked a violent reaction from William of Saint-Thierry. The schools of Cistercian charity confronted the schools of profane love; against the spurious master of spurious love they claimed and proclaimed the rights of the sole master and the sole Love—the Holy Spirit. Of what spirit was Ovid? Evidently it is useless to look in this direction.

Love, in the proper sense of the term, is one thing. There is another and kindred sentiment, to which the Ancients would seem to have transferred all those treasures of affection, nobility and disinterestedness for which they showed themselves so avid in this matter. This, it need scarcely be said, was friendship. In this field, let us add, we shall have no need to look far. Without denying that other influences might have been operative, even in the full assurance that they were so, we must admit it to be highly probable that none could compare in importance with that of the *De Amicitia* of Cicero.

For here at any rate, in the *De Amicitia*, the men of the twelfth century found much they felt able to borrow; either as it stood or adapted to their needs. Let us not be tempted however to multiply disputable analogies. Let us simply retain a small number of notions whose influence can hardly be denied.

I. Calling to mind Cicero's splendid eulogy of friendship (Cap. VI) we may expressly retain, as a point of technical importance, the identification of friendship with what he calls *benevolentia*. The English "benevolence" is hardly a satisfactory equivalent—"good-will" would be better. *Benevolentia* really means the sentiment that wishes the good of the beloved for the sake only of the beloved himself. Kinship can exist without it, but not so friendship. Hence we see how far friendship outweighs the family tie: "sublata enim benevolentia nomen amicitiae tollitur, propinquitatis manet" (Cap. V).

II. The source of friendship lies in love as opposed to practical utility. By this we must understand that *benevolentia* springs from an inward feeling of affection (*sensum diligendi*), a certain tenderness (*caritatem*), whereby we will nothing but the good of the beloved (Cap. VIII).

III. Hence advantage attends upon friendship, but cannot be admitted as its motive: "Sed, quanquam utilitates multae et magnae consecutae sunt, non sunt tamen ab earum spe causae diligendi profectae" (Cap. IX).—"Amare autem, nihil aliud est, nisi eum ipsum diligere, quem ames, nulla indigentia, nulla utilitate quaesita" (Cap. XXVII).

IV, Consequently the whole fruit of friendship lies in the very love of good-will which we bear our friend: "... sic amicitiam, non spe mercedis adducti, sed quod omnis ejus fructus in ipso amore inest, expetendam putamus" (Cap. IX). Cf. "Atque etiam mihi quidem videntur, qui utilitatis causa fingunt amicitias, amabilissimum nodum amicitiae tollere: non enim tam utilitas parta per amicum, quam amici amor ipse, delectat. . . . Non igitur utilitatem amicitia, sed utilitas amicitiam, consecuta est" (Cap. XIV). We shall eventually encounter in St. Bernard himself an almost literal reminiscence of Cicero: "fructus ejus, usus ejus."[4]

V. Friendship is the offspring of virtue, but no man becomes attached to another on account of his virtue unless he is virtuous himself. And so, when all is said, the deepest cause of friendship lies in likeness; for nature loves nothing so much as that which resembles it: "Quod si etiam illud addimus, quod recti addi potest, nihil esse, quod ad se rem ullam tam alliciat, tam attrahat, quam ad amicitiam similitudo: concedetur profecto verum esse, ut bonos boni diligant, addiscantque sibi quasi propinquitate conjunctos, atque natura: nihil enim est appetentius similium sui, nihil rapacius quam natura" (Cap. XIV).

VI. And let us add this last trait, to which at first we might fail to attach the importance we shall see it to have later on: the sentiment of friendship is essentially reciprocal. It is a mutual accord of wills, a "consensio".

Not one of these various elements but entered into the texture of Cistercian mysticism, and the more important of them, it would seem, had a certain influence on the courtly conception of love. Cicero's *benevolentia* bears a strong resemblance to the *bonne volonté* of Chrètien of Troyes; the doctrine of the disinterestedness of true love, in the

B

measure at least in which it is characteristic of both schools, is incontestably borrowed from Cicero.

But there is one thing, we must add, which our authors do not appear to have relished in the *De Amicitia*, and that is Cicero's definition of friendship. It makes its appearance, heavy, complicated, charged with Stoic undertones, in Chapter VI: "Est autem amicitia nihil aliud, nisi omnium divinarum humanarumque rerum, cum benevolentia et charitate, summa concordia." There are too many Stoic implications in that, and too much latent metaphysic, to please our authors. With the exception of Aelred, who set himself to re-write Cicero's treatise, no one, as far as I know, seemed to take any interest in the definition. Two others, however, engaged the attention of our mystics or theorists of love.

The first is also taken from Cicero, but not from the *De Amicitia*; it occurs in the *De inventione rhetorica*, lib. II, n. 55: "Amicitia est voluntas erga aliquem rerum bonarum, illius ipsius causa, quem diligit, cum ejus pari voluntate." The definition was indeed perfect in the sense that it completely summed-up the teaching of the *De Amicitia*. There in the first place we find recalled the note of "*benevolentia*", next that of disinterestedness, and finally that of the reciprocal character of love, of that "redamare" of which Cicero had said in the *De Amicitia* that nothing can be "jucundius" (Cap. XIV). Observe that the word "redamare", so familiar to St. Bernard, is used by Cicero as a kind of neologism: it was fully to establish itself in the Middle Ages, and eventually to become popular in the "sic nos amantem quis non redamaret".

To this definition we may perhaps add another text of the *De Amicitia*, which, while not providing a definition of friendship properly so-called, might eventually be made to serve the purpose: "Nam cum amicitiae vis sit in eo, ut unus quasi animus fiat ex pluribus. . . ." (Cap. XXV). We may notice a resemblance between these phrases and the *unitas spiritus* so dear to our mystics. It helps us to understand how, in data at bottom so alien to their own particular problem, they could yet find materials that went to its solution.

Necessary as it is to take these facts into account, they are far from explaining the origin of this wave of mysticism, whose power, already perceptible round about 1125, was to burst in full force upon the twelfth century. The birth of the movement is a problem as pressing as that of vernacular literature or of ogival art; it is just as much a part of history and in no way less difficult to solve. The truth is that problems of this kind are never open to any *one* solution because such movements depend on very complex material conditions, with which we are very imperfectly acquainted, and especially on spiritual conditions which are so much the more mysterious as their spirituality is the more pure. Let us say above all that before being effects these movements are events which suffice to themselves, until in the end they become causes. What we do know is this: that about 1120, in the Benedictine monastery of Saint-Thierry, the Liégeois, William, began to write, or at least to consider, a *De natura et dignitate amoris*, and that towards 1125 St. Bernard addressed to some Carthusians, in response to certain *Meditationes*, all burning with divine love, an *Epistola de Caritate* which he was soon to incorporate in his *De diligendo Deo*. Beyond the field of this theology, the passionate drama of Heloïse and Abelard, more fertile in ideas than one might suppose, riveted all eyes on the problem of love. There then, at any rate, we have so many events. For the rest we may still hope for some insight into the historical conditions which, if they did not determine, at least occasioned the movement. A new mystical springtide burgeoned in the twin gardens of Saint-Thierry and Cîteaux. Whence came the fresh sap that brought it to birth?

Everybody knows that the monastery of Cîteaux arose from a powerful effort to restore in all its purity the observance of the Benedictine Rule. Robert de Molesme and his successors, Alberic and St. Stephen Harding, had put their energy into the enterprise. It had already found its definitive orientation when Bernard and his companions joined the little band of their disciples. It is therefore very natural to suppose that the Rule of St. Benedict exerted a considerable influence on the thought of St. Bernard. It is not without good reason that Dom U. Berlière, at the opening of his book on *L'Ascèse benedictine*, writes of Cîteaux: "Its ascetic formation rests upon the Rule; the literature it produced is the exquisite flower, the savoury marrow of the ancient Benedictine teaching." The studies that here follow will confirm, on many points, the truth of this judgment. Let us add, however, that this is not exactly the point that concerns us here, for if it is easy to see at a glance that meditation on the Benedictine Rule produced the flowering of ascetic theology, it is not so immediately obvious how it was able to favour the birth of a mystical theology. St. Benedict, of his own free will, had remained on a humbler level; many had read him; before Robert de Molesme and St. Bernard there had been admirable Benedictines and Benedictine saints; the Order, if it stood in need of reform, had known its periods of spiritual brilliance even during the course of the Middle Ages; and yet at no time do we encounter an outburst of mystical activity in any way comparable to that of which the twelfth century was to be the astonished witness. How account for this phenomenon?

Apparently it can be done in one way only; namely, by referring all its force to the desire that animated St. Bernard

and his companions for the observance of the pure
Benedictine Rule. By that we must understand that a
perfect literal observance of the Rule did not suffice them.
That for which their souls were longing was not merely a
strictly regular Benedictine life, but also that very Christian
perfection itself to which this life has power to lead. Now to
be a true Benedictine it is enough to put into zealous practice
the first seventy-two Chapters of the Rule. That was
already no easy thing, and although St. Benedict had proposed to lay nothing excessively hard or painful on his
monks, it is easy to realize that many considered the effort
to be as much as could reasonably be demanded; if even
many fell short, historians seated comfortably at their work-
tables in the intervals between two long nights' rest and three
full daily meals, would judge them with no very good grace.
It remains true to say, nevertheless, that even for St. Benedict
himself, all that was insufficient to make a perfect Christian,
unless to this observance there should be added that of
the seventy-third and final Chapter. We have only to
read it and weigh its words and we shall realize it readily
enough.

LXXIII.—THAT THE WHOLE OBSERVANCE OF PER-
FECTION IS NOT CONTAINED IN THIS RULE

We have written this Rule in order that by observing it in
the monasteries we may show ourselves to have some degree
of goodness of life, and a beginning of holiness. But for him
who would hasten to the perfection of religion there are the
teachings of the holy Fathers, the following whereof bringeth
a man to the height of perfection. For what page or what word
is there in the divinely inspired books of the Old and New
Testaments that is not a most unerring rule for human life?
Or what book of the holy Catholic Fathers doth not loudly
proclaim how we may by a straight course reach our Creator?
Moreover the *Conferences of the Fathers*, their *Institutes* and their
Lives, and the Rule of our holy Father Basil—what are these but
the instruments whereby well-living and obedient monks attain
to virtue? But to us, who are slothful and negligent and of evil

lives, they are cause for shame and confusion. Whosoever
therefore thou art that hasteneth to thy heavenly country,
fulfil by the help of Christ this least of Rules which we have
written for beginners, and then at length thou shalt arrive, under
God's protection, at the lofty summits of doctrine and virtue
of which we have spoken above. Amen.[5]

End of the Rule.

End of the Rule, which means that the Rule has no end.
St. Benedict's *Amen* was understood. To see how it was that
St. Bernard came to add a mystical renaissance to all the
others that adorned the century we have only to realize
the irresistible appeal with which these last words echoed
through his soul. That they should have been so understood
is not in the power of the historian to explain; but he may
note the fact, and thereby put himself in the way, not
merely to elucidate the genesis of the Cistercian mysticism,
but also to introduce a certain amount of order into the
very difficult problem of its sources.

For the first question that arises is this: what was it
that suggested to William of Saint-Thierry and St. Bernard
the idea that mystic union with God is the crown of the
monastic life? I admit that if you take it in one way the
question looks a little naïve. I propose to take it in another.
True, the mystical life has other sources than books: and
unquestionably the world has never wanted for great
mystics who have remained quite unknown, who have
written nothing and read very little. But the case is different
if we look for the sources of a speculative mysticism, for then
we have to do with a theology, and no theology arises out
of nothing, or amounts to no more than a conceptual
transposition of a bare experience. Nor is it always the
same in the case of the mystical experience itself, for although
it may spring spontaneously in an isolated soul, it is commonly the reward of a long effort, the fulfilment of a promise,

the realization of a hope, or of an ambition born of example. What encouragements, what spurs, did William and Bernard receive? The rapture of St. Paul? Undoubtedly: but who would therefore dare to aspire so high? Some words of Tertullian's,[6] the commentaries of Origen on the Canticle of Canticles, known to St. Bernard but of another spirit than his[7]; the admirable doctrine of Gregory of Nyssa, which undoubtedly had its influence on St. Bernard through Maximus[8] but which he probably did not know at first hand—there is nothing in all that amounting to a formal invitation to the ecstatic life, or at any rate to an invitation that St. Bernard certainly heard. We can go farther and make the same remark as regards St. Augustine. Apart from the unique instance of the rapture at Ostia, personal mystical experiences are absent from the works of St. Augustine. Of all those who had read and meditated him before St. Bernard from the opening of the ninth century, none, not even St. Anselm, ever dreamt that a mystical doctrine could be gathered from his writings. Theological considerations, profound no doubt, but abstract, were insufficient to determine a movement such as the Cistercian. What was required was the inspiring contagion of example, and this it was precisely that St. Bernard and his companions found in the *Vitae Patrum :* the *Lives of the Fathers of the Desert.*[9]

To these they owed in the first place their acquaintance with a type of mortification that threw everything later attempted into the shade, as if it were no more than a moderate penance. The asceticism of Cîteaux, of the Chartreuse for that matter, is certainly derived from the Fathers of the Desert. In the former the cenobites of Egypt lived their lives over again in France, in the latter the hermits. Cîteaux and the Chartreuse were "deserts" peopled by the ascetics of the twelfth century, and

multiplying with incredible rapidity. To set out to observe
to the letter the Rule of St. Benedict, not omitting the last
chapter, is thus to follow in the footsteps of St. Antony,
of Macarius and Pacomius. The *Lausiac History* of Palladius
lay to hand, like a kind of wonder-book, to show what these
spiritual athletes could take upon themselves for the love
of Christ. In the presence of the assembled community
the stories of these mortified lives were read aloud. Inevitably, for souls so avid for perfection, they became so many
incitements to heroism. There they learnt the meaning of
the words of St. Benedict stamping the monastic life with
its essential character. "Ad te ergo nunc meus sermo
dirigitur; quisquis abrenuntians propriis voluntatibus, Domino Christo vero regi militaturus obedientiae fortissima
atque praeclara arma sumis."[10] Thus was their ascetic
ardour enkindled; but there too they found no lack of
pressing invitations to the mystical life.

For St. Antony himself had been a mystic, nor were
extraordinary graces unknown in the Egyptian deserts.[11]
Furthermore, in referring the monks to Cassian, the Rule
referred them to a master who had expressly described
ecstasy as the supreme reward of the ascetic life led by the
Fathers of the Desert. The influence of Cassian on the Benedictine school has been repeatedly affirmed, and with good
reason. Cassian, it has been observed, was St. Benedict's
spiritual book of predilection,[12] and in fact every critical
edition of the Rule refers again and again to these three
principal sources: Scripture, St. Basil, Cassian. Now the
doctrine of Cassian is not concerned only with asceticism,
were it only of the most heroic type. It considers the
purgative way as absolutely indispensable, but as an introduction, nevertheless, to the contemplative life, of which
the culminating point is the "Sight of God."[13] Meditation
on the Scriptures often passes into prayer, as with Origen,

and "pure" prayer is at times consummated in ecstasy: "Ad coelestes illos rapiebamur excessus. . . ." We need not reproduce the well-known texts in which Cassian describes these experiences.[14] The important fact to be noted is this: that in binding themselves to follow the Rule to the very end, St. Bernard and his companions put themselves to school with the master for whom ecstasy was the Christian's highest ambition.

St. Gregory the Great, who may with good reason be regarded as a Benedictine, could but confirm on this point the example of Antony and the teaching of Cassian. It is hardly an exaggeration to say that the writings of St. Bernard are impregnated with his doctrine and terminology almost as much as with those of St. Augustine. Nor is this at all surprising, since Gregory himself was full of Augustine. Long before St. Bernard he teaches that no one can attain to the summit of the spiritual life without ascending through a series of degrees. Fully to possess God we have to be perfectly detached from ourselves: "Tunc vero in Deo plene proficimus, cum a nobis ipsis funditus defecerimus."[15] The road to be followed is an orderly ascent in which St. Bernard's is already prefigured; in the first place, contempt of self and humility: *contemptus sui;* then the fear of God: *timor;* lastly love: *amor.*[16] Love moreover, is for him, as for Augustine, the motive power of the soul: *machina mentis,*[17] and this it is that leads us on to the mystical contemplation of God.[18] This contemplation can be nothing but joy and sweetness, like the love itself which it crowns.[19] None knows how the divine light penetrates the soul,[20] but we know at least that it sometimes inflames it to the point of complete separation from the flesh, and utter surrender to God. A brief and fleeting experience, an obscure mode of knowledge, ecstasy is not to be confounded with the beatific vision. It is merely, so to speak, a momentary effort on the

B*

part of the creature to attain to this vision without having yet passed through the death of the body.[21]

It may thus be maintained with every appearance of truth that the first invitation to the mystical life came to St. Bernard by way of meditation on the Rule of St. Benedict, and on the examples proposed by St. Benedict for imitation: *Collationes Patrum et Instituta et Vitas eorum.* But here we stand on the threshold of a road that is really interminable. For, this point decided, we have still to ask: What materials went to the making of St. Bernard's speculative mysticism—what earlier syntheses did he lay under contribution for the elements of his own?

An enquiry into the sources of St. Bernard's text would have to take account of all the formulae he borrowed, and all that brought him suggestions. Full of the Bible and the Fathers as he was, such a voyage of discovery would never end. Not that it would be therefore useless—far from that. We cannot hope to understand him without constantly referring to his sources in Scripture, where his thought may rather be said to bathe than to drink. However, if we are to make it our aim to reconstruct his systematization we cannot but think it preferable, for this particular purpose, to proceed in another manner. St. Bernard's mystical theology is an incontestably original creation, albeit altogether made up of traditional elements. It would seem to have arisen out of the combination of several knots (*blocs*) of doctrine, each retaining, even in the new synthesis, both its own proper structure and the evident marks of its origin.

For it almost looks as if St. Bernard were putting to himself a purely personal problem, but bargaining with himself at the same time that none of the materials entering into the solution should be alien to the Scriptural and Patristic tradition. He held to his bargain, let us add, and gained

his point. There, perhaps, lies one of the secrets of the
perpetual rejuvenation of Christian thought, of its inexhaustible vitality. Whenever a saint puts to himself a
new question, or an old question under a new form, the
Christian tradition stands ready with all the materials
required for the formulation of the answer; but of course
the saint has to be there to put it. St. Bernard put his:
How to make the Benedictine Rule avail for the realization
of this life of union with God in love for which his whole
soul thirsted? He turned to tradition, and it gave him the
elements of the answer. It had already provided him with
the elements of the answer in the case of quite another
question touching the means or the end of the Christian
life itself; but only he could order them into a synthesis
which should be the synthesis of his own spiritual life—
for his life was but the concrete realization of his doctrine,
and his doctrine the abstract formula of his life. Now first
and foremost, before everything else, we must put at the
source of his thought this first doctrinal bloc, namely the
group of Scriptural texts taken from the First Epistle of St.
John, Chapter IV, on union of the soul with God by love.
Undoubtedly St. Bernard found and cited many others
expressing the same doctrine; but we cannot escape the
impression that all his thought starts from that, and must in
the end come back to that. The only reservation to be made
would be in the case of St. John's own Gospel; but we have
to recognize, not that St. Bernard held it in any less authority
—the supposition would be absurd—but that even the most
outstanding passages of the Fourth Gospel on union with
God by love grouped themselves in his eyes around the
rich, complete and condensed synthesis which he found in
the First Epistle. Let us try to set out its essential factors.

I. UNION WITH GOD BY LOVE (I JOHN, IV)

1. In the first place we have the fundamental conception of God considered, not now as metaphysical cause, but as the end and means of the spiritual life: God is love, "Deus caritas est" (I *John*, IV, 8).

2. If then God is charity, it goes without saying that possession of charity is the necessary condition of any knowledge of God. We cannot load this text with all that speculative theology was to find there later on; but neither can we deny that the speculation was called forth, instigated, by the text. For there, in fact, we have the source of the doctrine, afterwards so famous, of charity as knowledge, or even as vision, of God. The least that can be said is that such a text supposes that the man who has nothing in himself of what God is in essence is incapable of knowing God. St. Bernard himself adds practically nothing to the text, indeed I believe he adds absolutely nothing, for he contents himself with merely making it more precisely clear that the "likeness" of man to God is the condition of our knowledge of God, and that this likeness is the work of charity. Whether or not this is to be taken as already understood in the Johannine text is a matter of small importance, and the basic idea remains: "Qui non diligit, non novit Deum, quoniam Deus caritas est" (I *John*, IV, 8).

3. If God is charity, and if charity must needs be in us if we are to know God, then charity must of necessity be given by God. There we have the origin of the distinction, so important in St. Bernard, between the Charity which is God, and the charity which in us is the "gift" of God. This distinction is suggested by the verse that declares that charity comes from God: "Caritas ex Deo est" (I *John*, IV, 7).

4. A new thesis, not less important, is added to the foregoing by the identification of the gift of charity with the gift of the Holy Spirit. That is a point which the Cistercian mystics always had in mind; it explains why the Holy Spirit always, in their doctrine, plays the part of the bond by which the soul is united to God and the spiritual life becomes a participation in the Divine life: "In hoc cognoscimus quoniam in eo manemus, et ipse in nobis, quoniam *de Spiritu suo* dedit nobis" (I *John*, IV, 13).

5. Another step; this presence in the soul of charity, which is a gift of the Holy Spirit, and alone puts us in a position to know God, is also for us the substitute for the sight of God which we lack. No one has ever seen God, but if charity dwells in us, then, since it is the gift of God, God dwells in us, and then our love for Him is perfect. In default, therefore, of a vision of God which is not vouchsafed us here below, there is a presence of God in the soul which marks the point of perfection of charity in us: "Deum nemo vidit unquam. Si diligamus invicem, Deus in nobis manet et caritas ejus in nobis perfecta est" (I *John*, IV, 12).—"Et nos cognovimus et credidimus caritati, quam habet Deus in nobis. Deus caritas est: et qui manet in caritate, in Deo manet, et Deus in eo" (I *John*, IV, 16).

6. The reason why we ought to love a God-Charity is clear; because He first loved us. It is doubtless needless to press the point and to go on to show that here we have the problem of St. Bernard's *De diligendo Deo* and its solution: "Nos ergo diligamus Deum, quoniam Deus prior dilexit nos" (I *John*, IV, 19).

7. By what signs shall we be assured that we have fulfilled this precept? How shall we know that the charity of God is in us? By two signs; of which the first is the love we bear our neighbour. For all men are brothers in Jesus Christ; if, therefore, anyone pretends to love God whom he does

not see, and loves not his brother whom he does see, that
man is a liar. We have here the starting-point of all the
developments where St. Bernard requires the love of the
neighbour as an indispensable moment of the apprenticeship of charity: "Si quis dixerit quoniam diligo Deum, et
fratrum suum oderit, mendax est" (I *John*, IV, 20).

8. The second index of the presence of charity in the soul
lies in the expulsion of all fear. For there, where charity
reigns, there at the same time is full confidence in the issue
of the Day of Judgment. This *fiducia*, offspring of charity,
is an essential factor in St. Bernard's doctrine. Penetrated
with charity, we become even in this world, in virtue of the
gift, what God is in virtue of His Nature; and how then
should we fear His judgment? "In hoc perfecta est caritas
Dei nobiscum, ut fiduciam habeamus in die judicii; quia
sicut ille est, et nos sumus in hoc mundo" (I *John*, IV, 17).
Hence we see why St. Bernard's contemplation moves by
way of consideration of the judgment, and how the precise
point where the fear of Divine chastisement gives way to
"fiducia" marks the entry of the soul into ecstasy. We see
also why, to put it more simply, the progress of love consists
in the passage from a state in which a man is a slave to fear
(*servus*) to another in which he purely and simply loves. For
love banishes fear: "Timor non est in caritate; sed perfecta
caritas foras mittit timorem, quoniam timor poenam habet;
qui autem timet, non est perfectus in caritate" (I *John*, IV, 18).

Here then, as we may easily perceive, we stand in the
presence of a doctrinal "bloc". It passed practically as it
stood, with all its essential articulations, into the mystical
theology of St. Bernard. Its influence, indeed, may be said
to be felt throughout like that of a solid rock that sustains
the whole edifice. Nevertheless it does not stand alone. On
this basis another doctrine had to be superimposed to explain
how it is that love brings God to dwell within us and makes

us dwell in Him. On this point St. Bernard appealed to a second source which, given the speculative nature of the question put, had to be theological rather than Scriptural. For a doctrine of ecstasy and the divinization of the soul by love he turned to Maximus the Confessor in the translation of Scotus Erigena.

II. DIVINIZATION BY ECSTASY

The influence exerted on the Cistercian mysticism by Dionysius is very difficult to estimate. It is remarkable that the Dionysian style has left no mark on St. Bernard's mode of writing, and even Dionysius' very characteristic language contributed practically nothing to Bernard's terminology. We meet with no superlatives, none of those heavy and embarrassed periods creaking with Greek terms thinly disguised in Latin. The word "theophany", almost inevitable in a writer familiar with Dionysius, and occurring at least once in William of Saint-Thierry,[22] seems to have no place in his vocabulary. We may ask, then, whether he ever read Dionysius, or rather we might have asked it if the thing, likely enough in itself, were not made the more so by the fact that he had certainly read, and in Scotus Erigena's translation, a text of Maximus the Confessor and turned it to good account. The fact is important, not only in itself, but for the history of Cistercian mysticism and the influence of St. Bernard. For he always had opponents, illustrious opponents among the rest, who addressed themselves with special preference to this defect in his armour. We shall have plenty of opportunity to realize that the defect was more apparent than real; but is it not precisely an opponent's proper cue to treat apparent defects as if they were real? Now it happened that Scotus Erigena, not content with translating Maximus, had passed into his own *De*

Divisione Naturae the very fragment from which Bernard himself had drawn inspiration. After that it needed only a step to suspect and accuse St. Bernard of Erigena's pantheism; nor did his opponents omit to take it. Without doubt, if they wanted to be just, they should first have assured themselves that Erigena himself was a pantheist, or that Maximus was such; or have established that no one has the right to draw inspiration from a non-pantheist text from the moment it was turned to account by an author accused of pantheism —and this whether the accusation is true or false, and whether he knows it or not. A heated controversialist does not bother himself with distinctions of this sort, and it is a fact that the presence of a Maximian "bloc" in the synthesis of St. Bernard occasionally damaged him in theological eyes. What chief factors does analysis here reveal?

1. Firstly, it is from Maximus (or from Dionysius, but we are not sure of him, and we are of Maximus) that St. Bernard seems to have borrowed the word that he uses to signify ecstasy: *excessus*. All things move towards God as towards the motionless Sovereign Good. The end of their movement, which is also their own proper good, is to attain this motionless Good. Natural things tend to Him in virtue of their very nature; intelligent beings by way of knowledge and love. Hence the ecstatic movement which bears them on towards Him: "Si autem intelligit, omnino amat quod intelligit; si amat, patitur omnino ad ipsum ut amabile excessum" (MAXIMUS, *Ambigua*, cap. II; P.L., CXXII, 1202 A).

2. The effect of this "excessus" is to make him who loves "fiat totum in toto amato" (*op. cit.*, 1202 A), in such a way that there now remains nothing for him to will of his own will. Circumscribed by God on all sides, he is as air flooded with light, or as iron liquefied in the fire: "Sicut aer per totum illuminatus lumine, et igne ferrum totum toto lique-

factum, aut si quid aliud talium est" (MAXIMUS, *op. cit.*, 1202 B). St. Bernard was to make use of the same images in his *De diligendo Deo*, X, 28; P.L., CLXXXII, 991 BC. The expression "liquescere" occurs there also: 991 B.

3. This liquefaction, or fusion, of the soul in ecstasy does not involve its destruction, quite the contrary. For the substance of the soul remains intact, and the *excessus* indeed confirms in it its own true nature: "Non conturbet vos, quod dictum est; non enim ablationem propriae potentiae fieri dico, sed positionem magis secundam naturam fixam et immutabilem, id est excessum intellectualem" (MAXI-MUS, *op. cit.*, 1202 CD).

4. The *excessus* can never be complete in this life; it will be consummated only in the next. In the meantime, this fusion of the soul in love is an analogical participation in future beatitude: "participationem per similitudinem solummodo accipimus" (*op. cit.*, 1202 B), and it is ineffable.

5. The *excessus* thus makes the soul like God because it remodels the image on its exemplar: "velut imagine redeunte ad principale exemplum" (*op. cit.*, 1202 D. Cf. 1207 B).

6. The upshot of this assimilation is a deification: *deificatio*: "magis autem Deus per deificationem facta" (*op. cit.*, 1202 D); "theosin" (1206 B); "et totus factus Deus . . ." &c. (1208 B).

We may remark here, as in the case of the First Epistle of St. John, that St. Bernard would seem to have exhausted all the resources which the text in question put at his disposal. The literal resemblance of certain phrases—the two comparisons taken from Maximus—strengthen the impression, already in itself irresistible, that this sequence of ideas, common to the two doctrines, really passed over from Maximus to St. Bernard. But we ought especially to add that in the act of borrowing, St. Bernard so welded it with the Johannine bloc that the two become altogether one. God is Charity; He gives us charity, and thus dwells in us and makes us to dwell in Him. How? By way of the restoration of that image, which each of us substantially is, to the likeness of its Exemplar; by stripping us of our own will thus to unite us to His, by liquefying us, so to speak, so that we may already pass into Him by ecstasy, while awaiting the day when we shall pass wholly into Him by glory; by no means there to be dissolved and lost, but confirmed for ever in perfection.

There then already we have sources of inspiration the importance of which it would be superfluous to underline. But that is not yet all, for if we need to know the end in view and the means to this end, no merely theoretical acquaintance will suffice; we still need to know by what practical methods these means may be brought into play and the end attained. Now St. Bernard was far from being without resources even here, for he had to his hand the whole treasure of the Patristic tradition. None better than he knew how to make use of it. It lay at his fingers' ends. As we read him we stand amazed at the easy mastery with which he chooses and marshals his Patristic materials, interprets them, adapts the teachings of the Fathers to his own purposes. It is none the less true that here also one special influence dominates all the rest and we can speak once more of a kind of doctrinal bloc that St. Bernard turned to account. This was the Benedictine ascesis.

III. THE BENEDICTINE ASCESIS

The *Regula Monasteriorum* is neither a treatise of philosophy nor a treatise of theology, whether mystical or even merely ascetic. It is a rule of monastic life, but one which resembles Scripture in this respect, that it provides us with endless food for thought. Let us remember, moreover, that it is charged with all the speculation of Cassian, resumes it, or is frequently inspired by it, and that anyone familiar with Cassian may very legitimately recognize his voice behind words suggesting his presencè. Certain things in this highly condensed text would seem to have particularly engaged the attention of St. Bernard. Let us try to set them out.

1. Retain, in the first place, this central idea which runs through all the Rule, that the first duty of anyone who would serve God is to renounce his own will: "Abrenuntians propriis voluntatibus" (*Regula*, Prolog., ed. Linderbauer, p. 13, l. 6–7). St. Benedict intends it in an altogether practical sense; what he would say, in effect, is that one cannot give oneself up wholly to the service of God without putting oneself under obedience to an Abbot, and, moreover, obeying him. That is just what the "Girovagi" do not do (*op. cit.*, I, p. 20, l. 23), but that is what one has to do in a Benedictine monastery: "Nullus in monasterio proprii sequatur cordis voluntatem" (III, p. 23, l. 33–34). The precept recurs again and again: "Abnegare semetipsum sibi . . ." "voluntatem propriam odere" (IV, p. 24, l. 7 and 32–33)— ". . . voluntatem propriam deserentes . . ." (V, p. 25, l. 9). Finally, for a text ending with a reference to Scripture, let us cite: "voluntatem vero propriam ita facere prohibemur, cum dicit Scriptura nobis: *et a voluntatibus tuis avertere*" (*Eccli.*, 18, 30) (VII, p. 28, l. 39–40). This is of the first importance for anyone who would understand St. Bernard and the part played in his doctrine by the systematic elimination of the *proprium*. But what now is the method by which this elimination is to be effected?

2. By way of the practice of humility, to which the whole seventh Chapter of the Rule is devoted. Here St. Benedict sets forth the twelve ascending degrees of this virtue. Our life is compared to a ladder—the ladder of Jacob—the two sides being the body and the soul, and the steps being the twelve degrees of humility which we have to mount by

our actions so to raise ourselves to God (VII, p. 27, l. 11–21). One may say without fear of mistake, since St. Bernard at the opening of his treatise says it himself, that the *De gradibus humilitatis et superbiae* is nothing but a theological commentary on this Chapter.

3. A third element of the Rule, particularly important since it rises almost to the plane of speculation, assigns to humility the very part that it was to play in the mystical doctrine of St. Bernard. In the first place, it is the introduction to charity: "Ergo his omnibus humilitatis gradibus ascensis monachus mox ad Caritatem Dei perveniet . . ." (VII, p. 81, l. 131–132). We should look in vain in St. Benedict for any explanation of the way in which humility introduces charity by renunciation of one's own will; it was to be precisely St. Bernard's task to explore this point and reconstitute the mechanism. What he found in the Rule was the statement of the problem to be solved and the indication of the solution. It was left to him to demonstrate its truth.

4. Passing beyond this point in the very phrase that introduces it, St. Benedict at once adds: "ad caritatem Dei perveniet illam quae *perfecta foris mittit timorem*" (VII, p. 31, l. 132). Thus, in one step, he rejoins the text of the First Epistle of St. John, IV, 18, already cited, which was thus doubly recommended to St. Bernard's attention. To seize the full import of this Johannine reference, in the passage where it occurs, we must remember that from the outset of the Rule St. Benedict has never ceased to insist on the importance of meditating the Judgment. Fear, and not merely fear of God, but fear of God's chastisements, plays a capital part in the apprenticeship to the spiritual life as he conceives it. It is so much the more important to notice that at the term of this apprenticeship charity is substituted for fear as the motive power of our acts: "per

quam (caritatem) universa quae prius non sine formidine observabat, absque ullo labore velut naturaliter ex consuetudine, incipiet custodire, non jam timore gehennae, sed amore Christi et consuetudine ipsa bona et delectatione virtutum" (VII, p. 31, l. 133–136). In adding, very briefly, that the Holy Spirit will demonstrate these effects of charity in the purified soul, St. Benedict completes the sketch of the synthesis for which St. Bernard was to supply the doctrinal justification: the substitution of love for fear by the Holy Spirit as reward for the long apprenticeship of humility —that in fact is the theme repeatedly developed in the *De diligendo Deo* and the Sermons on the Canticle of Canticles. Its place is at the very centre of the ascesis of St. Bernard, and since for its origin we must go back once more to Cassian we are still moving on the ground marked out by the Seventy-Third Chapter of the Rule: "necnon et Collationes Patrum et Instituta et vitas eorum . . .", let us read: *Collationes*, XI, 8 and *Instituta*, IV, 39.

If now we try to connect this third "bloc" with the two others we shall obtain a kind of skeleton outline of the mystical theology of St. Bernard. God is Charity; by the gift of charity He dwells in us and we in Him; already here below this union is effected by esctasy which is the crown of the life of charity uniting us to God by making us like to Him; but to attain to this beatifying union we must set out from the state of fear, divest ourselves, by way of humility, of all self-will, until at last, charity now taking the place of fear, we shall henceforth accomplish the will of God by love. Reconstructing the same synthesis in the inverse direction, starting from the "neque aliquid habere proprium" (XXXIII, p. 46, l. 10), we shall obtain a very serviceable schema of St. Bernard's doctrine.

True: but notice in the first place that here we have merely a kind of framework that will have to be filled up

if this collection of precepts is to become a genuine theology. [23]
Notice especially that the historian has no particular
difficulty in thus combining the materials borrowed by St.
Bernard to constitute the framework of his own doctrine,
since St. Bernard himself has shown him how to do it.
Should we ever have thought of linking them up in this
order if the synthesis he made of them did not exist? Evidently not. In the study of St. Bernard's sources this should
never be forgotten. For himself, he often gloried in having
advanced next to nothing in the way of doctrine that had
not been taught before, nor was this a mere show of mock
modesty on his part but the sincere expression of his habitual
attitude in the face of these problems; for so, he was convinced, it had to be. We might seek endlessly in earlier
writings for expressions and thoughts resembling his; even
outside the chief sources we have been analysing we could
always show that here he follows St. Ambrose, there St.
Augustine, [24] or again that he adopts suggestions from various
Commentaries on the Canticle of Canticles by Origen, for
example, or Bede; and after all we should have said no
more about him than has been said already. To extract
the mystical theology of St. Bernard from this heap of
scattered data in Scripture or the Fathers we should need
the spiritual life and speculative genius of St. Bernard
himself. Suppose we suppress it in imagination, what then
will remain to us in its place? The twelfth century made no
mistake on the matter; if, for ourselves, we hardly feel the
void that its absence would create, the contemporaries of
St. Bernard drank deep of the overflowing abundance of
its riches. For to set out to live to the end the Rule of St.
Benedict, even as to set out to live the Rule of St. Francis,
is to set out to live to the end the life of the Gospel; and
never will there be anything rarer than that, or more
original.

CHAPTER II

REGIO DISSIMILITUDINIS

THE study of the thought of St. Bernard is too often carried on in a fragmentary manner. It is not the best way of discussing the meaning of texts to begin by tearing them out of their context. This has happened notably in the case of his famous doctrine of the priority of egoistic or carnal love. Make it the starting-point of his whole system, as some are ready enough to do, and then it becomes easy to accuse St. Bernard of attempting to square the circle, that is to say of trying to excogitate a pure and disinterested love out of a love that by its very nature must needs be interested. The truth of the matter is altogether different; but we shall be able to perceive this only if we begin where St. Bernard himself began, that is to say with the question about what love ought to be, rather than with the question about what it is.

The sole true love, if you take it in itself, is the love of God; and if you ask why God should be loved, and how, St. Bernard's answer is the very same as that returned by Severus of Milevis to St. Augustine: the cause why we ought to love God is God Himself, and the due measure of love is to love Him without measure.[25] To the wise this deep word will be sufficient; but feeling himself, like the Apostle, a debtor also to the unwise, St. Bernard undertakes to set out the reasons that justify his thesis. Nothing could be easier than to justify it to Christians. For anyone who believes that God gave Himself to us for our salvation, it is very clear that He deserves our love and a love that knows no limit. But what shall we say when we come to the pagans? Now here St. Bernard's position is defined with the utmost clearness.

His demonstration is a systematic application of the method we have elsewhere called "Christian Socratism".[26] Look into yourself, seek to know yourself, and what do you find? Naturally in the first place the good things of the body, but besides these and far excelling them, the good things of the spirit. First we find what St. Bernard, in one word, calls the "dignitas", the human dignity *par excellence*, that is to say free-will. Why does it deserve to be called a "dignity"? For a two-fold reason: first because it raises man above all other living things, and then, next, because it gives him power to rule them and turn them to his own ends. Pre-eminent nobility, dominative power; such are the two characters that a man discovers in himself when, by way of this self-scrutiny, he becomes aware of his free-will.

But what are we to understand by that: to become aware of his free-will? To know himself free is obviously in the first place, to know. Thus man is unable to claim his own highest dignity without at the same time attaining to another, namely "science". But this science of our dignity would itself be incomplete were there not added the knowledge of Him from whom we hold it. The desire to discover the author of our dignity, and to cling to him firmly when found, that is precisely "virtue". And these three things must never be divorced. To be in possession of this dignity and to lack the science of it, that is to say to be free without knowing it—what glory is there in that? To possess both the dignity of free-will and the science, but without the virtue that prompts us to refer it all to God—that perhaps may be a kind of glory, but it would be better to call it a vain-glory, forgetful of the Apostle's word: "Quid habes quod non accepisti, quid gloriaris quasi non acceperis?" (I *Cor.*,

IV, 7). These three attributes of human nature would therefore lose all their own true nature if divorced.

And thus in the upshot it would be the man himself who would lose his. For he always stands in this two-fold peril, either of forgetting the "dignity" which constitutes his glory, or of forgetting that its source is not in himself. In the first case he forgets his glory, in the second he falls into vainglory. Now to forget that which invests him with his glory is to lose sight of the source of his own pre-eminence and power over the beasts of the field, and so in the end to become like them. For want of realizing his freedom he loses the prerogative of reason which distinguishes him from the other animals, and so exposes himself to the risk of becoming one of them himself. The first moment of self-knowledge, according to St. Bernard, lies in man's awareness of his own greatness: "And so it comes to pass that when a man no longer recognizes himself as a creature endowed with the high prerogative of reason, then he begins to be herded with the flock of beings without reason. Not knowing his own glory, which is all from within, the soul is led away by its own curiosity, and conforming itself to sensible things without, it becomes but one of the rest, not understanding that it has received more than the rest."[27]

Man then stands in grave peril when he forgets his greatness, but when he falls into the opposite error and forgets from whom his greatness comes, he stands on the brink of the abyss. "Utrumque ergo scias necesse est, et quid sis, et quod a te ipso non sis: ne aut omnino videlicet non glorieris, aut inaniter glorieris."[28] In the first case we lose our own true glory, in the second we glorify ourselves on account of that which is not ours. Now it is very noticeable that St. Bernard, following St. Paul, takes the greatest care to mark the universal obligation that lies on all men to come to the knowledge of God. *Ut sint inexcusabiles :* so that not only Christians, but even the very infidels, can and ought to know themselves as pre-eminent creatures, but, nevertheless, as creatures. The *Nosce te ipsum* is a precept that binds all the world. Every man, whether Christian or non-Christian, can and ought to know himself free—and that is his greatness, to be free and to know that he is so—but he ought also to understand that he is himself the author neither of his being nor his liberty, nor of his knowledge of the one or the other. And thence arises for every man equally the strict obligation to love God with his whole soul and his whole heart, and above all things, whether he be Christian or not. We have no need to know Christ to recognize this duty, we have only to know ourselves: *meretur ergo amari propter se ipsum Deus, et ab infideli ; qui etsi nesciat Christum, scit tamen seipsum.*[29]

It goes without saying that what is true of mankind in general is so much the more so of Christian man. Neither Jews nor pagans know themselves to be loved as the Christian knows himself to be loved; they know themselves created, but they do not know themselves redeemed, nor the price paid down. Every Christian therefore sees himself twice a debtor for himself to God, knowing himself made and remade, given to himself and given back: *datus et redditus, me pro me debeo et bis debeo.* There then he stands, not merely now in the same position as the pagan, but face to face with an issue still more difficult. Bound, as a man, to love God above all things, he is bound, as a Christian, to pay back to God the price of this infinite love wherewith He gave Himself for our salvation. How can he, a finite creature, quit himself of such a debt? We have therefore good reason indeed to say that the motive for loving God is God, since it was He who first loved us; and that the measure of our love for Him should exceed all measure. In default of an infinite love we owe Him at least a total love, a love without reserve, a love that exhausts all man's capacity for loving.

We see then what would have been the normal condition of our love if the Fall had not intervened to spoil it in all men whatsoever, and if the neglect of Christians themselves did not make them deaf to the call of grace. If, then, we would understand St. Bernard we must very carefully distinguish the definition of the love that man owes God, from the mere description of the love that in fact men offer Him. All that has just been said is true and remains true of a nature unfallen, or of a nature which, although fallen, still listens to the promptings of grace. All that we are about to say is true of the will of a fallen nature, forgetful or rebellious, in any case of a nature not yet restored. The necessities of fact which weigh upon us so heavily henceforth are moral necessities, which in no way diminish the metaphysical necessity of the primacy of divine love.[30]

That is why, having defined the love of God as the first love due from man, Bernard says elsewhere that love must needs develop progressively by way of a certain number of degrees, the first of which is egoistic as by definition. He calls it—and we should retain the name because it has something of a technical significance—*carnal love*. Its definition runs thus: "carnal love is that love by which man loves himself, for his own sake and before all else."[31] The assertion of the anteriority of this love, and even its priority with respect to every other, is constant in St. Bernard. It involves a very difficult problem of interpretation, for if we have here a necessity that is really inscribed in the very nature of man it is not easy to see how we can ever be rid of it. In such a case he would be doomed by his own nature to give place to the love of self before the love of God. Now, as we have already said, man is bound to love God before all things. To demand, then, that he give place to another love before that with which his very nature compels him of necessity to begin, would seem to place him in an impossible situation. St. Bernard, however, so often asserts both the necessity and the demand that he cannot have failed to see the difficulty. Let us go a step further: this very difficulty is itself the whole *raison d'être* of his doctrine; for if man's love were directed to its proper object of its own spontaneous impulse, then no problem of love would arise at all. St. Bernard could hardly have failed to recognize the very question he was so unweariedly engaged in discussing. We must therefore try to see in what sense each of these two loves is first with respect to the other. There is no room for doubt about the answer. The love of God is first in right, and carnal love is first in fact. How to return from the state in which we stand in fact, and recover the state in which we ought to stand as of right? There lies the whole question.

Let us note in the first place that in affirming the priority of carnal love Bernard is guaranteed in his position by the authority of St. Paul. Again and again in his sermons he recalls the famous text: *prius quod animale, deinde quod spirituale* (I *Cor.*, XV, 46). It is important to note this doctrinal filiation at the outset, so that we may orientate our interpretation of the Cistercian texts in the right direction. Here, as everywhere when we are dealing with medieval citations, we must look upon the latter as a summary indication intended to refer us to the whole passage in which it occurs.[32] It runs thus: "Yet that was not first which was spiritual, but that which is natural: afterwards that which is spiritual. The first man was of the earth, earthly: the second man from heaven, heavenly. Such as is the earthly, such also are the earthly: and such as is the heavenly, such also are they that are heavenly. Therefore as we have borne the image of the earthly, let us bear also the image of the heavenly. Now this I say, brethren, that flesh and blood cannot possess the kingdom of God; neither shall corruption possess incorruption."[33] What Bernard therefore especially wants to recall is that if man is to receive the immortality which Jesus Christ has promised to bestow, and of which His own resurrection is the pledge, then he must needs submit to a transformation which shall raise him from carnal things to spiritual; but that if this transformation is a necessity, it is so because there is something that has to be changed in man, and what has to be changed must be there before that which changes it. The earthly man, that which is earthly—there precisely is the thing that is to receive the heavenly man and so to be renewed to the image of God. In us, then, animality comes first; but in what sense?

In a twofold sense; first in that of a natural necessity, for the rest heavily aggravated by sin, and then in the sense of a morbid inclination, not natural therefore at all, but there by way of addition to the necessity of the nature. Let us draw out the distinction; and first as to the natural necessity. It arises from the fact that man is not a pure spirit, but a being composed of a soul and a body. In this connection the word "flesh" is first to be taken in the immediate sense of "body." From this standpoint, the anteriority of carnal love with respect to the love of God means simply that man finds himself compelled first of all to take thought for the needs of the body. And that is what happens in fact. The new-born infant is wholly preoccupied with the body, and so remains for years before there can be any question of turning his desires towards the things of the spirit. And the adult is in similar case; for, finally, not even the rudest ascetic can give himself up to the contemplation of divine things for any longer than the flesh allows. This primary necessity throws ramifications over the whole field of human life, giving rise to the arts—of clothing for instance, of building, of curing bodily ills, and in short all those major occupations that absorb most of the energies of the human race. It is needless to run through the list;

we have but to live to become aware of the imperious
demands of this necessity: *ipsa nos erudit experientia, ipsa
vexatio dat intellectum.* The true name for this love of the
body is *necessity.* And so, in St. Bernard's thought, there
is very certainly a question of a purely natural necessity,
compelling us, before everything else, to serve the needs
of the body.[34] Carnal love, taken in this sense, is opposed
to the love of God only as an infirmity inherent in the animal
nature, especially when fallen; man may suffer from it,
he may hope to be delivered from it in another life, but it
is a congenital weakness not to be overcome in this life,
and for which he cannot hold himself responsible.

The question begins to wear a rather more complicated
aspect when we consider that although this necessity is
not in itself a fault, it weighs upon us much more heavily
as a result of original sin. And that is a fact, but a fact
to be interpreted; for this chastisement of a fault is not
itself imputed to us as a fault. Men, as we may admit,
could hardly be born adult, and so would need in any
event to pass through a period of merely animal existence
which would leave the problem intact. The constitutive
animality of human nature being out of our power to
eliminate, the anteriority of animal life with respect to
spiritual life in the human being is in the same case. St.
Bernard says no more than that when he asserts, in this
first sense, the anteriority of carnal love with respect to
every other love. The fact creates a difficulty, an embarrassment, doubtless it makes it practically impossible for the
love of God to expand freely in this life, but it implies
no essential subjection of soul to body in man such as would
prevent him from preferring the soul to the body it animates,
and still less from preferring God to self.[35]

St. Bernard's terminology, moreover, is much more
technical than one might suppose. Whenever this first

form of carnal love is present in the text it is always easily recognizable. Its distinguishing characteristic is expressed by the word *necessitas*, and its mode of action on the will by the term *urget*. It is therefore easily distinguishable from. the other form of carnal love which we have now to examine, and which arises from concupiscence; for the technical terms that refer to it, whether in itself or in its effects, are not the same. Its distinguishing characteristic is expressed by the word *cupiditas*, and the manner in which it acts on the will by *trahit*. Thus the necessity of the nature, and the needs it engenders, are always to be opposed to cupidity and the allurements it brings in its train.

As the normal state of the body is health, so the normal state of the heart is purity: *sicut autem corporis natura est sanitas, ita cordis est puritas*. It is unhappily a fact that human desire only very rarely observes the limits of either. Instead of remaining canalized in the bed of natural necessity the will goes off in pursuit of useless pleasures, that is to say of pleasures not desirable because required for the due exercise of the functions that preserve life, but pleasures simply desired for their own sake and as pleasures. That the will has overstepped the limits of natural necessity may be recognized by this sign: that it no longer sees any reason to keep its desires within bounds. St. Bernard has described this quest of pleasure and the weariness that goes along with it, in pages on which the historian of ideas may regret that he is not called upon to comment; for they are as beautiful as they are clear.[36] What, on the contrary, has to be emphasized is the new sense in which the priority of carnal love over all other love is here to be taken. For in fact St. Bernard often puts down this anteriority, not now to the account of natural necessity, but to that of this cupidity just referred to. Why, in this second sense, is the will compelled to yield first to carnal love? Here once more

St. Paul will furnish the answer: because we are carnal and born of the *concupiscence* of the flesh. If the animal precedes the spiritual in this second sense, it is not now because nature demands it, but because, on the contrary, this nature has been corrupted by sin.[37]

Here occurs the only point on which we have to note a certain lack of precision in St. Bernard's terms, and it is undeniably awkward. He uses the same word *necesse* to designate two distinct states of the will, without distinguishing the two meanings it then covers. The natural is the normal. Morally, it is natural for man to love above all things God, Who is the author of nature; and this he did spontaneously before transgression, when the Divine likeness was not yet effaced in him by sin. In fact, on the other hand, he has of necessity to begin by taking care for his bodily subsistence, and in this sense it is true to say that carnal love must necessarily take precedence over every other love; but that does not mean that man's love for his body consists naturally in preferring it to God. There can be precedence without preference, and in such a case the love in question is not culpable; or again, if concupiscence be mingled in it, there may be precedence with preference, and in that case the preference is necessary but against nature. If then, as occasionally happens, St. Bernard refers to the necessary character of the love of concupiscence, he uses the word in the sense of moral necessity, as St. Augustine also commonly does, to designate the nature, not now in its essential definition, but as in the state of fact in which it finds itself placed in consequence of original sin. If we fail to distinguish these two types of necessity we entangle St. Bernard in inextricable difficulties. We may introduce them into his system under colour of this imprecision of vocabulary, but manifestly they were never in his thought.[38]

Cupidity, thus distinguished from nature, involves a

complete inversion of the order of values,[39] and ruins the hierarchy of goods established by God. Not content with beginning with the flesh, it gives place to it before all else because it prefers it. St. Bernard very well marks the distinction between the two cases when he observes that we cannot even ask God to deliver us from the necessity which keeps us bound to the body; all we can do is to ask Him to deliver us from "our necessities", that is to say to make it possible for us to satisfy them one by one as they make themselves felt. To be freed from *the* natural necessity, that, for us, would be to cease to be men, or at any rate terrestrial men, for then we should no longer be in possession of our bodies. To ask, on the contrary, to be freed from cupidity is a perfectly legitimate prayer, since this cupidity is no part of our nature, but a deformation of the nature. "The soul begs its bread of another because it has forgotten how to eat its own; it runs after the things of earth simply for lack of meditating the things of heaven."[40]

This adventitious, and, so to speak, accidental character of concupiscence goes far to explain why it is always baulked of its satisfaction. For it conforms itself neither to the nature of things, nor to the nature of man. The body is pampered with more than it needs; and once the sole natural limit has been overstepped there is no longer any limit to be looked for from the side of things. On the other hand, that to which concupiscence looks for satisfaction is, by definition, incapable of giving it, since it is not the thing for which the will is made. It has committed itself, therefore, to a false path; and liberation is not to be effected by going further down it, but only, on the contrary, by disengaging itself altogether from these blind alleys. Now that is not to be done except by a movement of "conversion".

A movement, for the rest, to which everything invites us; for man has no choice between that and the deepest

c

misery. St. Bernard never ceases to insist on the inevitable
distress to which we condemn ourselves when we walk in
the ways of cupidity. Whoever gives himself up to that
enters upon what St. Bernard, in another of these Scriptural
metaphors which for him have an almost technical significance, calls "the circle of the impious". For they revolve
in a vicious circle. Continually urged on by desire, they
naturally go in search of all that may serve to slake it, but
always they pursue it by running endlessly round and round
the same circle, instead of breaking out of it once and for
all, and entering the straight way that would bring them
nearer to their end. No longer now to one of these false
ends where we consume and are consumed, but to the
end where we are consummated: *fini dico non consumptioni
sed consummationi*. What we have to do, instead of running
about the world and trying first one thing and then another,
is rather to seek to attain to the Lord of the world. A man
perhaps might begin to think of that when he had satisfied
his desire for the whole earth, and come to be possessed at
last of all things—of all things, that is, save the Source of
all. Then, by the very law of his own cupidity, whereby
he always wearies of what he has and hungers for what he
has not, he might perhaps at last despise all earthly goods
and cling to the one thing that would now be lacking:
God. But the world is great, and life is short. Why follow
a road so hard and circuitous? The sole remedy for the evil
is to allow reason to take charge of sense instead of trailing
miserably after it.[41] For what in fact does reason teach?

    That the very impotence of our desire to achieve satis-
faction must needs have a positive significance. This
strange restlessness that moves a man to abandon the good
he possesses in order eternally to go in search of another
he lacks—this, besides being a fact, is it not also a question?
Undoubtedly; and here is the answer—we are attracted by

the Good. The restlessness, the instability of desire, are nothing but the excess of a love too great for the thing that it loves, because mistaken in its object. How can it halt at any finite good, this love that can be satisfied by nothing short of an infinite good? Created by God and for God, our human love may refuse with good reason to break off its unfinished quest until at last it shall have found the sole Object that can finally set it at rest.[42] Here, then, we hold the key to the mystery; all that remains is to see why it arises. Whence this madness? Why this stubborn will of the impious man to turn for ever in the "circuit" where his strength is spent, desiring without knowing, and nevertheless rejecting, the thing that would bring him to his end? Cupidity is but a love of God become unaware of itself. But why, then, is man in this state?

The reason is, to adopt a comparison more than once employed by St. Bernard, that man is an exile. He no longer inhabits the land of his birth. We might say, in terms but slightly different, that he lives in a climate that is not his. As God made him, he was a noble creature—*nobilis creatura*—and he was so because God created him to His own image. Disfigured by original sin, man has in fact exiled himself from the Land of Likeness to enter into the Land of Unlikeness: *Regio dissimilitudinis*. There we have the first inversion of order from which all the evil has arisen. Conversion reversed, conversion for ever "execrable", by which man exchanged the glory of the Divine image for the shame of the earthly image, peace with God and with himself for war against God and against himself, liberty under the law of charity for slavery under the law of his own self-will. We might go still further and say that man, by that conversion, has exchanged heaven for hell; a word in which all the foregoing is summed up, for hell is at once self-will, and its consequence, unlikeness to God, and war set up between creature and Creator. Now this evil that

Adam brought into the world is hereditary, and the proper
object of the Christian life is to wage war on its effects.
We are born corrupt: "Engendered in sin, we engender
sinners; born debtors, we give birth to debtors; corrupted,
to the corrupt; in slavery, to slaves. . . . We are crippled
souls from the moment when we enter into this world, and
as long as we live there, and we shall still be so when we
leave it; from the sole of our foot to the crown of our head
there is no health in us."[43] If cupidity draws us on endlessly
and inevitably from finite goods to finite, this is because
man's nature is no longer in the state in which it ought to
be; each man born henceforth is born deformed.

At once the question rises in the mind—is the evil irremed-
iable? No reply is possible except by way of a closer analysis
of the nature of the Divine likeness, also of the ravages
left there by sin. As soon as we follow St. Bernard into this
field we come at once face to face with a doctrine in which
the combined influences of St. Augustine and St. Anselm
are easily recognizable, while its profoundly original
character is none the less evident. He borrows; but all that
he borrows is ordered in such a way as to prepare the solution
of his own particular problem, namely: to give a coherent
doctrinal interpretation and a complete theological justification of the Cistercian life, so that the doctrine, born of and
nurtured on this life, may nurture and give it life in its turn.

In full accord with St. Augustine, St. Bernard places the
image of God in the mind of man: *mens* ;[44] but while Augustine seeks it for preference in intellectual cognition where
the Divine illumination attests the continuous presence of the
Creator to the creature, St. Bernard puts it rather in the
will, and very especially in freedom. However, here again
we have to distinguish. Scripture says that God made man
"to His image and likeness" (*Gen.*, I, 26). Each of these words
has a weight of its own and they have to be separately defined.

God created man that He might associate him with His own beatitude; all our history begins with this free decision. Now to be happy we have to enjoy; in order to enjoy we require a will; this will enjoys only by laying hold of its object by an act of consent; and to consent is to be free. That is why, creating man in order to associate him with His own beatitude, God created him with the gift of free-will (*liberum arbitrium*), and it is chiefly on account of his freedom that man is this "noble" creature, made to the image of God, and capable of entering into society with God.

This gift of liberty made by the Creator to His creature is, furthermore, complex, for it implies three liberties, one of them being immutable, inalienable, and the other two not. Consider free-will in itself. It may be resolved into two elements, namely voluntary consent and a power of moral decision. The liberty of free-will is to be identified in the first place with the power of consenting or refusing consent, a power inseparable from the will as such. A voluntary agent is able to accept such and such a thing or to refuse it, to say yes or no, and this in virtue of the sole fact that he is gifted with a will. It is this natural liberty, inherent in the very essence of volition, that is called "freedom from necessity"—*libertas a necessitate*. The expression therefore signifies above all that the idea of the voluntary is radically incompatible with that of constraint, and that is why it is also sometimes called "freedom from constraint"—*libertas a coactione*. For whatever the external circumstances may be which contribute to bring a decision to maturity, when nevertheless the decision is taken it is very certainly the will that consents, and it is strictly contradictory to suppose that anyone can "consent in spite of himself". So utterly inalienable is this privilege of freedom from every voluntary agent that it can in no wise be less in us than it is in God Himself: "Freedom from necessity belongs to all

reasonable creatures, whether good or bad, equally and
indifferently with God. Nor is this freedom lost or diminished
either by sin or by misery, nor is it greater in the righteous
than in the unrighteous, or more complete in the angels
than in men. For just as the consent of the human will,
when grace turns it towards the good, becomes thereby
freely good, and makes the man free in doing good, that is
to say leads him to will it and does not force him to it in spite
of himself—so also the consent of the will, when spontaneously turned aside to evil, no less makes a man as free as
spontaneous in evil doing, since he is brought to it by his
will and not made evil by any coercion. And as the angels
in heaven, and indeed God Himself, remain good freely,
that is to say of their own will and by no extrinsic necessity,
so in just the same way the devil fell headlong into evil and
there remains freely, that is to say in virtue of a voluntary
movement and not of any external compulsion. Freedom of
will subsists therefore even where thought is enslaved, and
as fully in the wicked as in the good, although in the latter
in a better ordered state; it remains also as complete after
its own mode, in the creature as in the Creator, though in
Him it is more powerful."45

We see then well enough how radically St. Bernard is
opposed to any doctrine of a slave-will. If, in his affirmation
of freedom, he goes so far as to maintain its existence even
in the damned, that is because it is indestructible by any
wickedness whatsoever. And if it be objected that this
henceforth inefficacious free-will is now only a word void
of meaning, we are confronted with this further fundamental
thesis which makes of the free-will of man, even after sin,
even in damnation, an analogue of the free-will of the blessed
in heaven, of the angels, and of God Himself. It is a point
on which we cannot sufficiently insist: this freedom from
necessity, whatever may now be its miserable condition

among us, amounts to no less in the human act than it does in the act of the angel. Taken in itself, independently of the conditions that qualify it, the will of the just who adhere to good, of the sinner who consents to evil, or of the damned who confirms himself in it for ever, lays hold of its object no less efficaciously than does the will by which God eternally wills His own perfection and His own beatitude. That is why this freedom from necessity, which is altogether one with the faculty of consent, and consequently with the will, far from being, or being able to become, a negligible factor in our constitution, is on the contrary a rightful title of honour, of which no reasonable creature, in whatsoever state he may be, can ever be deprived. The creature may so act as to degrade it, but can never lose it without thereby also ceasing to exist. And that also is why this freedom, inalienable, indestructible, is that whereby we are chiefly made in the image of God. This image also therefore is inalienable, indestructible, like the freedom from constraint and the will itself: "Hence it is, perhaps, that free-will alone suffers no defect or diminution of itself, because it is in this free-will above all else that there seems to be impressed a kind of substantial image of the eternal and unchangeable Godhead. For it had indeed a beginning, but it will know no destruction; neither will it be in any way increased by righteousness or glory, nor suffer diminution from sin or from misery. What, save Eternity itself, could bear a greater likeness to eternity?" [46]

Up to this point all is clear. We have only to add this inevitable complication, that if all we have just been describing in free-will is inalienable, there is nothing else in us that is. Now there are other things in us. Suppress freedom from necessity and you suppress the will, you suppress therefore the man himself. But although we cannot imagine a man incapable of willing, we can very well imagine one incapable of willing the good. Let us suppose him in fact incapable of willing the good, that does not prove that he now lacks free-will, but something else that remains to be defined. Suppose even that he is capable of willing, and of willing the good, but incapable of doing the good that he wills—in that case too he still retains his free-will, but now a third thing is wanting. [47] What then is the missing element?

To settle that point let us resume and complete our analysis of free-will (*liberum arbitrium*). It is in the first place, as we have said, a freedom coessential with the will itself, a freedom to consent or not consent; and this is what is expressed in the word *liberum*. But next, it is a power to bring a judgment to bear upon our consent, that is, on our will itself, and to declare it good if it be good, evil if evil; and this is what is expressed in the word *arbitrium*. In a sense we might say that it is the will that judges itself, nor would this be at all incorrect, since the will is a will only in virtue of its close association with the reason; otherwise it would be no longer a will, but an appetite. It remains true, none the less, that strictly speaking it is the *liberum* that consents and the *arbitrium* that decides. Now to decide (*arbitrer*) is to judge, and just as every man, as man, is always capable of willing, so is he always capable of bringing a judgment to bear upon his voluntary decisions. St. Bernard, who here undoubtedly has St. Paul's *ut sint inexcusabiles* in mind, shows himself extremely firm on this point: that what we should nowadays call the voice of conscience is never extinguished in man. Always capable of distinguishing good from evil, we are always capable of judging our own decisions, and we have therefore always with us our free *arbitrium*. Only, to consent and to judge the consent is not yet all. We can will evil and know it to be evil, and choose nevertheless to do it. To the "judgment" there is therefore added a

"choice", and this act of choosing (*eligere*) is itself the upshot
of a deliberation (*consilium*). Now, as a result of original
sin, we are not of necessity always capable of choosing the
good or of avoiding evil, even when reason has judged them
as such. We must therefore say that if the *liberum arbitrium*
is never lacking, we can nevertheless, and without ceasing
to be men, lack the *liberum consilium*. And supposing further
that knowing what is good we choose to do it, we can still
want strength to carry it out. If this strength fails us we
shall indeed retain the *liberum arbitrium* and the *liberum
consilium*, but, along with the *posse*, it is the *liberum complacitum* which will have disappeared. [48]

There then we have man, a complex structure, and one
in which all the component elements are far from being
equally indestructible. The central point in St. Bernard's
doctrine is that the Image of God in us can never be lost,
and that is why man remains man, after transgression as
before: *ipse liber sui propter voluntatem, ipse judex sui propter
rationem;* but the Likeness to God in us can be lost, and
that is why, when he lost the virtues bestowed on him by
God in order that his deliberations, his choices, and his
actions might follow the judgment of reason, man lost also
his Divine likeness. Always gifted with free-will, he has no
longer either the liberty of choosing which would set him
free from sin, or that of acting in accordance with his choice
which would set him free from the misery of an impotent
will. In short, the *libertas a necessitate* remains to us, but we
have lost the *libertas a peccato* and the *libertas a miseria*.
By abusing the first, man has lost the other two; he has
preserved the Image, and the two Likenesses have disappeared. [49] Why? Because, unlike the former, the two
latter kinds of freedom are susceptible of degrees. Man
could therefore receive them in a certain measure, according
to a certain proportion, which might have been greater

C*

and could also become less. He would have received them in a
supreme degree had he been so totally exempted from sin and
from misery that he could not possibly fall into them at all.

God might have created man in this state, and in that
case, favoured with these two freedoms in their fullness, he
could never have lost them. Then, from the first moment
of his creation, he would have been confirmed in good as
are the angels to-day, and the blessed in heaven. But there
is another and lower degree, consisting in the power to sin
or not to sin, the power to suffer or not to suffer; and this
was precisely the state in which God in fact created him.
Human nature, by its own fault, has fallen from the possibility in which it stood of not sinning into the impossibility
of not sinning, and from the possibility of not suffering into
the impossibility of not suffering. A fault freely committed,
for which therefore man is wholly responsible, and which has
stripped him, by an inevitable consequence, of those virtues
which would have enabled him to avoid, had he willed it,
both sin and misery.[50] Now, as we have said, these two freedoms constitute the Divine likeness in man; when therefore
man lost them he lost the likeness and drove himself into exile,
into the desert of unlikeness, through which there still wanders
to-day the crowd of disfigured human beings. Let us try to
make clear the precise nature of the ill that afflicts them.

Man is made indefectibly to the image of God. However,
he is simply *made* to the image—one alone *is* this Image
Itself, namely the Word, because the Word alone is an
adequate and subsistent expression of the Father. Albeit
therefore man's greatness consists in bearing the image of
God, this greatness is nevertheless there by way of gift.
An exalted creature, capable of participating in the Divine
Majesty—*celsa creatura in capacitate majestatis*—his dignity does
not belong to him as of full right. To express the manner
in which the soul's greatness appertains to its nature without

being identical with it, St. Bernard adopts a terminology rather apt to give us pause. This greatness, he says, is the "form" of the soul, and no form is that of which it is the form, in spite of the fact that it remains inseparably bound up with it. The thing, then, that he calls "form" is evidently not Aristotle's essential form; and we know, on the other hand, that neither can it be a simple accident, for accidents are separable from the substance—as, for instance, the Divine likenesses we have lost. Accordingly, the "form" here in question can only be a *proprium*, that is to say a qualification inseparable from the subject in which it resides and from which it remains nevertheless distinct.[51] Thus the thing affected by the diminution of stature imposed on man by sin cannot be his "greatness". There remain for consideration the likenesses.

One word may serve to designate them: man's "rectitude" —erection, uprightness[52]. The soul is "great" inasmuch as it is capable of participation in the Divine life, but it is "upright" inasmuch as it desires to participate in this life. The soul's uprightness, like its greatness, is distinct from the soul, but uprightness and greatness are furthermore distinct from each other, and the proof of this is that although the soul's greatness is inseparably bound up with the soul, its uprightness is not so. Incapable of ceasing to be great and to God's image under pain of ceasing to exist, it can nevertheless cease to be upright and to His likeness without being destroyed. To cease to be that it has only to lose its virtues, that is to say to lose its love for eternal things and to begin to prefer earthly, temporal, perishable things. Now what is eternal is God's portion, remaining essentially His even when offered to us: what is temporal, earthly, is man's share, remaining man's even when God invites him to a higher heritage. Rejecting the divine for the sake of the earthly, man accordingly demands his own portion in preference to God's, and, in so doing, loses his upright stature, stoops, bends down, turns away from heaven to which God had erected him, to bow himself down to earth to which his animal nature attracts him. Now what exactly is his new state?

From "recta", which once it was, the soul has now become "curva"—another technical term which was to have a considerable vogue later on.[53] However, in virtue of the distinction introduced above, the loss of its rectitude does not involve the soul in the loss of its greatness. Stripped of that love of eternal things which constituted its uprightness, it still remains capable of it nevertheless; were it not so, then, after trangression, no hope of salvation would remain. Happily that is not the case. Just as Adam was apt, as an image of God, to receive also from God His likeness in addition, so also do we remain capable of receiving it anew, if it should please God to restore it. And this has to be thoroughly understood because it forms, so to speak, the bed-rock of all the Cistercian mysticism, it is from this point that the soul has to set out "ut ad amplexus Verbi fidenter accedat".[54] The thing that so disfigures us is the earthward curvature, the loss of all relish for Divine things, which is charity; instead of being moved by love we are henceforth subject to fear, and not only to the fear of God, which is needful in any event, but to the fear of God's chastisements, which we might have avoided. Nevertheless, the unlikeness has not effaced the image; fear has not annihilated love, servitude to sin has not destroyed our natural freedom; in short, the ills we suffer by our own fault are not simply substituted for the good things that God has heaped upon us, but rather cover them over as with another vesture; they hide, but do not eliminate. Underneath this hard crust that conceals it, indeformable, indestructible, there still subsists the image, that is to say human nature itself, arrayed in its noblest character— freedom.[55]

Let us now dive more deeply into the human heart, since St. Bernard himself would not refrain but would probe with his scalpel into the very hidden ulcer that consumes us. What precisely is this "curvature" which turns us aside from God and twists us back upon ourselves? How shall we recognize it and trace out its effects? We have but to examine the particular movements of our will. They are of two different types, and we may say accordingly that the will is two-fold: *common*, or *proper*. These terms of course do not mean that we have two different faculties of willing, but they imply on the other hand that there are two different modes of willing, the first being called *voluntas communis* and the other *voluntas propria*. They stand in opposition *recta fronte*, and this antithetical character will enable us to define the one in terms of the other.

Voluntas communis, the common will, is nothing else than charity. For the chief characteristic of charity lies in an eagerness to share with others the good things that it enjoys.[56] To share them is not to lose them, but on the contrary to keep them the more surely and even to increase them, as we shall have further occasion to note. The contrary of this *voluntas communis*, that is to say the *voluntas propria*, is therefore a refusal to have anything whatsoever in common with others, a decision to will nothing save for ourselves and for our own sake. A wise decision as it might appear, but really foolish; for when a man's heart is filled with this "proper will", then, making shipwreck of charity, his will becomes alienated from God's will, and by that very fact he shuts himself out from participation in the Divine life. The "curvature" of the soul is therefore this "proper will", that is to say the twisting back upon self of a charity which has degenerated into cupidity.[57]

The ground of the opposition of "proper will" to charity is now apparent. God is charity; the "proper will", setting itself up against charity, wages therefore a relentless warfare against God. First, by becoming "proper", by turning back on self, it withdraws itself from the dominion of Him Whom it ought to serve as its Author. Furthermore, it seizes upon and makes a spoil of all that belongs to God; it would lay hold of the whole universe had it the power, and we may be quite sure that not even the whole universe would serve its turn. Not content, moreover, with grasping at God's creation, it turns round upon God to deny and abolish Him as far as in it lies. It cannot make Him not to be, but wishes at least that He were not, for when man harbours a hope that God takes no notice of his sins, or lacks the will to punish him, or the power, what is this but to want to see God deprived of His knowledge, His justice, or His power, that is to say to want Him to be no longer God? "Malice most cruel and detestable, hoping that God may lose His power, His wisdom, and His justice.[58] An abominable wild beast, the worst of wolves, the fiercest of hyenas. This is a most unclean leprosy of the soul for which we ought to plunge ourselves forthwith into Jordan and imitate Him Who came not to do His own will: *non mea voluntas*, as He said in His Passion, *sed tua fiat!*"

Nevertheless there is a leprosy that is more pernicious still, since it is one that touches free-will in its rational constituent itself. It consists in "proper counsel"—*proprium consilium*. For we have seen that free-will is, at one and the same time, a power of voluntary consent, and a power of rational judgment. Now the pathology of the soul is rigorously modelled on its anatomy, and St. Bernard, who is but little disposed to be curious in sterile questions, here, where the issue so deeply concerns the interests of the spiritual life, displays a very remarkable power of systematization. The disorders of the "proper will" depend immediately upon the voluntary constituent in our freedom; now this is none other than the freedom from necessity, that is to say it is the image of God in the soul, which we know to be indestructible. It is therefore evident that the disorders of which the will is the seat, since they can in no way touch its essence, must be of a secondary character; their cause, of which they are but repercussions or effects, must lie elsewhere. But neither can we hesitate about where to situate this basic disorder. Man lost his likeness to God in losing his virtues; these virtues resided in that which brings into our freedom the element of *liberum consilium*; it is therefore in the *consilium* that the root of the evil is to be found; and the hidden source of our "proper will" can be nothing but *proprium consilium*.

The evil is formidable, for the more we are wedded to our own opinion (*sensum proprium*), the worse we are and the more we believe ourselves righteous. There is no disposition of the soul that more easily brings with it an illusory sense of righteousness, for it sins not by lack of zeal, but by lack of knowledge; it is in truth a misdirected zeal. It is this that we see openly flaunted in the abetters of heresies and schisms. True, it exalts righteousness—not God's however, but its own. "It works in those who are zealous for God but not according to knowledge; they become obstinate in error to the point of refusing to listen to anyone. These are the destroyers of unity, the enemies of peace; void of charity, swollen with vanity, full of self-complacency and great in their own eyes, they ignore the righteousness of God, and would set up their own in its place. What greater pride hath the heart of man than thus to prefer his own judgment to that of the whole congregation, as if he alone had the Spirit of God?"[59] At bottom, then, this *sensum proprium* is idolatry, self-adoration, and revolt against God.

There, then, is the root of all the evil. Reason, setting itself above God, has perverted its own power of choice, warped its capacity to rejoice only in the good and introduced disorder into the will. Inasmuch as the *consilium* and *complacitum* of reason are diseased, there can be no health for free-will. That is why, losing uprightness of counsel, and, in consequence, the Divine likeness, man's will has lost its *libertas a peccato;* and losing the uprightness of the *complacitum*, man is henceforth incapable of rejoicing in good even when his will would accomplish it, that is to say he has lost his *libertas a miseria.* That moreover is why ascesis and a mortified life remain painful even to him who embraces them with a good heart. We are able, with the aid of grace, to overcome the flesh, but the soul suffers, because she no longer knows how to accomplish in joy what before the first transgression she would have done without effort.

Such is the condition of those who live in the Land of Unlikeness. They are not happy there. Wandering, hopelessly revolving, in the "circuit of the impious" those who tread this weary round suffer not only the loss of God but also the loss of themselves. They dare no longer look their own souls in the face; could they do it they would no longer recognize themselves. For when the soul has lost its likeness to God it is no longer like itself: *inde anima dissimilis Deo, inde dissimilis est et sibi ;* [60] a likeness which is no longer like its original is like itself no more. It is true that it remains an image. In the deepest abyss of its misery this truly divine thing, freedom of will, continues to sparkle at its centre like a jewel in gold. But that only fills up the cup of its wretchedness, since, feeling itself at one and the same time both the same and yet different, an image still but incapable of regaining its lost beauty, it remains capable of passing judgment on its own deformity. Let then the impious man consider himself, let him look steadily at this diseased countenance all corroded with leprosy; will he then still dare to pretend that he bears the likeness of God? Much rather would he cry out with the

Psalmist: "Lord, who is like unto Thee?" (*Ps.* XXXIV,
10). Thus in this man the indestructible image of God
passes judgment on the ruined likeness, thus the eternal
likeness mourns the likeness lost: *nam manet prima similitudo,
et ideo illa plus displicet, quod ista manet.*[61] How arise from
this depth of wretchedness, how recover the likeness to God?

The reconstitution in the human soul of these three kinds
of freedom demands the extinction of the "proper will";
this proper will can be extinguished only if the "intention"
yields itself up to the guidance of charity; but the rectification
of the intention demands that man be no longer wedded
to his own opinion (*proprium sensum*) and that reason should
submit herself to the light of truth. Charity in the intention,
truth in the election; gentle as doves, but prudent as serpents;
prudence in the first place: *oculus videlicet cordis, non solum
pius qui fallere nolit, sed et cautus qui fallere non possit*[62]—such
are the first counsels of St. Bernard to the soul that seeks
herself in God. The "blindness" of the reason is the first
ill to be cured for whosoever would find a remedy for the
"perversity" of the will.[63] And what then will light up
the inner eye and bring it back to upright counsel? Faith;
not conviction merely, but faith, and the true faith. "All
that is not of faith is sin" (*Rom.* XIV, 23). If we accept
this faith it will deliver us to truth, a knowledge much more
sure than that of which Abelard's reasoning goes in pursuit;
lighting up reason, it will eliminate *consilium proprium;* the will
now opens itself to charity, which drives out *propria voluntas*,
and the Divine likeness shines out anew in the soul so lately disfigured. The remedy is sure, but the cure is long. It may be
taken in hand wherever you will, but there are certain places
of special predilection where it may be brought about more
easily than elsewhere. These are the monasteries. Bernard
looks about him for the one place where it may be brought
about most easily of all. He does not hesitate. It is Cîteaux.

CHAPTER III

SCHOLA CARITATIS

WHAT was it then that Bernard and his companions were asking of Cîteaux when they knocked at the door of the monastery in 1112? It is not to be supposed that they brought with them any ready-made doctrine, that is to say the one that lies before us to-day in the writings of the Abbot of Clairvaux. Quite the contrary. These young men came to be instructed in the principles of the Christian life and to learn to put them into practice. At any rate we can say that it was not without serious reflection, or without knowing what they were doing, that after their months of retreat at Châtillon-sur-Seine they addressed themselves to Cîteaux. The anonymous monk of Clairvaux who drew up later on the *Exordium magnum Ordinis Cisterciensis* has given us so clear an explanation of the meaning of the Cistercian life for those who embraced it in those early years that if we would understand the motives that actuated them we can do no better than to turn to him.

As its originators conceived it the Cistercian reform was in no sense an innovation on the Benedictine life, the Benedictine life was no innovation on the Christian life. For true followers of Christ there is no longer anything left to be invented, but there may be, and too often there is, a good deal that needs to be recovered. That is what Bernard, Stephen Harding and Robert de Molesme were doing. They returned to St. Benedict, and by way of St. Benedict to the form of the perfect life as practised in the primitive Church. No one, even in the twelfth century, entertained any naïve illusion about a primitive Church in which all the members were perfect Christians. The number of the saints had always been small. The Gospel, since it was preached to all the world, had never been received save in the measure of the capacity of the recipients; but it was precisely on that account that even from the earliest days there was formed a small inner group of perfect imitators of Christ, whose presence, acting like a leaven, worked through the whole lump and kept it from corruption. Immediately after the death of Christ the Apostles themselves would seem to have formed a group of this kind, that is to say a school of masters whose very life was a lesson, who, for the rest, taught nothing save the Gospel offered to all, and whom few nevertheless cared to join precisely on account of the rigorous way in which they put its teachings into practice. "And they were all with one accord in Solomon's porch. But of the rest no man durst join himself to them, but the people magnified them" (*Acts* V, 12-13). These then were the first monks, and from their example we learn what from the first had always been the meaning of the monastic life: that is, the life of an élite who, by preaching and by example, maintain the full spirit of the Gospel in a world unable to bear it.[64]

The name attached to this group by the author of the *Exordium* is typically Benedictine; it is a school, the School of the Primitive Church: *schola primitivae Ecclesiae.* Already at the outset of his Rule, St. Benedict had proclaimed that he intended to open a school of the service of the Lord, *dominici schola servitii.*[65] The Cistercians had many good reasons of their own for adopting the expression and investing it with new significance. Twelfth-century France was filled with schools of profane science and ancient letters. There was not only Saint-Vorles, where the young Bernard pursued his studies, with a programme that might well

astonish, not to say disquiet, a soul so eager for Christ—
there were Paris, Reims, Laon, Chartres, so many other
famous names but always the same masters; Cicero, Vergil,
Ovid, Horace, eloquent spokesmen of a world that had never
read the Gospel. Why not invoke another master, the only
master who has the words of eternal life? *Unus est enim
magister vester* (*Matt.* XXIII, 8); for man has but one master,
Christ: *magister vester unus est, Christus* (*Matt.* XXIII, 10).
Cîteaux, Clairvaux, and Signy were then to stand over
against Reims, Laon, Paris and Chartres, schools against
schools, and to vindicate in a Christian land the rights of a
teaching more Christian than that with which the minds
of guileless youth were wont to be poisoned.

There is nothing in that to cause surprise, for Cîteaux
and Clairvaux were themselves but daughters and con-
tinuators of this School of Jerusalem founded by the first
Apostles, or of the School of Antioch that acknowledged
the illustrious Paul and Barnabas for masters. The proper
name for their scholars was simply "Christians"; nothing
was taught there but the doctrine of Christ, and it was this
that was always put in the foreground whenever a new school
arose. Antony, Pacomius, Macarius, Paphnutius, Basil,
never pretended to do anything else than to turn back
their disciples to the life of perfection as lived in the primitive
Church.[66] Benedict himself appealed to these in drawing
up this Rule where all perfection is summed up in the love
of God and the neighbour.[67] Cîteaux, in its turn, had no
other ambition than to re-establish in all its rigour the
observance of the Benedictine Rule, that is to say of the
Christian life, which is the life of charity.[68] If we add that
the unknown monk who reports all this could not forbear
to quote Horace twice and Ovid once,[69] we shall have a
very apt picture of the state of mind which led these young
athletes to the cloister. They fled from the world, but the

strongest temptation that assailed the most detached amongst
them all had been to become a man of letters;[70] and he
found ways to become a saint even when he succumbed.
In spite of all his formidable asceticism St. Bernard was no
puritan when it came to literature. The walls of his
monasteries were bare,[71] but his style was not bare; nobody
writes like William of Saint-Thierry or Aelred of Rievaulx[72]
and just by chance. These Cistercians have renounced
everything save the art of good writing; each and all of
these hardy ascetics carried in his bosom a humanist who
by no means wanted to die.

In spite of all that, it remains nevertheless true to say
that the Cistercians entertained no merely scholastic conception of the monastic life, but rather, on the other hand,
a monastic conception of the scholastic life. They reduced
the School to the Cloister, and whenever they went on to
compare the Cloister with the Schools it was to show that
it took their place and dispensed with them, just as faith
takes the place of philosophy and dispenses with it. In effect,
the Rule of St. Benedict is proposed to all but imposed upon
none. Nobody is obliged to profess it, and one can save one's
soul without it. Nevertheless if once embraced it is a powerful
aid to salvation—with this proviso, that thereafter it is
faithfully followed. No one who has not taken it upon
himself is in any way bound by it, the will remains entirely
free to take it or to leave it; but once a man has freely made
profession, then what was optional becomes obligatory.
The monk therefore assumes the Rule freely, but then he is
bound of necessity to follow the law he has freely espoused.
A happy necessity for the rest, that necessitates us to perfection! In any event, the articles of the Benedictine Rule,
once it has been undertaken, are no longer counsels but
precepts—*ante professionem voluntaria, post professionem neces-
saria*[73]—and every really grave infraction is a crime. Now

what the Rule prescribes is essentially all that has to be done to acquire and preserve charity, which is the end of the Christian life[74]. All that, and nothing but that, to be thoroughly well learnt only in the cloister and in no wise in the schools. Why then be solicitous about what is unavailing at the risk of losing what is indispensable? Look at Abelard, the professor *par excellence*—what does he teach?

Errors, only too often, which imperil the life of faith, errors into which he falls by dint of trying to substitute philosophy for faith. Even when his teaching is not false it is animated by a dangerous spirit. It is pride, always pride, that prompts reason to set out to understand what we ought rather humbly to accept by faith; to evacuate mystery is to evacuate our merit, since it is to refuse the act of humility that God requires of us if we wish to attain some day to the truth. The thing that makes Abelard's attitude so dangerous is therefore more especially his claim to see everything face to face and to give free rein to reason in dealing with mysteries that exceed its powers.[75] The intentions of these professors moreover are seldom pure, and Abelard unfortunately is not the only one of his species. Some of them learn in order to know; others in order that it may be known that they know; and others again in order to sell their knowledge. To learn in order to know is scandalous curiosity—*turpis curiositas*—mere self-indulgence of a mind that makes the play of its own activity its end. To learn for the sake of a reputation for learning is vanity. To learn in order to traffic in learning is cupidity, and, what is worse, simony, since it is to traffic in spiritual things— *turpis quaestus, simonia.*[76] The only proper thing to do is to make our choice between the sciences with a view to salvation, that is to say so that we may acquire charity, just as one chooses one's food with an eye to health. Every science so chosen, so acquired, is "prudence", all the rest is "curiosity". You will not learn to choose rightly in the school of Abelard, but only in the school of St. Benedict, in the school of Christ.

To determine which of the sciences are likely to prove useful we have only to consider the people that teach them: "Peter, Andrew, the sons of Zebedee, and the rest of their fellow disciples, were not chosen in a school of Rhetoric or Philosophy, yet it was through their ministrations that the Saviour brought the work of redemption to fulfilment in the midst of the world."[77] The reference to the school recurs again and again in St. Bernard's writings, and always with the same significance: "Gaudeo vos esse de hac schola, de schola videlicet spiritus, . . . ubi bonitatem et disciplinam et scientiam discatis. . . . Numquid quia Platonis argutias, Aristotelis versutias intellexi, aut ut intelligerem laboravi? Absit, inquam, sed *quia testimonia tua exquisivi.*"[78] What the Cistercian learns in this school is the most important of all the arts, the art of living, and he learns it directly from Christ: "Tu es enim magister et Dominus, cujus schola est in terris, cathedra in coelis. . . . Exultaverunt gigantes Philosophi non ad currendam viam tuam, sed ad quaerendam vanam gloriam."[79] But Christ also makes use of assistants in His school, for what He teaches Himself is charity, a thing that He alone can give, while the other masters teach the fear of God, respect for the Rule, the life of penance, and, in a word, all that purifies the heart and prepares it to receive charity: "*In schola Christi sumus;* we are in the school of Christ"—it was at Clairvaux that these words were uttered—"and there we learn a twofold doctrine: one which the only and true Master teaches us Himself, and the other through His ministers. Through His ministers, fear; from Himself, dilection.[80] That is why, when the wine fails, He commands His ministers to fill the urns with water, and still to-day and every day, if charity grows cold, the ministers of Christ fill the urns with water, that is to say our minds with fear. And not without good reason is 'water' interpreted as 'fear', for as water quenches fire, so fear quenches libidinous desires, and as water washes away the stains on the body, so does fear remove the stains on the soul. Let us therefore fill this urn with water, that is to say our minds with fear, for he who fears neglects nothing, and well is that mind filled where neglect cannot enter. But water dulls us and fear afflicts; let us hasten therefore to Him who changes the water into wine, who changes fear and its affliction into love, that we may hear His own teaching concerning dilection. For He says: *These things I command you, that you love one another*, and that is to say: Many things I enjoin on you by the mouths of My ministers, but this especially and by My own mouth I bid you, that you love one another. And elsewhere He says: *By this shall all men know that you are My disciples, if you have love one for another.* Let us therefore love one another, and so prove that we are disciples of the Truth. And in this mutual dilection let us be careful of three things, for God is charity—*Deus caritas est*—and we should be anxious about nothing but charity: that it may come to birth, that it may grow, and that it may be preserved".[81] This lesson was not lost on the companions of St. Bernard, and in the works of William of Saint-Thierry it received a splendid development.

For the famous *Letter to the Brothers of Monte Dei*, which is very certainly one of his masterpieces, rests wholly upon this conception. Written for the Carthusians, this treatise is the work of a monk addressing himself to monks and seeking above all else for the true meaning of the monastic life. The wise of this world, full of the spirit of this world, aspire to the highest wisdom, but they lick the dust; let us leave them to it while they find the wise way down to hell.[82]

Quite other is the life of the monk, for he is concerned not simply with serving God but with adhering to God: "Others believe in God, know, love and reverence God, but to you it belongs to enter into the wisdom, the understanding, the knowledge and joy of the Lord. A great thing, a difficult thing." [83] But why, after all, does a Carthusian shut himself up in a cell? Because, says our Cistercian, he would give himself up to the contemplation of God, he would enjoy God. Doubtless this ideal is not to be attained without effort, but then the Abbot is there to give encouragement and counsel. For the Abbot teaches; he is a genuine professor and the novices are his pupils: "Primumque docendus est rudis incola eremi, secundum apostolicam Pauli institutionem . . . Rursumque docendus est cavere . . ." "Deinde docendus est animalis incipiens et Christi tyrunculus Deo appropinquare."[84] "Docendus est etiam in oratione sua sursum cor levare." School of the apprentices rather than of the students of Christ, for in that school the exercises are acts; especial school of charity—specialis caritatis schola—where charity is studied, its problems discussed, their solutions determined, not so much by reasonings as by reason, and the very truth of things, and experience.[85] Why and how to teach the lesson of love—that is what we have now to determine.

Our problem is: how to restore to man, now disfigured, the lost divine likeness? If the Benedictine Rule, as interpreted by the Cistercians, aims above all at the acquisition and preservation of charity, that is because it is a rule of life, and because, as the soul is the life of the body, so is charity the life of the soul. The bond of union between soul and body is very different from the bond that unites it to God; for the soul animates this portion of matter to which it is united by "necessity", and that moreover is why we have said that its love begins "of necessity" by being carnal.

It is otherwise with the love that it bears to God, for as conscious of itself and voluntary, this love is free. Where the soul loves there it is. Unable not to love its body, it cannot but be in its body; but it is not in God unless it loves God. If it loves Him, then it is at the source of its true life as soul; if it does not love Him its spiritual life is dead, for now cut off from the source that gives it life, it withers. Now the soul loves God by charity;[86] it is therefore by charity that it communicates with the source of its life, and the first thing we have to do, if we would bring it back to life, is to enter it on the apprenticeship of charity.

What then will be the first moment of this apprenticeship? Clearly, the initial obstacle to be overcome is our immoderate love for the body, holding back the soul from God; and here we have the explanation of the severity of Cistercian asceticism.[87] Not that the body is to be killed, for that would be to kill the man; but at least we can try to bring the soul back within the bounds of natural necessity, and subject its cupidity to the pruning-knife. We must do something more than that. Contentment with natural and necessary pleasures may be Epicurus' programme, but it cannot suffice for the Cistercian; possibly it might serve well enough in the case of a nature which was still what it was when God made it, unspoilt as yet by original sin. But our fall is always with us along with its heavy chastisement, concupiscence; so that nature must first of all be rectified before it can be safely taken as guide. That is why the Cistercian mortifies this body which so frays our charity with its perpetual exigencies.[88] To mortify it we must withdraw it well within the limits imposed by natural necessity, and attempt rather to save it from death than help it to live. That involves the holding of a somewhat delicate balance; but Bernard succeeded in holding it till his sixty-third year. The first thing to be aimed at, therefore, by whoever would live the life of charity, is not merely to limit indulgence of the body to a sufficiency for health, good and desirable as this may be in itself, but to subject it to a rude discipline. That is the price the soul has to pay for its liberty.

This corporeal asceticism, filling but a few lines in precept but lasting a lifetime in practice, is nevertheless merely the indispensable condition for an ascesis of the mind, now in turn to be described. This is the more easily done since, apart from the inevitable variations on a familiar theme so frequently resumed by St. Bernard, the order he recommends for its due execution remains constant throughout. It arises moreover from the very nature of the case. *Recole primordia, attende media, memorare novissima tua : haec pudorem adducunt, ista dolorem ingerunt, illa metum incutiunt.* What invests the execution of this programme with its properly Cistercian character is the fact that it supposes the application of that method of psychological analysis which St. Bernard, as we have already said, made one of the foundations of his mysticism. The root idea of it is announced, immediately after the words just cited, by an appeal to the Canticle of Canticles, I, 7: *Si ignoras te, O pulcherrima mulierum.* To know whence we came, where we stand, and whither we go is to know what we were, what we are, and what we are to be; in short, it is to know ourselves. The first thing to be done then, by whoever would walk in the ways of charity, is to learn to know himself; and that is the true science, the only one the Cistercian needs, the one that in his case should supply for all the dialectical quibbles of Plato and all the sophisms of Aristotle. From the outset of his teaching, therefore, Bernard enters on the consideration of man, and his doctrine turns aside from speculative philosophy only to dive more deeply into the study of the interior life of the soul, wherein he had been preceded by St. Augustine and was to be followed later on by Pascal and Maine de Biran.

In thus imposing on the man who would turn to God the duty of first knowing himself St. Bernard was the heir of a long tradition formed among the Greeks, but modified in its course by the Fathers of the Church.[89] As far as it is possible to judge, the sources whence he imbibed the idea himself were St. Augustine and the teacher St. Augustine had heard at Milan, St. Ambrose. It can easily be shown that the text of St. Ambrose was familiar to St. Bernard's intimate friend, William of Saint-Thierry. The latter, in the preface to his *Epistola aurea*, mentions that among his own works was a commentary on the Canticle of Canticles entirely made up of texts bearing on this subject scattered through the works of St. Ambrose. What St. Ambrose had omitted to do for himself, William will do for him. Nothing could be more natural in one whom we know, like St. Bernard, to have held the Canticle to be the initiation *par excellence* into the mystical life. It is unnecessary then to say that St. Ambrose should be regarded as one important source of the Cistercian mysticism. Now in the Ambrosian commentary compiled by William we find brought together a long series of texts on the indispensable necessity, for Christians, of acquiring self-knowledge,[90] and on the reasons that underlie it.

We have only to let St. Bernard speak for himself and we shall see at once how he understands this self-scrutiny and what he expects to gain from it. To know ourselves is essentially, in his view, to recognize that we are defaced images of God: "Is it not shameful to lift up thy head, thou who dost not lift up thy heart—to stand erect in body whose desire crawls upon the earth? For to savour of the flesh, to desire carnality, to run after what is carnal, is not this to crawl upon the earth? Nevertheless, since thou wast created to the image and likeness of God, thy life, now become like to that of the beasts in losing its likeness, is still the life of an image. If, therefore, even when thou wast clothed in thy greatness thou didst not understand that thou wast slime of the earth, at least now take care, now thou art sunk into the slime of the abyss, not to forget that thou art the image of God, and blush to have covered it over with an alien likeness. Remember thy nobility and take shame of such a defection. Forget not thy beauty, to be the more confounded at thy hideous aspect."[91] A passage of wonderful condensation in which the whole of the Cistercian asceticism is contained. Misery of man: to have lost the divine likeness; greatness of man: to have kept the divine image; to strip away the alien likeness with which sin has covered it over—that is what the novice learns first at Cîteaux. But, to strip it away, he needs must recognize it; that is to say, learn to know himself for what he has become.

If now we turn to the rule of life of which the Cistercian makes profession we see that this precisely is the first thing that it sets out to teach, for to learn to recognize his misery is to accomplish the apprenticeship of humility. St. Benedict has set forth its twelve degrees disposed as so many rungs of the ladder, not merely to be enumerated but attained; a ladder of which the two sides are the body and the soul, which lifts up towards God our life upon this earth, since it is by humbling oneself that one exalts oneself to God. On this theme St. Bernard builds the whole doctrine of his *De gradibus humilitatis*,[92] and here we see how deeply his thought is rooted in the soil of the Benedictine life. What he borrows from the Rule is at once the fundamental conception of humility and the goal to which it tends, that is, charity. "Having ascended all these degrees of humility, the monk will presently arrive at that charity of God which, when perfect, casteth out all fear (I *John* IV, 18), whereby he will

begin to keep without labour, and as it were naturally and
by custom, all those precepts which hitherto he had observed
through fear—no longer through dread of hell, but for the love
of Christ, and of a good habit and delight in the virtues."[93]
The displacement of fear by charity by way of the
practice of humility—in that consists the whole of St.
Bernard's ascesis, its beginning, its development and its
term. It was likewise Cassian's and Basil's; it is the discipline by which St. John's promise may be realized:
*Timor non est in caritate, sed perfecta caritas foras mittit timorem,
quoniam timor poenam habet; qui autem timet, non est perfectus
in caritate.*

How does the gradual acquisition of humility bring
a man to this goal? By bringing him to the truth,[94] and,
above all, to the truth about himself. *Humilitas est virtus
qua homo verissima sui cognitione sibi ipse vilescit.*[95] To humble
ourselves is therefore essentially to prove by acts of body
and mind that we are aware of our misery, and pass judgment
on ourselves. A familiar theme of meditation continually
recalled to mind by St. Bernard, and a common property
of the whole Cistercian school, but one, nevertheless, which
he alone knew how to justify down to its ultimate theological
roots. For it presents a problem which his genius could
not fail to perceive and scrutinize. Every spiritual director
knows that we must humble ourselves. St. Bernard knew
and expressed more; he discerned and shows us the profound connection between self-knowledge and judgment
of self, and between judgment of self and charity.

Charity, as we have already noted, is the "common will"
as opposed to the "proper will"; to speak precisely, it is
the will common to man and God. It reigns therefore in
the heart when our will desires what God's will desires.
What in fact does a man do when he practises humility?
He proves that he knows his misery and judges it; he judges

himself then as God judges him. Already the rectification
of the *consilium* begins, inasmuch as he begins to know
himself by process of reason as God Himself knows him.
On this lower but quite indispensable level, the man can
already say that he knows himself as he is known. That
this may be said of him hereafter in glory it must first be
said of him in his misery. Of the man who humbles himself,
and of him alone, can this be said. Judging himself miserable,
as God judges him miserable, he knows the enormity of
his wickedness, and knows that he deserves to be punished.
The punishment is already there in the hideous disfigure-
ment of a soul so deformed that it dare no longer look itself
in the face; but it is not yet consummated, and he knows
that it will be unless grace should come to his aid. To know
it, however, is not enough; he accepts it, wills it, inasmuch
as he deserves it; and it is to witness that he wills it that
he chastises himself up to the limit of his strength by way
of mortification. Rectification of a nature in revolt, the
Cistercian asceticism is therefore also the proof that the
man goes half way to meet the punishment that he knows
he deserves. So doing, he unites not only his judgment with
God's judgment, but also his will with God's will; and that
is why, if we take it in its essence, humility is already charity.

This first step, the indispensable beginning of the
restoration of the ruined image, very soon involves another.
The original transgression has entailed the same consequences
on all the sons of Adam.[96] My history is also your history;
my state is also your state. When a man knows himself
miserable, guilty, under condemnation and deserving to
be so, then he knows also by that very fact that all men are
in the same condition. To know the truth concerning oneself is therefore to know the truth concerning one's neighbour, and it is indispensable to know it, not this time to
pass judgment, as we have to do in our own case, but that

we may have compassion. This compassion will express itself outwardly in almsgiving, but its inward source lies in the very heart of the Christian. We must consider it in both aspects, beginning with what is outward.

Cistercian almsgiving is undoubtedly Christian almsgiving, but it has a particular nuance of its own. Not for nothing are almsdeeds called "works of charity", for alms are the fitting expression of compassion; now compassion for the neighbour arises out of knowledge of our own misery, this self-knowledge is humility, and humility is already charity. St. Bernard's charity to the poor was ardent; we hesitate to say, but it has to be said, that it was fierce: and this accounts for the violence of his invectives against the luxury of the Cluniac abbeys. It is difficult to read them without being shocked when one remembers the motives that animated the parties accused. The "luxury for God" of the Cluniacs was also in its own way a very Christian sentiment, beautiful in itself, and an inexhaustible source of beauty; but one of the essential reasons that provoked St. Bernard's indignation was that in pouring out silver and gold for the ornamentation of their churches they left Christ to suffer in the person of those that wanted bread: "The walls of the Church are indeed resplendent but her poor go in need. She clothes her stones with gold and leaves her children to run naked. The eyes of the rich are flattered at the expense of the poor. The delicate find the wherewithal to gratify their taste, but the miserable find nothing to satisfy hunger."[97] Here was deep feeling without a doubt, and violent passion; but then, also, ideas. Now what were these ideas?

Being carnal, man is linked with his body in bonds of necessity. He has no right to more than this necessity demands, and it would be a praiseworthy prudence to stop a little short of its normal requirements. However, as a necessity it creates a right, and in relation to this right, since the needs of men are much the same, all men are equal. Born equal, they would still in this respect be so, were it not that cupidity had tempted the greater part to transgress the bounds of natural necessity, and to rush in pursuit of a much greater share of this world's goods than they can really consume. Suppose that original sin had not corrupted man's will, and that everybody was content with necessities, then we should see that there is more than enough for all. A true Cistercian is entitled to say these things, for he lives on little, and working with his own hands on the monastic farm, the little he consumes he also produces. Indeed, he produces enough to give out of his meagre superfluity to those who lie under like necessities. Very different is the attitude of those who live in the world. Filled with cupidity, they never have enough. When nature is satisfied, then, to satisfy passion, they proceed to seize on what should be left for the needs of others. Filled with pride, urged on by their "proper will", they seek themselves and for their own sake; suppressing their "common will", they exalt themselves as masters above those whom God made their equals. For "nature made all men equal"—*et quidem omnes homines natura aequales genuit*—"but as the natural order of good living has been overset by pride men have become impatient of this equality, and try to raise themselves above others, vieing with each other as to who shall be the greater". That is just what the monk renounces by practising obedience in his cell,[98] that is to say by renouncing his "proper will"; and, so renouncing it, he recovers the "common will", which is charity.

He recovers it in both senses, materially and spiritually, the one carrying the other with it. Understood as above defined, an almsdeed is an act whereby cupidity surrenders its superfluities so that others may not want for necessities.

D

Thus it re-establishes the divinely-willed order of things; by this exterior act it gives proof that even in its secret depths the will is now accordant with the Divine will; it is thus the concrete expression of an inner communion between our willing and God's willing, and this is spiritual charity itself. And that moreover is why, even on this lower plane of carnal love where we are still moving, God commands us to love our neighbour, and to love him as ourselves but for love of Him; for we cannot love our neighbour as ourselves without abandoning superfluities and re-entering the limits prescribed by natural necessity; but when we do that we do more than merely re-establish our own personal justice, for we re-establish social justice. Whoever wills that all God's creatures shall have their necessities does more, in sacrificing superfluities, than merely to lift a perilous burden from his own soul; knowing his own misery, he knows also his neighbour's, and if he strips himself of useless goods that others may not want for what, by his own experience, he knows to be necessary, then he is refusing to arrogate to his own proper use what God has willed shall be in common. The Cistercian who thus strips himself does not give, he, makes restitution. To re-establish social justice is, for him, to unite himself in will with the Divine will to justice; and he truly loves his neighbour as himself for the love of God.[99] That is *social* carnal love. Thus, under the blows of ascesis, this *consilium proprium*, source of all the evil, begins to crumble. Nor is that all. If, in thus rising from the individual order to the social order, carnal love already goes far in the life of charity, it is doubtless because knowledge of self at once involves knowledge of all others, but especially because knowledge of our misery, for a Christian, passes beyond knowledge of man. From the day when Jesus Christ was made flesh and dwelt amongst us, our misery has become God's.

What an example! But, above all, what a transfiguration of carnal love, and what an infinite deepening of the knowledge of self! Truly a glorious apprenticeship is that of the young novice who in learning to know himself discovers Jesus Christ, and knows henceforth that he would not know even himself without Jesus Christ. For we have but to call Jesus to mind and we behold the perfect image of humility, and understand that the end of humility is compassion. This infinite humiliation, the Incarnation of the Word—this is something that God desired for Himself and desired for our sake; and these two desires are one.

We may look at it from either side. As God, the Word from all eternity knew our misery. He knew it better than we do, He knew it perfectly; but He did not know it as we know it, since He had not experienced it; and He could not experience it save by becoming man: *sciebat quidem per naturam, non autem sciebat per experientiam*. That is why this impassible God abased Himself to suffering; taking the form of a servant, He put our misery and subjection to the proof, that He might put mercy and obedience to the proof; obedience in submission, human misery in His Passion. He had no need of this experience to enrich His knowledge—for He knew all things—but He willed it that He might humanly feel the suffering that He divinely knew. In this sense it is no exaggeration to say that God had something to learn by His Incarnation; what Christ, in virtue of His divine nature, knew already, that He wished to feel, that is to say to know it *otherwise*, in His human nature; and He wished to know it for our sake to the end that we, through His sufferings, might be brought nearer to Him from Whom we had wandered so far.[100]

For God, if the expression may be allowed, had no other resource left. He could do no more than make this last incredible experiment: Himself to undergo the misery we suffer for having sinned against Him, *experire in se quod illi faciendo contra se merito paterentur.*[101] If, while His justice chastises us, His mercy submits to our chastisement that we may be saved from it, that is because He had made trial in vain of everything else, or at least of all that it was possible to try, in order to reclaim a creature like man, moved by the simplest and most elementary passions: fear, cupidity, and love.

It would have been easy—nothing easier—to subjugate the heart of fallen man by fear; but that would not have been to gain it. Carnal as we have become, we nevertheless remain these "noble" creatures, men: free beings therefore, spontaneities, and fear is the very negation of spontaneity. "I would regain, said God to Himself, the heart of this noble creature, man: but if I force him against his will, I shall have but a stubborn mule, not a man, for he will not come to Me of himself, nor with good-will." Something else then was required. God might still think of tempting man's cupidity, and did so too as only God could do it; for in exchange for good-will He promised the infinitely greater gain of eternal life. A splendid promise, none more apt to tempt the heart of man, for if he loves gold he loves life more, and now he is promised eternal life. The thing is obvious, even painfully obvious. Unhappily, life eternal is hereafter and gold is here to hand; cupidity for the eternal was not yet strong enough to prevail over cupidity for the temporal. "Seeing then that all this availed nothing, God said to Himself: but one thing is left, for the heart of man does not harbour fear and cupidity alone, but also love; and no attraction is stronger than love". That then is why God made Himself man and suffered death—to gain our love by letting us *see* His own.[102]

Thus knowledge of self, already expanded into "*social*" carnal love of the neighbour so like ourself in misery, is now a second time expanded into a carnal love of Christ, the model of compassion, since for our salvation He has become the Man of Sorrows. Here, then, is the place occupied in Cistercian mysticism by the meditation on the visible Humanity of Christ. It is but a beginning, but an absolutely necessary beginning. In this humiliated God we behold humility; in this Mercy we behold mercy; this "Passion by compassion" teaches us to have compassion. Thus to habituate our will to pass over from ourselves to our neighbour, from our neighbour to God, is therefore to uproot the cupidity which tethers us to our own flesh and to set erect again the bent and stiffened will which was no longer able to shake itself clear of self. In man, become carnal, the apprenticeship of charity must needs begin with that.

Charity, of course, is essentially spiritual, and a love of this kind can be no more than its first moment. It is too much bound up with the senses unless we know how to make use of it with prudence, and to lean on it only as something to be surpassed. In expressing himself thus Bernard merely codified the teachings of his own experience, for we have it from him that he was much given to the practice of this sensitive love at the outset of his "conversion"; later on he was to consider it an advance to have passed beyond it; not, that is to say, to have forgotten it, but to have added another,[103] which outweighs it as the rational and spiritual does the carnal.[104] Nevertheless this beginning is already a summit.

This sensitive affection for Christ was always presented by St. Bernard as love of a relatively inferior order. It is so precisely on account of its sensitive character, for charity is of purely spiritual essence. In right, the soul should be able to enter directly into union, in virtue of its spiritual powers, with a God Who is pure spirit. The Incarnation, moreover, should be regarded as one of the consequences of man's transgression, so that love for the Person of Christ is, as a matter of fact, bound up with the history of a fall which need not, and should not, have happened. St. Bernard furthermore, and in several places, notes that this affection cannot stand safely alone, but needs to be supported by what he calls "science". He had examples before him of the deviations into which even the most ardent devotion can fall when it is not allied with, and ruled by, a sane theology. However, it is quite indispensable, and God Himself has judged it to be so, since He became incarnate and suffered in the flesh precisely that He might touch the hearts of sensitive creatures by means of this sensible spectacle. We should therefore misapprehend the place it occupies in St. Bernard's conception of the spiritual life if we thought that on this score it might be neglected. To pass beyond it is not to destroy it, but rather to preserve it by completing it with another. And it would be but an empty pretence to claim to rise to this other unless we had already passed through this preparatory experience, which, moreover, should still go hand in hand with a purely spiritual charity when this has been attained. The spiritual outweighs the carnal, and the latter therefore is no more than a beginning; but we shall see that even from this beginning the soul already attains a summit.

For it cannot indeed be doubted that sensitive devotion to the Person of Christ will be rewarded with clearly marked mystical states.[105] The Church, that is to say here the souls of Christians, as distinct from those of Jews or pagans, is pricked by motives unknown to the rest when she stands in the presence of this testimony of an infinite love, vouchsafed to her and to her alone. In the face of this spectacle, which none but she can contemplate, of a God dead on the cross for her salvation, she can but cry out with the Bride of the Canticle: *vulnerata caritate ego sum*. That is why meditation on the Passion, and on the Resurrection that crowns it, from the very fact that it elicits a more ardent outpouring of love, is accompanied by an expansion of charity that prepares the soul to receive the visitation of the Word. Then she passes directly to union by compassion: *Compatimini et conregnabitis.*[106] We have only to read attentively the third chapter of the *De diligendo Deo* to be assured that here we have to do with well-marked states of mystical union: "Gaudet Sponsus caelestis talibus odoramentis et cordis thalamum frequenter libenterque *ingreditur* . . .; ibi profecto adest sedulus, adest libens . . . Oportet enim nos, si crebrum volumus *habere hospitem Christum*. . . ." Such expressions, and others easily verified, leave us in no doubt about the nature of these visitations.

We have said that they are the first mystical fruit of the life of charity, but we added that sensible meditation of Christ, carnal affection for His humanity, must subsist throughout the whole life of the Christian man, even then when another and more spiritual love has begun to grow up in the soul. We are and we remain carnal beings, and our sensibility always claims its rights. Purely spiritual meditation demands a tension which becomes in the end insupportable; the mind must unbend, and this it does by re-descending to carnal love of Christ. This recourse to meditation on the Passion ought even to be frequent if our love of God is not to grow lukewarm: "Haec mala, hi flores, quibus Sponsa se interim stipari postulat et fulciri, credo sentiens facile vim in se amoris posse tepescere et languescere quodammodo, si non talibus jugiter foveatur incentivis." This text, from the same Chapter III, serves for introduction to the very important idea that the *memoria* —and by that let us understand the memory, the sensible recollection of the Passion of Christ—is in us the condition and herald of the *praesentia*, that is to say, in the full sense of the term, of the beatific vision in the future life, but also already of these visitations of the soul by the Word in this life. "Dei ergo quaerentibus et suspirantibus *praesentiam,* presto interim et dulcis *memoria* est, non tamen qua satientur, sed qua magis esuriant unde satientur." Here, as we see by the whole context, we are concerned with the *memoria passionis.* Whoso finds frequent meditation of the Passion a burden, how should he sustain the presence of the Word when He comes to judgment? "Verbum modo crucis audire gravatur ac *memoriam passionis* sibi judicat onorosam; verum qualiter verbi illius pondus *in praesentia* sustinebit?" Quite otherwise will it be for him to whom the remembrance of the Passion is dear and familiar. "Ceterum fidelis anima et suspirat *praesentiam* inhianter et in *memoria* requiescit suaviter." Here therefore we encounter a theological theme which has become celebrated in the history of medieval Latin poetry, thanks to the famous *Jesu dulcis memoria.* We see at the same time that if this poem was not written by St. Bernard himself, it very directly depends on his influence, and expresses one of the most important aspects of his mystical doctrine. And, what is still more useful, we can now fix its exact meaning. It describes the movement by which the soul rises from- remembrance of the Passion of Christ to mystic union, while awaiting the day when it shall be united to Him for ever in eternity. The opposition of *memoria* to *praesentia* has always in fact a technical import in the writings of St. Bernard and of those who appeal to his doctrine. The other poems traditionally attributed to St. Bernard, and which are so many meditations on the sufferings of Christ on the Cross, might also be connected with this same doctrinal point. The *Salve caput cruentatum,* if not from his pen—and it seems but little likely that it is— is certainly inspired by his- thought, or a thought closely allied to his. In attributing them to St. Bernard tradition

CARNAL LOVE OF CHRIST

has probably fallen into a material error, but to fail to see the deep truth hidden beneath the error would be another and a worse one.[107]

To pass beyond the *carnalis amor Christi* would be to emerge from the apprenticeship to the life of charity, since it would be to pass from carnal love to that spiritual love of which it is the prelude. In the meanwhile, before this passage is effected, the renunciation of one's own will begins to bear its fruit. Contempt of the world, which at first was but the effect of a will in violent reaction against it, is now transformed; for now it has become the spontaneous distaste of a will tending henceforth to other things. The soul loves elsewhere, and its contempt for the rest is already no more than the obverse of its love for God.[108] Thus, under the influence of grace, the *libertas consilii* is re-constituted, for reason now begins to know what it ought to prefer above the rest. But at the same time the *libertas complaciti* begins also to reappear, for it is quite whole-heartedly now that the will turns away from the world and towards the suffering Christ, to Whom it would henceforth render love for love. Everything, even the life of mortification itself, begins to take on a new character. Certainly there can be no question of its ever becoming a pleasure; it would cease to exist if it ceased to involve effort and suffering. The flesh is and remains wounded by sin; it is therefore always in revolt against the will, and against the discipline the will would impose on it. If "proper will" could be wholly extirpated from man in this life, charity would no longer find anything to chastise in the body. In reacting against it in union with the Divine punitive decree, she sides with the justice of God against a flesh turned rebel, and, since the flesh will always make its protests heard, the penitent will never abandon his self-imposed sufferings. It is none the less true that he will find henceforth a heartfelt

D*

joy in mortification. The pains he inflicts on the body he
wills out of desire to associate himself with the sufferings
of Christ on the Cross. In his turn, he collaborates by means
of his own affliction in the ransom of the sinner; his sufferings
have become, in the fullest sense of the term, a *compassion*
with the Passion of Christ; he associates himself with the
work of redemption, and thereby begins to re-establish a
state in which the will shakes itself free from the misery
into which it has fallen since the first sin. To chastise oneself
for love is no longer to be chastised in fear; now this accord
of the will with the actual state in which man finds himself
placed is precisely *libertas a miseria.* And that is so true
that if the damned in hell could do what man can still do
in this life, that is to say if they could lovingly embrace
the torments which Divine justice inflicts, they too would
soon cease to suffer this frightful excess of misery, hell itself
would cease to exist: *cesset voluntas propria et infernus non
erit.*[109] For the novice, at any rate, who in this sensible
remembrance of the Passion and in carnal love for Christ
enters on the apprenticeship of divine love, mortification
is henceforth enveloped in sweetness, and the yoke of the
Saviour, without ceasing to be a yoke, becomes lighter.
The Carthusian in his cell sets himself to love its solitude.
The burden, perhaps still heavier, of the common life,
begins to be cherished by the Cistercian like a friendship:
Ecce quam bonum est . . .; emerging gradually from the Land
of Unlikeness to draw nearer to the Land of Likeness, he
emerges from this analogue of hell, which is the world, to
enter into this analogue of heaven, a monastic life of union
with the Divine Will: *paradisus claustralis.*

CHAPTER IV

PARADISUS CLAUSTRALIS

THE beatitude of heaven is union with God Who is Charity. Therefore, to restore in the heart of fallen man the life of charity which ought never to have been extinguished in it, is to bring him nearer step by step to the life eternal which is to be. The cloister, the school where charity is taught, is truly the antechamber of paradise.

Everything of course depends on the answer to the question whether divine love can be taught, and, if so, how. And there is a very particular question as to whether this teaching is really possible according to the method proposed by St. Bernard. Doubts have been cast upon it. We shall henceforth be compelled, if we wish to grasp his thought, to force our way through a whole thicket of artificial obstacles erected around it. How ignore them? Doubtless here lies the whole positive contribution of history to the understanding of St. Bernard's mystical theology. Let us then try to make out the path on which his thought travels, and the goal he aims at.

The first difficulty encountered in the attempt to establish the inner coherence of his doctrine lies in an apparent contradiction between its starting-point and its goal. The latter is a pure and disinterested love of God introducing us to a state analogous to that of the beatific vision. The starting-point is a love that is egoistic, even "a narrow self-love, a vicious self-love, characteristic of a sinful nature."[110] How be surprised, after that, to find St. Bernard in a certain difficulty when he tries to demonstrate love as

85

a simple and continuous movement? To succeed, it would seem, he would have to show that disinterestedness is the characteristic of self-love and that charity is the characteristic of cupidity. Evidently the bargain will not hold.

True; and just on that account St. Bernard never entered into it. The problem foisted on him, along with a challenge to solve it, is evidently insoluble; but then it is not the problem he proposed. Undoubtedly the starting-point of his analysis of the degrees of love is always the love of self; but here we have to recollect that this cupidity, this concupiscence, this carnal love, with which we begin as a matter of fact, does not constitute the true beginning of the history of love. Were it a question of transforming an "essential cupidity" into charity the task would evidently be contradictory; but what we really have to do is simply to restore a love of God, corrupted into love of self, to its original state of a love of God. The problem therefore is altogether different. I do not say that it is as simple—in fact it needs Divine grace to resolve it—but certainly, when put in this way, it is not contradictory. In short, the problem which St. Bernard is accused of having vainly attempted to solve would consist in seeking how the divine likeness could be restored to man without taking any account of the fact that he has retained the divine image. What is taken for the starting-point of the operation is, in reality, only its second moment; far from being an essential character of man, this "vicious self-love" is an adventitious corruption, and it can, in consequence, be eliminated. It will be so by grace.

Failure to perceive this point entangles the historian in inextricable difficulties, unless indeed he proceeds to father them on St. Bernard. It is quite true to say that "there is but one sole current of human appetition, and it is this that has to be canalized"; but it is not true at all to say that *cupiditas* was conceived by St. Bernard "as the very spring of the natural appetite, which *caritas*, while giving it its proper direction, will maintain in force".[111] To put the matter thus is to tear a whole chapter out of the story of Cistercian love and then to imagine that the story begins there. No, the unique current that here has to be canalized is not *cupiditas*: it is the divine love which, accidentally led astray in us under the guise of cupidity, demands only to be put back into its normal and primitive channel. The starting-point of the analysis is therefore for St. Bernard, as it should be for us, the factual state of man, without which indeed the question would not arise, no problem would be there to solve; but this problem consists in restoring health obscured by an overlying malady, not in so successfully canalizing a malady that it becomes a kind of health.

It is true that St. Bernard expressed himself occasionally as if that were his intention. Charity, says he, will never be free from fear, nor free from cupidity, but it brings them into due order; in short there is no question of ever succeeding in ceasing to love ourselves, but rather of succeeding in no longer loving ourselves save for God's sake.[112] Does not that amount to this alleged common basis of never-to-be-wholly-uprooted cupidity, which it is proposed to canalize into charity? The objection is so much the stronger inasmuch as it can be reinforced by the celebrated analysis of the degrees of love as we find it in the *De diligendo Deo*, or rather in the *Epistola de caritate* addressed to the Carthusians which forms the concluding part of this treatise. For St. Bernard there distinguishes four degrees of love: at the first, man loves himself for himself and is in a state of almost pure cupidity; at the second, man begins to love God, because, becoming aware of his own misery, he realizes that he needs divine aid to escape it. To love God thus is still cupidity; but observe that in fixing on the proper object of love, cupidity prepares the healing of the ill that afflicts us and sets itself on the road to charity. That which it loves still amiss it loves nevertheless with good reason, even if amiss, for only in this way can it eventually succeed in loving it better. For this second degree soon leads on to a third, and a higher one. By dint of turning to God out of need, the soul soon begins to feel that to live with God is sweet: then she begins to love Him for Himself, yet without ceasing to love Him still for herself; so that she hesitates, alternating between a pure love and a self-interested cupidity, well-ordered though it be. It is in this state that the soul remains for the longest time, nor indeed can she ever wholly emerge from it in this life. To pass altogether beyond this mixture of cupidity and disinterested love and to rise to pure love of God, would be to pass out of this life and to live already the life of the blessed in heaven. Let us carefully note this point, which is one to which we shall have to return, and altogether essential: never, in any state, is human love for God in this life an absolutely pure love— and that is why there will always be a clearly defined breach between even the most sublime of mystic states and the beatific vision. But let us add this second point, not less important: the difference between the third state of love and the fourth does not lie in this, that the third carries with it still a certain self-love from which the fourth would be exempt. The difference lies of necessity elsewhere, since love of self subsists even in the beatific vision. St. Bernard expressed himself quite clearly on this point: pure love of God is not a state in which man would cease to love himself, but a state in which henceforth he loves himself only for God's sake: "Iste est tertius amoris gradus, quo jam propter se ipsum Deus diligitur. Felix qui meruit ad quartum usque pertingere, quatenus nec seipsum diligat homo nisi propter Deum."[113]—Have we not here then, in this persistence of a cupidity we might have hoped to eliminate, that very contradiction in terms which we denied to exist in St. Bernard's statement of the case?

Contradictions in terms are not dangerous when they are contradictions merely in the terms; for we have only to explain the terms and the contradictions disappear. To reply to the question thus put we shall have to take up again and explore the whole problem of the life of charity as led in a Cistercian cloister, for never shall we completely explain a love thus conceived without defining the relation in which love stands to its different objects. Now mystic union is nothing but the final crown of all our love of God in this life; and here therefore the whole interpretation of Cistercian mysticism is certainly involved.

The source of all the difficulties seems to lie in the tendency, common unfortunately among certain historians, to define the terms employed by theologians or philosophers in the abstract, instead of in function of the concrete problems they are directed to solve. For example, the definition of love, in St. Bernard, is not to be considered as one of the possible answers to the abstract question: what is love? For St. Bernard, that question was already answered: God is love. It is useless therefore to consider the consequences to which his formulae might lead in a doctrine in which God would not be love—for He is so, and that suffices. The case is the same when we turn to the other factor in the problem, the nature of man—what it was and might still have been, what it is and may re-become. Man, for St. Bernard, is another given fact, namely a divine image that has lost his likeness to his Original, but can nevertheless recover it if God should please to give it back. If we attempt, independently of these facts, to interpret formulae which, unless read in their light, are meaningless, then we shall certainly find ourselves entangled in endless difficulties. We must try to avoid them.

Let us return therefore to the concrete situation of the Cistercian who, under the direction of his Abbot, has just made the apprenticeship of charity. As we have defined it, charity is a liberation of the will. We may say in this sense that by way of charity our willing gradually shakes itself free of the "contraction" imposed on it by fear, and of the "curvature" of self-will. In other words, instead of willing a thing out of fear of another, or of willing a thing out of covetousness for something else, it is now enabled, having chosen the sole object that can be willed for itself, to tend towards it with a direct and simple movement, in short with a "spontaneous" movement. Let us understand by *spontaneous* a movement explicable without the intervention of any factor outside this movement itself, a movement which, on the contrary, contains in itself its own complete justification. To desire a thing for fear of another would not be a spontaneous movement; to desire a thing in order to obtain something else would be a movement determined from without; to love, on the contrary, is to will what one loves, because one loves it; and herein spontaneity consists. If, then, spontaneity is the manifestation of the will in its pure form, we can say that love, making it spontaneous, makes it also voluntary, restores it to itself, makes it become once more a will.

We have said on the other hand that the sole proper measure of man's love for God is the absence of all measure. Where then on the road of love will the loving will come to a halt? Or let us rather put it thus: what can be the nature of the end pursued by such a will when it proposes to love it without measure? To attain to God, without doubt, to possess Him; but how, in what sense, under what form? That is the question we have to determine before we go on to ask in what sense love is disinterested or is not so; for only in relation to a determinate end will its nature appear and become intelligible. Let us therefore try to set out precisely the nature of this end.

Note in the first place that the cloister is *a* paradise, it is not yet *the* paradise. We may put the term of the mystical life and the object of love as high as we like in this life, never is it to be confounded with the beatific vision. Ecstasy is often said to be a foretaste of beatitude, and although the expression is not false it is nevertheless a metaphor. It is of the essence of beatitude to be eternal, for what would be a beatitude which was threatened with loss from moment to moment—what could it be but a misery? The ecstatic, even he who is rapt to the third heaven, remains no less an inhabitant of the earth. It would be a contradiction to imagine him as in some way or other temporarily elect; and it is consequently true to say that the term of love, in this life, cannot be the vision of God face to face, nor the possession of the Sovereign Good as it is in Itself, how brief soever such vision and such possession.[114]

However, it remains true to say that the term of the life of charity, even here below, is to reach God by direct contact, to see Him, in a certain sense, with an immediate sight; to taste Him or to touch Him. To appreciate the extent to which this claim of the Cistercian mysticism is seriously put forward we have only to remember the very strongly marked "spiritualism" that characterizes the doctrine. St. Bernard considers—and we shall have to return to the point—that union of the soul wi.h God is possible in virtue of the absolute spirituality of God and the spirituality of the human soul itself. It is because there is a question of two spirits that their contact, their union, even their fusion, is a possibility; whence it follows at once that the soul cannot attain to God save after transcending every material reality and every corporeal image. St. Bernard, then, would not be content with anything in the nature of a mystic dream, or even of a supernatural apparition, were it that of God Himself. These, undoubtedly, would be graces of a very high order, which no one would be mad enough to despise, but it is not after these that St. Bernard seeks or would have us seek. The goal of his mystical ambition here below is a state of union with God which would not indeed be the beatific vision, for God does not reveal Himself in it as He is, but one nevertheless in which He reveals to us something of what He is.[115]

To grasp the nature of states of this kind, the name St. Bernard gives them, and the way in which he describes them, the essential thing is to recollect that the primary condition of any mode of cognition whatsoever lies in a certain mode of being. Faithful to the ancient Greek doctrine that only like knows like, St. Bernard affirms that the necessary condition of the soul's knowledge of God lies in the likeness that it bears to God. The eye does not see even the sun as it really is, but only as it illuminates other objects, such as air, hills, or walls; it would not even see these objects did it not in a measure participate in the nature of light in virtue of its transparency and serenity; and pure and transparent as it is, finally, it sees the light only in the measure of its purity and transparency.[116] These are mere comparisons, but we may adopt them if we are careful to retain their properly spiritual sense. For they signify that the immediate condition of the beatific vision will be a perfect likeness of man to God; that this likeness is at present too imperfect to justify any pretension to the beatific vision; and, finally, that the more our likeness to God increases, so much the more does our knowledge of God. The stages therefore on the road by which we approach Him are those of the spiritual progress of the soul in the order of divine likeness. This progress is the work of the Holy Spirit, but takes place in our spirit, and thanks to it we draw nearer and nearer to this divine state in which the soul will see God as He is, because it will now be, not indeed what He is, but such as He is.[117]

Porro jam praesentibus non aliud est videre sicuti est, quam esse sicuti est, et aliqua dissimilitudine non confundi. Sed id tunc, ut dixi. This formula is of capital importance. It explains in the first place why union with God must be exclusively spiritual. Based as it is on an interior transformation of the soul, it is not to be effected by any knowledge of God in the mirror of creatures, nor even by any vision of God clothed in sensible images; that this union may be effected demands no less than that the soul itself shall be interiorly changed, purified, clarified, and restored to the likeness of its Creator.[118] Here then everything must be effected from within, nothing can supply for this interior purification of the soul which makes it akin to its object. But we see at the same time in what this indispensable transformation consists, namely a progressive elimination of unlikeness to God, enabling us to know Him in the measure in which it re-makes us in His likeness.

These unifying transformations and progressive assimilations have been several times set forth by St. Bernard. It is very difficult to tell whether he would classify the various mystical states in a definite hierarchy, and what this hierarchy would be. The two principles to which he holds firmly are the superiority of purely "spiritual" states over those in which images still have a part to play, and the essentially diverse character lacking in common measure, of individual mystical experiences. On the former we have already commented. The second is equally connected with the other basic idea we have noticed, namely that God cannot, in this life, be seen as He is. For it follows from this that God cannot be seen save as He Himself may will to make Himself seen; and since He has absolute liberty in the matter of distribution of graces, we cannot possibly argue from the nature of one mystical favour to that of another granted by God under different conditions or to a different subject.[119] That indeed is why the nature of the divine union does not lend itself to generalized descriptions valid for each particular case. Experience alone can apprise us of these states, and the experience of one is not applicable to another. Let every man drink from his own well.[120]

Probably it was this very strongly marked individuality of the mystical states that deterred St. Bernard from attempting a systematic classification. For it is impossible to classify without comparing, and this very decided partisan of the *Nosce teipsum* showed always the greatest distaste for making comparisons between his own experience which he knew, and that of others from which he was naturally shut out. At times he dwells on the theological conditions required for union with God, and sets himself to describe the economy of the Divine graces which prepare the way for it; at others he tries rather to follow the trace of the action of these graces in his own soul, and to pass from the effects to their cause. We may try in our turn to follow him in both these efforts; and first let us enquire into the conditions under which union of the soul with God by love is possible from the side of God.

In the Holy Trinity, the Father generates the Son, and the Holy Spirit proceeds at once both from the Father and from the Son. He is therefore the bond of Union between the Father and the Son. But the Holy Spirit is charity— and it is on that account moreover that He is bond—so that it may be said that, as charity, the Holy Spirit assures in some sort the unity of the Trinity.[121] This is what is meant by saying that charity is the *law* of God. It signifies two things: first, that God lives by charity, and then, next,

that all who would live with the life of God can do so only
by living by this same charity, that is to say by receiving
it from God as a gift. In God the supreme and ineffable
unity is preserved by this substantial bond as by its law—
but here let us recollect the essential character of charity.
It is by definition the common will: chaste, that is to say
disinterested; immaculate, that is to say unclouded by any
shadow of self-seeking or "proper will": *lex ergo Dei immacu-
lata caritas est, quae non quod sibi utile quaerit, sed quod multis.*
Divine charity would therefore communicate itself: substantial in God, it will be, in the creature, a quality, *qualitatem*, or a kind of accident, *aliquod accidens*. Thus "charity is
rightly called both God and the gift of God. That is why
Charity gives charity, the substantial the accidental." But
in virtue of this gift whereby God bestows charity on man,
that charity which was the law of God becomes the law of
man. "This then is the eternal law, that creates and rules
the universe. All things indeed were made through it in
weight, number, and measure, and nought is left without
law, since the very law of all is not without law, though this
be none other than itself, by which, although it created not
itself, it nevertheless is its own rule."[122] Formulas these of
most extraordinary condensation, ruling the whole economy
of the liberation of human love.

For consider the case of a will still "contracted" by fear,
or "bent" by cupidity. We know that even God Himself
lives by a law—*nec absurdum videatur quod dixi etiam Deum
vivere ex lege*—much more then will the slave and the hireling
have a law of their own. These are the laws they have made
to themselves. They do not love God. Since God loves
Himself alone, and loves Himself with a total love, the slave
and the hireling do not live by the Divine law; but instead
of living by charity they live under another law, the law
of fear or the law of cupidity. Here we see clearly in what

the perversity of the "proper will" consists; it prefers its
own to the common and eternal will; and worse, it professes
to imitate this will by doing what only the Creator can do,
by setting itself up as its own sole law, ruling itself, making
its own will its own law. But then, by a just retribution, the
will, withdrawing itself from the sweet yoke of the law of
charity, remains under the changeless and necessary order
of the eternal law. To punish man God has no need to
inflict on him any supplementary chastisement, it suffices
to leave his proper will to itself, and that carries with it
its own chastisement. In place of the light yoke of charity,
the slave and the hireling must submit to the unbearable
yoke of their own proper will; a heavy yoke, because if
charity is spontaneity and freedom, self-will is servitude;
instead of making man *spontaneus*, it makes him *invitus*,
incapable of acting by a simple and direct movement of
love, condemned on the contrary to will nothing save out
of fear or out of cupidity. God therefore remains in the
changeless joy of His own liberty, but abandons us to the
servitude that we have chosen. In contradiction with
ourselves, divided against ourselves, we can do no more
than offer up to God this prayer: "O Lord my God, *why
dost thou not pardon my transgression, and why dost thou not take
away mine iniquity?*—that, having cast off the heavy load of
mine own will, I may breathe under the light burden of
charity; that I may be no more constrained by servile fear,
nor enticed by hireling cupidity, but may be led by Thy
Spirit, the spirit of liberty, whereby Thy sons are led, and
it bear witness with my spirit that I too am one of Thy
sons, since the same law is mine as is Thine, and, as Thou
art, so I too may be in this world. For as to those who do
as the Apostle says: *Owe no man anything, but love one another,*
assuredly even as God is, so are they too in this world;
they are neither slaves nor hirelings but sons."[123]

For whoever carefully follows St. Bernard's deduction it once more clearly appears that his doctrine of liberty is one of the essential factors in his mysticism. There can be no question for man of seeking this liberty in the refusal of all law, for even God lives by His own; but, on the contrary, he must voluntarily submit himself to the only law that really liberates, since this is the very law of God, who is liberty. This is the sense in which we must understand St. Paul's expression (I *Tim.*, I, 19): *justis non est lex posita.* It does not mean that there is no law made for the just, but that their attitude to the law is such that it no longer lies on them like a burden, or cumbers them like a fetter. That, moreover, is why God Himself says: *tollite jugum meum super vos* (*Matt.*, XI, 29), as if He said: I lay it not on you, this yoke, but do you take it up for yourselves, so that, although never without law—*sine lege*—yet nevertheless you will not be under the law—*sub lege*—.[124] In short, what St. Bernard asks us to do is to renounce all claim to set up our own law, and to accept God's, to put our liberty on its only true basis by assimilating it to God's.

The apprenticeship to the true love therefore consists in passing beyond the sphere of sensitive love, to achieve union with the purely spiritual life of Divine charity. The best way to ascertain under what conditions the passage is possible is to consider first the extreme case in which we may be sure that it has been achieved, that is to say the case of divine "transport" or *raptus*. This word properly signifies those extraordinary states in which the soul is raised, even in this life, to the sight of God. Scripture bears the promise of it and lays down its essential condition as far as concerns man himself: *beati mundo corde, quoniam ipsi Deum videbunt* (*Matt.*, V, 8). It is thus clear that purity of heart is required of all who would rejoice in the sight of God; but we may also add that to those whose heart is pure this beatifying sight is promised. Why then, and how, will it be granted?

The answer is that the apprenticeship of charity is a progressive assimilation with the Divine life, and that the soul that achieves purity has arrived at that point of the progress where the secrets of God may be revealed to it. Let us resume in order the stages already passed. First, the practice of the Benedictine Rule, as observed at Cîteaux. That is the apprenticeship of humility, that is to say a life in practical union with the life of Christ, who manifested Himself as Humility Itself in His Incarnation. Now Christ is the Son of God, the Second Person of the Holy Trinity, that One of the Three in whom the Trinity is least inaccessible, since He became incarnate precisely in order to open a way of access to the unsearchable depths of a God who otherwise would have remained entirely hidden from us. On the other hand, Christ has revealed in humility the mystery of mercy; for He teaches by His own example how man may find compassion for the misery of others in experience of his own. Now compassion is charity, and charity is the Holy Spirit, the Third Person of the Trinity. Thus is man led to a more and more intimate and complete union with the life of the Three Divine Persons, and, we may add, he is now ready for the supreme initiation, should it please the Father to bestow it on him.

For henceforth the way is open for the Father to agglutinate with Himself (*conglutinat*) this illuminated reason, this will enflamed with charity. The heart of man has now become a "pure" heart, in the technical sense of the term as used by St. Bernard, a heart purged of all "proprium", that is to say wholly emptied of self. Reason now knows the man and judges him, as God knows and judges him. The will, clearing itself of cupidity, as reason has just sacrificed its self-opinion, now loves the neighbour with the love of compassion, for the love of God. In the measure in which this purification has been brought about the soul has recovered its lost likeness. It has already re-become such that God is able to recognize Himself in it once more; so recognizing Himself, He begins to dwell on it with complacence, for He cannot love Himself without at the same time loving that which, by way of image and likeness, is, as it were, another self.[125] Loving it, or, what comes to the same thing, loving Himself in it, God would now unite it with Himself. That, precisely, is the meaning of the expression St. Bernard so often employs when he says that the soul has now become God's "betrothed". With him the metaphor always indicates a well-defined state, that of a soul which God can henceforth seek to make His spouse because He recognizes Himself in it, and because nothing now remains in it to which His love cannot be given.

At the point at which we have now arrived nothing can replace St. Bernard's own text,[126] for we must learn to substitute mentally for the images he employs the definite concepts for which they are merely symbols.

I. RECTIFICATION OF REASON BY THE WORD

"Thus then the Son of God, that is to say the Word and Wisdom of the Father, first sought out this intellectual faculty of ours which is called reason, oppressed by the flesh,[127] a captive to sin, blinded by

[126] For the passage from St. Bernard which here follows the present translator has to acknowledge his debt to the translation of Barton R. V. MILLS (S.P.C.K., 1929), but he has by no means followed it exactly.

[127] CARO (synonym: *corpus*); the body to which the soul is united. But it is united to it in two different senses which it is important to distinguish; for here the second only is in question.

First. The soul is united to the body by a bond of natural necessity. Obliged to serve the needs of the body, it finds itself placed on a lower plane than that of the pure spirits; but this is the normal human situation, and, in this sense, the body does not "oppress" the soul, does not drag it down beneath its state as soul, which always implies union with a body. If the soul loves

ignorance,[128] and given up to things external. In His mercy
He took it up, by His power He raised it, by His wisdom He
taught it, and drawing it inwards, in a marvellous manner
made use of it as His representative to sit in judgment on
itself; so that for reverence to the Word with whom it was
associated, it might act as its own accuser, witness and judge,
thus executing upon itself the office of the Truth. From this
first association between the Word and reason is born humility.

II. RECTIFICATION OF THE WILL BY THE
HOLY SPIRIT

"We now come to that other faculty called will, con-
taminated indeed by the poison of the flesh,[129] though this

---

its body as it should it will make it, on the contrary, its auxiliary, and the
two together, mutually helping each other, will attain to their common end,
which is heavenly glory. See ST. BERNARD, *De diligendo Deo*, XI, 31;
P.L., CLXXXII, 993–994: "Bonus plane fidusque comes caro spiritui
bono. . . ." (*In Psal. Qui habitat*, X, 3; P.L., CLXXXIII, 222 D).
   Second. The soul is also, not exactly "united", but "subjected" to the
body by sin. This state is not natural, but against nature, since the soul
is superior to the body. In this sense the body is a "burden", which "weighs
down" the soul and "oppresses" it. This then is the sense in which *caro* is
used here, as always when it implies any bondage of soul to body. Cf. "Traxit
animam corpus in regionem suam et ecce praevalens opprimit peregrinum
[on *peregrinus, peregrinare*, see Chapter III, p. 68, note 88]. Factum est namque
talentum plumbi, non aliunde tamen, nisi quia sedet iniquitas super illud.
Corpus enim aggravat animam, sed utique quod corrumpitur," (ST.
BERNARD, *In Festo S. Martini episc.*, Sermo III; P.L., CI XXXIII, 491).
   In connection with the passage now under consideration, Mr. Barton R. V.
Mills (*Select Treatises of St. Bernard of Clairvaux*, p. 105, note 20) refers with good
reason to two important texts: *De praecepto et dispensatione*, XX, 59; P.L.,
CLXXXII, 892; *In Ascensione Domini*, Sermo III, 1; P.L., CLXXXIII, 304–305.
   SCRIPTURAL THEME: "Corpus enim, quod corrumpitur, aggravat
animam, et terrena inhabitatio deprimit sensum multa cogitantem" (*Sap.*,
IX, 15).
   [128] Blinded by ignorance of its own misery. This ignorance is itself due
to the fact that the soul turns towards things and conforms itself to them,
instead of seeking to know itself (Theme: *Si ignoras te* . . .). It is in this
that *curiositas* consists, the first degree of pride: "Quia enim seipsam ignorat,
foras mittitur, ut haedos pascat" (ST. BERNARD, *De grad. humilitatis*, II,
10, 28; P.L., CLXXXII, 957 C). The literal commentary on the text may
be found in the *De diligendo Deo*, II, 4: "Fit igitur ut sese non agnoscendo
egregia rationis munere creatura, irrationabilium gregibus aggregari incipias,
dum ignara propriae gloriae, quae ab intus est, conformanda foris rebus
sensibilibus, sua ipsius curiositate abducitur: efficiturque una de caeteris,
quod se prae caeteris nihil accepisse intelligat" (P.L., CLXXXII, 976).
See Appendix I, pp. 155–157.
   [129] See above, page 99, note 127.

had already been in a measure counteracted by reason. This the Holy Spirit honours with a visit, sweetly purifies, and fills with ardour making it thereby merciful,[130] so that after the fashion of a skin stretched by the application of an ointment, the will, now all suffused with the heavenly ointment, is expanded with affection even towards its enemies.[131] And of this second association between the Spirit of God and the human will is born charity.[132]

III. PASSAGE TO MYSTIC UNION

"Of these two faculties of the soul, that is to say reason and will, the one is therefore taught by the Word of Truth, the other inspired by the Spirit of Truth;[133] the one is sprinkled with the hyssop of humility,[134] and the other is set on fire by charity. And now become a perfect soul

[130] Passage of humility, by way of knowledge of its own misery, to compassion for the misery of another. See above, Chap. III, p. 73.

[131] AFFECTUS: One of four fundamental emotions out of which all the others are composed. These are: *amor, timor, gaudium,* and *tristitia.* Here, evidently, love. Cf. *De diligendo Deo,* Cap. VIII, 23; P.L., CLXXXII, 987. *In Cant. Cant.,* Sermo LXXXV, 5; P.L., CLXXXIII, 1190. Cf. W. WILLIAMS, *ed. cit.,* p. 41, note 9.
Affectus must often be distinguished from AFFECTIONES.
AFFECTIONES: The various affections of the soul relating to God. They are five in number, each determining a distinct relation of man to God.
Timor, state of a *servus.*
Spes, state of a *mercenarius.*
Obedientia, state of a *discipulus.*
Honor, state of a *filius.*
Amor, state of a *sponsa.*
See *In Cant., Cant.,* Sermo VII, 2; P.L., CLXXXIII, 807.
The *affectiones,* taken in the true sense, are complex emotions made up of the various fundamental *affectus* (see *Affectus*). However, St. Bernard often enough uses *affectiones* in the sense of *affectus,* and then follows the received usage; when he classifies the *affectiones* in the manner above set out, he follows none but his own.

[132] Charity is the "common will", common to man and to God; it is born of the association of our will with the Holy Spirit, the common love of the Father and the Son. See above, p. 94.

[133] On the "teaching" function of the Holy Spirit, see ST. BERNARD, *In Festo Pentecostes,* Sermo I, 5; P.L., CLXXXIII, 325.

[134] Hyssop is one of St. Bernard's symbols for humility. Now hyssop purifies, and so we read immediately afterwards that the soul is without stain. Scriptural theme: "Asperges me hyssopo et mundabor" (*Ps.* l, 9).

from which humility has removed all stain,[135] in which
charity has left no wrinkle,[136] in which the will no
longer resists reason,[137] nor does reason trifle with
truth,[138] then does the Father unite it closely with Himself as His glorious Bride; in such wise that reason is no
longer allowed to think of itself, nor may the will think
of the neighbour, but the entire delight of that blessed
soul will be to say: *introduxit me Rex in cubiculum suum*
(*Cant.*, I, 3).

"Fitting indeed it is that when the soul shall emerge
from this school of humility[139] wherein, under the tuition

The symbolism of hyssop is commented in this sense in *In Cant. Cant.*, Sermo
XLV, 2; P.L., CLXXXIII, 999–1000. It is complicated, moreover, by the
addition of a trait taken from symbolic botany: hyssop is a "humilis herba
et pectoris purgativa humilitatem significans" (*ibid.* and *In dedicatione Ecclesiae,*
Sermo II, 4; P.L., CLXXXIII, 520 B).—As one symbol never excludes another,
humility may be represented also by nard, to which the same medicinal
properties are attributed: *In Assumptione B. Mariae virginis*, Sermo IV, 7;
P.L., CLXXXIII, 428 D (Scriptural theme: *Cant. Cant.*, I, 11); cf. *In Cant.
Cant.*, XLII, 6; 990 B)—by the dove (*In Cant. Cant.*, XLV, 4; 1001)—by the
dawn (*De diversis*, Sermo XCII, 3; 711 D).

[135] The stain is sin; sin is the "proper will"; humility is the "common will"
because it is submission to and union with the will of God. Therefore humility
removes the stain of sin and makes the soul immaculate. Cf. preceding note,
and Chap. III, p. 71.

[136] I know of no text containing an express commentary on this image.
Perhaps we might bring it into connection with another, common in St.
Bernard, which describes cupidity or "proper will" as an "affectus contractus"; *Sine ruga* would thus mean that charity, eliminating the contraction
of the soul, in some sort smoothes it out, takes away its wrinkles or rough-
nesses. St. Bernard, moreover, has just said that charity spreads ointment
on the soul "ita ut more pellis quae extenditur, ipsa quoque . . . per affectum
dilatetur". Here, then, very probably, he wishes to express this smoothing
out of the soul's contraction.

[137] Mr. Barton R. V. Mills (*ed. cit.*, p. 106, note 18) interprets these words
as signifying the *liberum consilium*. I should rather say that they refer to the
liberum complacitum, that is, the will's acceptance of the judgments of right
reason. St. Bernard would say: "the will no longer resists reason, because its
proprium complacitum has been eliminated."

[138] Reason no longer, trifles with truth because, thanks to humility, the
proprium consilium has been eliminated and the *liberum consilium* recovered.
Since the *consilium* and the *complacitum* are certainly contemplated in these
two clauses of the sentence, and since the second cannot apply to the *complacitum*, it follows that this is referred to in the first. For remember that it is
by reason that man judges himself: "Judex sui propter rationem."

[139] Theme: *Regula monasteriorum*: "schola divini servitii"; "schola caritatis";
see Chap. II. The Son, example of humility in His Incarnation, is our Master
in this school.

of the Son,[140] she has learnt to enter into herself in accordance with the warning: *si ignoras te, egredere et pascere haedos tuos (Cant.,* I, 7)—fitting it is that now, under the guidance of the Holy Spirit, she be introduced through affection[141] into the store-rooms of charity,[142] by which assuredly we must understand the hearts of her neighbours.[143] There, stayed up with flowers, compassed about with apples, that is to say with good habits and holy virtues,[144] she may

[140] That is to say, instructed by the Word-Wisdom, Who has taught it to know itself and to judge itself as it really is, in accordance with the principle of Christian Socratism. Scriptural theme: *Cant. Cant.,* I, 7. See above, p. 35.

[141] *Affectionem* in the sense of *amor*, love. Cf. p. 101, note 131.

[142] Second stage: from humility, learnt under the tuition of the Son, the soul passes to charity, under the guidance of the Holy Spirit.—CELLARIA: places where the fruits of the field or garden are kept, and whence their perfumes float like an invitation (ST. BERNARD, *In Cant. Cant.,* Sermo XXIII, 1; P.L., CLXXXIII, 884 B).
The Canticle of Canticles, I, 3 (cf. II, 4), has this: "Introduxit me Rex in cellaria sua"; the Vulgate: ". . . in cubiculum suum." Bernard retains both terms, and gives each an appropriate meaning. He adds a third: *hortus,* whence come the flowers and fruits gathered into the *cellaria.* These terms are defined *loc. cit,* 3; 885 D, and *De diversis,* Sermo XCII; P.L., CLXXXIII, 714–715. The constant element throughout our three texts, as Mr. Barton Mills (*ed. cit.,* p. 106, note 22) very justly observes, is that the meaning of *cellarium* is moral, while that of *cubiculum* is mystical: "Sit itaque hortus simplex ac plana historia; sit cellarium moralis sensus; sit cubiculum arcanum theoricae contemplationis" (*loc. cit.,* P.L., CLXXXIII, 885 D). In fact, in the passage we are engaged in commenting, the *cellaria* are the virtues bestowed by charity, and constituting the way to the *cubiculum,* where the mystical union, in the proper sense of the term, takes place.

[143] By charity we enter the hearts of others, because it brings compassion on their misery, which we recognize by means of our own. See p. 73.

[144] Scriptural theme: "Fulcite me floribus, stipite me malis, quia amore langueo" (*Cant.,* II, 5).
Mr. Barton Mills (*ed. cit.,* p. 107, note 6) observes: "Cf. a better interpretation of these words (*Cant.,* II, 5) in *De diligendo Deo* (see notes there) . . ." On which we have two remarks to make:
First. The editors of St. Bernard, attentive and careful as they are in their commentary, seem to be haunted by the question whether these interpretations of the Biblical text always respect the letter. It hardly needs to be said that St. Bernard's interpretation is a mystical one and should be treated as such, at least if we wish to understand it as he understood it.
Second. The interpretation of these words in the *De diligendo Deo* may possibly be better, but the chief thing is that it is different. In the latter work the pomegranates are the fruits of the Passion, and the flowers are those of the Resurrection (*op. cit.,* III, 8; P.L., CLXXXII, 979 AB). The text, then, is concerned with meditation of the life of Christ, and indicates the reasons for our "amor carnalis" for Him. It is a lower degree of mystical contemplation, but it is, nevertheless, a degree. Here, in the *De gradibus humilitatis,* the interpretation of the same words is moral. St. Bernard sees in them a description of the state of a soul prepared for ecstasy, but not yet entered on ecstasy. It is quite common to find the same text interpreted by one and the same author, first "moraliter" and then "mystice".

at last find entrance into the chamber of the King, for whose love she longs.[145]

IV. MYSTIC UNION

"There, when silence has been made in heaven for a space,[146] it may be of half an hour,[147] she rests calmly in those dear embraces,[148] herself indeed asleep, but her heart on the watch[149] how while the time lasts she may look into

[145] LANGUOR.—The state of the soul in the absence of the beloved (*In Cant. Cant.*, Sermo LI, 3; P.L., CLXXXIII, 1026 B).—Synonyms: *languor animi, mentis hebetudo, inertia spiritus.*—Scriptural theme: *Cant.*, II, 5.
This state may consist in desire, not yet satisfied, for the *osculum*, or in the interval between two mystic unions (*In Cant. Cant.*, Sermo IX, 3; P.L., CLXXXIII, 816). This is the case in the text with which we are concerned. It may also be the chastisement inflicted by God for some movement of pride (*In Cant. Cant.*, Sermo LIV, 8; 1042).
[146] MODICUM.—This word is often used by St. Bernard to express the brevity of the mystic union. Cf. "O modicum et modicum! . . ." (*In Cant. Cant.*, Sermo LXXIV, 4; P.L., CLXXXIII, 1140 C).
Scriptural theme: "Modicum et non videbitis me; et iterum modicum, et videbitis me" (*John*, XVI, 17).
[147] Scriptural theme: "factum est silentium in coelo, quasi media hora" (*Apoc.*, VIII, 1).—Cf. WILLIAM OF SAINT-THIERRY, *De contemplando Deo*, IV, 10; P.L., CLXXXIV, 372 D.—Mr. Barton Mills (*ed. cit.* p. 107, note 6) observes: "It is difficult, e.g., to trace the relevance of the silence made in heaven (a clear allusion to *Rev.*, VIII, 1) to the slumbers of the Bride. . . ." The connection, however, becomes clear if we note that St. Bernard is here thinking of Gregory the Great, and that he had undoubtedly in his mind the mystical commentary on the same text given by this saint. Gregory compares the soul of the righteous to heaven; the silence in heaven is therefore the cessation of active life which yields to the peace of contemplation in the righteous soul. See below, p. 219, note 21. Gregory the Great's text is resumed by D. Cuthbert BUTLER, *Benedictine Monachism*, Ch. VII, pp. 82-86.
[148] AMPLEXUS.—Spiritual conjunction between God, Who desires to enter into union with the purified soul, and the soul into which He is infused by grace.—Scriptural theme: *Cant.*, II, 6; VIII, 3.
I have not succeeded in finding any express definition of the term in St. Bernard, even in the sermon in which he comments on *Cant.*, II, 6. On the other hand, the state designated by *amplexus* seems to me to be described, in so far as it can be, in *In Cant. Cant.*, Sermo XXXII, 6; P.L., CLXXXIII, 943. It is therefore a Scriptural metaphor indicating ecstasy, as analysed by St. Bernard in his commentary on *Cant.*, II, 7: the slumber of the soul in the Divine embrace (*In Cant. Cant.*, Sermo LII, 2; P.L., CLXXXIII, 1030 C). St. Bernard has not specially commented on the "amplexabitur" of *Cant.*, II, 6, probably because the whole of Sermon LII, which bears on II, 7, is a commentary on it.
Note a definition of the term (at once of the human *amplexus* and the divine *amplexus*) in WILLIAM OF SAINT-THIERRY, *De contemplando Deo*, Prooemium, 3; P.L., CLXXXIV, 366 BC.
[149] Scriptural theme: *Cant.*, V, 2.—*Dormitio*, generally commented in connection with the terms:
SOMNUS, SOPOR.—A state characterized by a two-fold effect of grace:

the hidden secrets of truth, on whose memory she will feast as soon as she returns to herself. There she beholds things invisible and hears things unutterable, of which it is not lawful for man to speak.[150] These are things that surpass all that knowledge which night showeth unto night.[151] Yet day unto day uttereth speech, and it is permitted to us to speak wisdom among the wise and to express in spiritual terms those things that are spiritual".[152] (*De grad. humilitatis*, VII, 21; P.L., CLXXXII, 953).

First. The soul is freed from the use of the bodily senses; this constitutes ecstasy properly so called. In this sense it may be said that the first moment of this mystic slumber is *Extasis*. It is the state that came upon Adam at the moment of the creation of Eve: "corporeis excedens sensibus obdormisse videtur." Bernard's remark leaves no room for misconception of his meaning: "Ille soporatus videtur prae excessu contemplationis." The death of Christ was another slumbering of this kind, for the life of the senses was suspended in Him, not by an excess of contemplation, but by an excess of charity (*In Septuag.*, Sermo II, 1-2; P.L., CLXXXIII, 166-167). Second. Nor is this all. The slumbering of the external senses is accompanied, in the mystic slumber, by an "abduction" of the internal sense. By that must be understood that without falling asleep, but on the contrary remaining watchful, the internal sense is carried away by God, who illumines it. This state therefore has all the appearance of a sleep, but is quite the opposite of a torpor: "Magis autem istiusmodi vitalis vigilque sopor sensum interiorem illuminat, et morte propulsata vitam tribuit sempiternam. Revera enim dormitio est, quae tamen sensum non sopiat, sed abducat" (*In Cant. Cant.*, Sermo LII, 3; P.L., CLXXXIII, 1031).

[150] ST. PAUL, I *Cor.*, II, 9-10; 2 *Cor.*, XII, 1-4. The ineffable character of ecstasy is immediately due to the state of "abduction" in which the senses are as long as it lasts.

[151] *Ps.*, XVIII, 3.—St. Bernard comments elsewhere on this text, but in a different context (*De diversis*, Sermo XLIX; P.L., CLXXXIII, 671-672). Our passage probably means: "They surpass all that knowledge whereby human understanding would communicate with another understanding. And yet God can utter these things to the illuminated soul, and to the wise we may speak wisdom. . . ." &c. See Sermo XLIX, *loc. cit.*, for the assimilation of day to God, and *ibid*, 672 A, for the meaning of the word "eructat".

[152] ST. PAUL, I *Cor.*, II, 13. A text invoked by St. Bernard when he would remind us that images expressing mystical union must be taken in a spiritual, not in a material sense. Cf. ST. BERNARD, *In Cant. Cant.*, Sermo XXXI, 6; P.L., CLXXXIII, 943 B *init.*

We see then that what Mr. Barton Mills (*ed. cit.*, p. 107, note 6) calls "a strange medley of metaphor and Scriptural allusions" is open to explanation. In the first place all the metaphors, as far as I can see, are Scriptural allusions. Here therefore we have no mixture, but Scriptural texts understood in a mystical sense. Furthermore, the procedure, seeing that we are in the Middle Ages, is not in the least strange, but on the contrary quite classical (see E. GILSON, *Les idées et les lettres*, pp. 154-169). Finally, when we take these metaphors in their technical sense, the train of thought at once appears: "The righteous soul, in which reason maintains silence for a short time, now

This doctrinal synthesis would seem to have presented itself to St. Bernard's mind as a personal discovery of his own. Perhaps it was but a re-discovery; but if that was the case he was not himself aware of the recollection, and the opening of the Chapter seems even to betray an effort to seize some confused intuition about to escape his grasp.[153] However this may be, the three stages here described may easily be brought into conformity with the celebrated text of St. Paul, on which St. Bernard's is a kind of doctrinal commentary. St. Paul tells us that he was "caught up" into the third heaven. Note that he says *"caught up"*, not *"led up"*. For the Son indeed leads the soul to the first degree—that is, the first heaven—which is that of humility; the Holy Spirit leads it up to the second degree— that is, the second heaven—which is that of mercy; but to pass from the second to the third needs something more than a leading: a carrying away and a catching-up is indispensable. One who is led moves of himself, co-operates in the movement, and we ourselves thus labour to acquire humility and mercy, under the guidance of the Son and the Spirit. St. Paul, then, could let himself be led up to the second heaven, but to attain to the third he would need to be caught up: *rapi oportuit.*

That is the exact sense of the word *raptus.* It means, therefore, that the soul thus ravished has no part of its own to play in the operation, which is effected in it without its co-operation. The trait, moreover, is characteristic of the operations of the Father. The Son became Incarnate and came down among us to save us; and it was therefore with

reposes in the longed-for slumber of ecstasy. She sleeps; but her deepest sense, which is love, remains watchful within her, and gazes into the inner-most recesses of truth, the memory of which will be her food when she returns to herself. There she sees the invisible, and hears secret words which man may not utter to man. But God may utter them to the soul, and we may speak of them among the wise, giving our words a spiritual meaning to convey spiritual things."

us, and from the midst of the world that He effected our salvation. And the Holy Spirit too, descends from heaven, whence He comes on "mission". It is therefore fitting that the first and second stages should be traversed by us under their guidance. But the Father never came down from heaven, nor was He ever sent among us. He is everywhere of course, but in His own Person He is never to be found save in heaven. It is in this emphatic sense that the words of the Lord's Prayer are to be understood: *Pater noster qui es in coelis.* The Person of the Father is there, in heaven, and there remains. St. Paul therefore could not have been led there by that Person; he must needs have been caught up. Moreover "those whom the Son calls by humility to the first heaven, the Spirit brings together by love in the second, and the Father raises by way of contemplation to the third. In the first they are humbled by the truth and say, *in veritate tua humiliasti me.* In the second they rejoice together in the truth and sing, *ecce quam bonum et quam jucundum habitare fratres in unum,* for of charity it is written: *congaudet autem veritate.* In the third heaven they are carried up into the innermost recesses of truth and say, *secretum meum mihi, secretum meum mihi*".[154]

In this analysis of *raptus* we might perhaps be tempted to see the description of a state of soul specifically distinct from the *excessus* which will occupy us henceforward. I would not venture roundly to assert that St. Bernard was unconscious of any difference between the two cases, but I have not succeeded in finding any text that authorizes a clear distinction, still less any attempt to arrange them in hierarchical order. If they are described in different terms that, perhaps, may be due to the difference between two standpoints from which states of this kind may be viewed: on the one hand that of the theologian who is to determine *ex professo* their conditions, as St. Bernard has been doing,—

E

and, on the other, that of the mystic explaining himself, drawing on his own experience in an attempt to describe what passes in his own soul, as he is now about to do for our benefit. To deny the basic unity of the states he describes once the plane of visions and images has been frankly abandoned, would be to undertake to prove that there exists for St. Bernard a mode of union between the soul and God which is other than an assumption òf the soul by the Father, following its restoration by the Son and the Holy Spirit. Now we are about to see that this is precisely the characteristic trait of what St. Bernard describes as his own personal ecstasy. If he seems to arrest his description at the point where the soul, already filled with charity, exulting in the voice of truth, implores God to "reach out His right hand to the work of Thy hands", so to unite it with Himself,[155] is it not simply because from that point on all is mystery? Even for the subject undergoing it the *excessus*[156] is lost in the ineffable as soon as it becomes an accomplished fact. How then are such states of soul to be represented?

Their first character consists in being immediate and direct contacts with God, and therefore the first condition required is that such contacts should be conceivable. Now they are so; for inter-communion of this kind is made possible by the immateriality of the soul on the one hand, and the absolute purity of the spirituality of God on the other. There are four orders of spirits: animals, men, angels, and God. The animal is not without a spiritual principle, but it is essentially body, and its *spiritus* has such slight capacity to exist apart from a body that it dies with it. Man is different. He possesses a body, and needs it moreover for the acquisition of that knowledge without which he would never be able to arrive at any conception of God. St. Paul's famous phrase: *invisibilia Dei* . . . clearly signifies that although we are spiritual beings, the body is necessary for the acquisition of this science of God without which it would be impossible to hope for beatitude. It may be objected, perhaps, that baptized infants who die without coming to the use of reason nevertheless see God; but this is a miracle of Divine grace, *et quid ad me de miraculo Dei, qui de naturalibus dissero?* As long as we hold to the natural order the body is so necessarily a part of man that it is no less than the cognitive instrument without which we could never attain our supernatural end. Bernard then, as we may perceive, would have raised no fundamental objection against the epistemology of St. Thomas Aquinas.

Angels too at times have bodies, but these are no part of their nature since they do not need them for their own sake but only for ours. Bernard will not decide the question whether these bodies are "natural" or "assumed", for he knows that the Fathers were divided on the point, but he clearly affirms that angelic cognition is in any event wholly free from sensible elements; the bodies of angels do not help them to know but help them to minister to us, their future fellow-citizens in the celestial City. However, spiritual as we are and they too are, they cannot enter into direct union with our spirit, nor we with theirs. Faithful to the Augustinian principle of the inviolability of spirits, the law of mutually closed consciousnesses as we may call it, Bernard maintains that no spirit can enter into union with another spirit directly and without the intermediation of signs. The angels are impenetrable to each other and to men, and men are impenetrable to each other and to the angels; only God can penetrate them. "This prerogative must therefore be reserved for the supreme and uncircumscribed Spirit, Who alone, when He imparts knowledge either to angel or to man, does not need that we should have ears to hear or that He should have a mouth to speak. By His own power

He penetrates our souls, by His own power He makes Himself known; and being Himself a pure spirit, He is apprehended by the pure."[157] In this sense, then, it may be said that God alone is absolutely spiritual; He needs a body neither to exist, nor to know, nor to act.[158] Nothing then prevents the Holy Spirit, should He wish to do so, from directly penetrating our spirit.

A second condition required before this union can be effected is this: that between the Spirit and our spirit the Word should serve as intermediary. That, it would seem, is no necessity on the side of God, nor is it even one due to the essential characters of human nature; but it would appear to have arisen from the depravation of this nature by sin. The Son became incarnate in order to redeem us, that is to say to re-open the way, which the Fall had closed, for love to pass between man and God. For us, therefore, He has become the indispensable condition of divine union. We can go even farther. Is not indeed the God-Man a kind of concrete ecstasy in Himself, an ecstasy in which the Word assumes man and Man is assumed by God? He is therefore the Kiss *par excellence*, the *Osculum* of the Canticle of Canticles, and it is through Him that we may hope for the favours of the mystical life. The point has so important a bearing on the sources of the mystical doctrine of St. Bonaventure,[159] that we must mark the absolute character of this exigency. No man, how great soever he be, can pretend to more than what is asked by the Bride of the Canticle: *osculetur me osculo oris sui*, that is to say not with His mouth itself, but only with the kiss of His mouth. "Christo, igitur, osculum est plenitudo, Paulo participatio: ut cum ille de ore, iste tantum de osculo osculatum glorietur."[160] Christ therefore, in Whom human nature is assumed by the Divine nature, is Himself the Divine Kiss. Man can hope for no more than to receive the kiss of this

Kiss; that Ecstasy which was the Christ is the model and the source of all ecstasy, and any other is a mere participation.

It will suffice to recall briefly, as a third condition, that the soul that aspires to divine union must have cast away the fear of the slave and the cupidity of the hireling; but it is of moment, on the other hand, to make it precisely clear that she ought now to wish to go farther than the obedience of a disciple, or the piety of a son. In her is no place any more for anything less than love, for now she has become the Bride—*sponsa*—that is to say *anima sitiens Deum*, a soul thirsting for God.[161] Let us understand by that that the desire of the soul, at this point on her journey to perfection, excludes all that is other than the kiss of the Word. She who asks this kiss is she who loves: "quae vero osculum postulat, amat"; and she who loves is she who asks this kiss, and asks naught else: "Amat autem quae osculum petit. Non petit libertatem, non mercedem, non denique vel doctrinam, sed osculum."[162] In short, the love of God, when brought to this degree of intensity, has something of the character of heavenly beatitude, inasmuch as it is an end in itself, the possession of which dispenses with all the rest because it includes it. Nor is this without good reason, for we shall soon have to define mystical union as a foretaste of this beatitude. But before we come to this point we must first of all enumerate the marks of so absolutely exclusive a love. They may be resumed in three words: the soul that loves thus, loves *caste, sancte, ardenter*.

That its love is chaste is very evident, for we know that "chaste" here means *disinterested*. Now Whom the soul loves she loves then for Himself, and for the sake of nothing else whatever, not even for any one of those gifts He has to give. She manifests all that direct simplicity of love properly so called, which distinguishes it from cupidity.

The soul then goes straight to its object and seeks in it nothing but itself: *quae ipsum quem amat quaerit, non aliud quidquam ipsius.* Being chaste, this love is also holy. Let us thereby understand that it is just the opposite of an affection of concupiscence, since it consists in the longing for a union of will between man and God. What the soul desires in the kiss is precisely the infusion of the Holy Spirit, Whose grace will unite her with the Father. St. Bernard affirms it so often that here there is no room for doubt about the meaning of his formulae: ". . . *ab osculo, quod non est aliud nisi infundi Spiritu Sancto"; "non erit abs re osculum Spiritum Sanctum intelligi"; "dari sibi osculum hoc est Spiritum illum."*[163] And finally this love is ardent, in the sense that it excludes all other affections from the soul, not by destroying but by absorbing them. This is particularly true of these two other primary human emotions, fear and concupiscence. So important are the consequences of this transformation that we must pause to consider them.

A love of sufficient ardour is a kind of inebriation;[164] and so it must needs be in order that the soul may have the mad audacity to aspire to the divine union. How, were it otherwise, could it ever dare to pretend to it? Were reason to remain judge, it would prudently conclude it absurd for a creature to aspire to such an honour, especially senseless on the part of a fallen creature, so often sunk in vice and entangled in the mire of the flesh. The mere thought of the infinite majesty of God is enough to fill the soul with fear if she be impure, with reverence if she be pure. Fear and adoration—there we have the only feelings which can normally find place in the human soul as long as it holds to reason for guide, even if this be accompanied by a certain lukewarm love.

It falls out quite otherwise when love attains to the highest degree of ardour of which it is capable. Transfiguring fear and cupidity, it leaves the soul free to pass beyond them. Fear is then no longer terror, but rather this profound reverence for the thing that it loves, which accords the loved object all its worth and makes it only the more desirable. Cupidity too is re-absorbed into the love of the Beloved Himself, Who becomes at once both the means of love and its end. The mere vehemence of this affection, simply because it leaves no room for any other, naturally produces in us an audacity, a confidence—*fiducia*—which carries it away of its own spontaneity beyond all that would restrain it from aspiring to divine union did we listen only to the voice of reason. Modesty, reverence born of fear, majesty of God—the soul forgets them all in this inebriation: *"quae ita proprio ebriatur amore, ut majestatem non cogitet . . ."*; *". . . desiderio feror, non ratione . . . pudor sane reclamat, sed superat amor."*[165] This "confidence" is precisely the deliverance of the soul, in which in place of misery now begins to reign freedom from misery, because there dwells in her the Spirit of charity, Who is the spirit of Charity.

The soul that reaches this point is ready for the mystic marriage. She does not reach it without grace, or without long co-operation with grace by her own zeal (*industria*), but it seems indeed that in St. Bernard's mind, when the soul has arrived at this point in the life of grace and of penitence, the marriage to the Word and her assumption by the Father are violences done to Heaven, which Heaven suffers from those who love it with an ardent love. To perceive to what extent it is legitimate to hope for them we have only to remember Who the Holy Spirit is: the reciprocal love of the Father and the Son, their mutual benignity, the goodness of the One for the Other.[166] In asking to be united to the Word, the soul therefore asks to be united to Him and to the Father, by the mediation of the Holy Spirit, Who is the Bond of the One and the Other. And this is done by the Son; He reveals Himself to whom He will and reveals the Father, in giving the Holy Spirit. Such, at least provisionally, seems to be the schema of the operation: "In giving the Spirit by whom He reveals, He reveals also Himself, in giving He reveals, and in revealing gives, and since this revelation is effected by the Spirit, it not only illuminates the soul's faculty of knowing, but also enkindles her to love." Two points are here to be considered: first, the content of the revelation, and then the reason why it is given.

As regards the first we must particularly note that the marriage of the soul to the Word, although effected by love, carries with it nevertheless a certain cognitive element. It is true that knowledge itself, as St. Bernard conceived it, is very profoundly impregnated with affectivity. But it would be an excessive simplification of his thought to over-look the rôle of knowledge in his doctrine. Even the sensitive love of Christ, as we have seen, needs to be controlled by theological science, and when this love that mediates union with the Word has been attained St. Bernard will still give knowledge a part to play. When love has come to this degree of vehemence there cannot but be union with the Word, but the soul is not to be united with the Word, Who is Wisdom, without receiving increase of her own wisdom. We must therefore hold to both aspects of the case: know-ledge has a part to play in the marriage of the soul to the Word first because, without knowledge, the soul would have nothing to love, and next because, in such a union, she gains direct experience of this Object; but it is equally true to say that it is because she savours her object in the act of experiencing it that her knowledge is wisdom: "She invokes the Holy Spirit so that through Him she may receive at once the taste for knowledge and the seasoning of grace to accompany it. And well is it said that knowledge given

in a kiss is received with love, since a kiss is the sign of love."
Both knowledge and love then are required if the union of
the soul with God is to be complete: "Let no one think that
he has received this kiss if he understands the truth without
loving it, or loves it without understanding, for in it is no
place either for error or lukewarmness." In short: "The
grace of the kiss conveys both the one and the other gift
(scil. of the Holy Spirit), both the light of knowledge and
the unction of devotion. For He is the Spirit of Wisdom
and Understanding; and as the bee bears both honey and
wax, so also he bears in Himself both that which enkindles
the light of knowledge, and that which infuses the savour
of grace."[167] The ardent love of the soul unites it therefore
with the Holy Spirit by the Word, and this implies impregna-
tion with an infused light which is indivisibly the charity
of understanding and the understanding of charity. But
why then does this union take place?

The answer may be put in a few words, and in fact it has
already been suggested. A love of Christ which is truly
ardent to the point of becoming exclusive puts the soul in
such a state of conformity with the mutual love of the
Divine Persons that it leaves the way free for the marriage
of the soul to God. That is what we have now to explain
in order to see how the objections directed against the
doctrine of St. Bernard, arising on a plane wholly alien
to that on which he moves, disappear at once if we adopt
the standpoint which is his.

Let us return to the soul in that state in which we had
left it before divine charity had restored it to something of
its lost liberties. Defaced, divided against itself, it looks
upon itself with horror because it feels itself to be, at one
and the same time, both itself and another—a likeness
destroyed in an indestructible image. Let us now compare
what it then was with what it has now become. Charity,

E*

taking up its abode in the soul, has eliminated the *proprium* and has substituted a will common to man and to God. Now the *proprium* is unlikeness. The immediate effect, therefore, of the love of God is to restore in the soul the lost divine likeness. Thence flow consequences of capital importance for our understanding of the doctrine.

In the first place, since the soul has now recovered her own true nature, she recognizes herself once more in all the fullness of her being. Image as she has always been, she now moreover re-becomes a likeness, which sin had made her cease to be. The interior conflict which was tearing her to pieces has now an end, at least in such measure as that is possible in this life. Peace is re-born, misery becomes supportable, and now that she has re-become herself, a living love of God, the soul is able once more to delight in the sight of her own countenance. Such then is the first aspect of this new life, of which peace of conscience makes a kind of paradise.

Nor is this all. When a divine likeness, thus restored, knows herself again in herself, then she recognizes in herself the God whose likeness she bears. Seeing herself, she sees Him. St. Paul teaches that God may be known through His creatures. How much more easily then can He be known by way of this creature He has made to His own image and likeness![168] And note well that the fact has its consequences on the side of God as well as on the side of man. Self-scrutiny in the deformed soul reveals nothing but her own deformity, God is no longer to be discerned there; but neither is God able to recognize Himself in the soul's pollution: He sees Himself in us no more than we see Him. But as soon as charity reigns in the soul, then God recognizes Himself in us as we recognize Him in ourselves. Hence two further consequences.

The first is that the supposed antinomy between love of

self and love of God vanishes. On the side of God, in Whose eternal love for Himself is no shadow of change or alteration, we can say that all remains the same. He loves Himself; the soul, making itself unlike Him, is withdrawn from the love wherewith He loves Himself—she has, so to speak, retired from the field of the changeless Divine love. No longer seeing Himself in her who resembles Him no more, He no longer loves Himself in her. Then emerges the full meaning of St. Bernard's expressions; "peregrinating" in the Land of Unlikeness, man wanders endlessly through the circle of the reprobate, in the shadows of a world withdrawn from any ray of the Divine love. On the contrary, as soon as the soul recovers the divine likeness, God once more sees Himself in her, and loves Himself once more in her, with the same love as that with which He has never ceased to love Himself.

By the ways of the unstable creature man arrives at the same result. When there triumphed in him this "proper will", this love of the unlikeness as such, he could not love God in loving himself. To love himself then was to love a detestation of God. Suppose on the contrary that the likeness has been restored in the soul, then what she loves in loving herself is a divine likeness. Now to resemble God is to love God for God's sake, since God is this love itself. Impossible then to ask St. Bernard to define the supreme degree of love in any other way than that in which he defines it; to love oneself no longer save for God. It is impossible to eliminate the love of self, not merely because along with it there would disappear the created being from whom it is altogether inseparable, but also because God loves us, and we should cease to be like to Him if we ceased to love ourselves. It is equally impossible to strike out the clause "save for God", for since God loves neither Himself nor us save for Himself, we should cease to be like

Him were we to love ourselves otherwise than He loves us, that is to say only for Himself. Let us add finally that since God's love for us is englobed in His love for Himself, to love us exclusively for Himself is identical with what in Him it is to love Himself exclusively. At the ideal limit, inaccessible in this life but prefigured in ecstasy, there would be perfect communion between God's will and ours. Just as the love that God bears us is but the love that He bears Himself, so the love that we bear ourselves would then be naught but the love that we should then bear God.

The second consequence is this: that in according to the conception of image the central place that it occupies in this doctrine, we are thenceforward on the way to understand why every life of charity tends of its own accord towards the mystical unions. To love oneself, once one knows oneself to be a divine likeness, is to love God in oneself and to love oneself in God. And for God, when He complacently beholds Himself in an image ever more and more perfect of Himself, that is to love Himself in her and to love her in Himself. Like always desires its like; man therefore desires this God Whom he represents, and God covets, so to speak, this soul in whom He recognizes Himself. How should the betrothed not ardently desire to become the Bride, and how should the Bridegroom not desire to enter into union with this betrothed, whose whole beauty is the work of His love? That is why it sometimes happens that from the first or the second heaven the Father ravishes the soul to the third; that is how it comes about that, yielding to the impetuous desire of a soul that tends towards Him only out of the love that He bears Himself, the Spouse allows this impetuous stream for a time to rejoin its source: Love gives Himself to love as He wills to give, anticipating the hour for which He created it, when He shall give Himself to it as He is.

CHAPTER V

UNITAS SPIRITUS

THE foregoing analyses have put at our disposal all the materials required for the solution of a certain number of essential problems. Above all things they must be taken in some kind of order. In what order? I am almost tempted to dismiss the point as unimportant; but order at any rate there must be if we are to keep clear of these circular deductions in which St. Bernard's critics so often involve themselves—not observing that when they arrive at their conclusion they have not yet quitted their starting-point.

First of all then let us examine the question of "pantheism" or the supposed "pantheistic tendencies" of the Cistercian mysticism; observing at once that while, as a matter of right, the very conception of a pantheistic Christian mysticism is a contradiction in terms, the mysticism of St. Bernard, as a matter of fact, is in radical opposition to all pantheism.[169]

As regards the first point, its settlement obviously depends on our definitions. Mysticism may be conceived in an endless variety of ways, some wide enough to embrace in their scope the vague poetical emotions of a Wordsworth or a Lamartine, others leaving no room for anything save the rigorous terms of a St. Thomas Aquinas or a St. John of the Cross. That is so much the more reason for taking up a position—we must offer our opponents a clear concept to discuss. Now in the present instance it is of the first importance to grasp that wherever there is any trace, how slight soever, of pantheism, there the problem of Christian mysticism ceases to arise.

By way of hypothesis, let us admit one of these poetico-metaphysical states,[170] in which is effected a sort of fusion of the soul and God, as if the two substances were henceforth one, were it only in a certain respect. Explain their nature as you will, such states always presuppose that the divine being is in no real and irreducible transcendence with respect to the human being. No one doubts, of course, that even for the poet or metaphysician who sets his face in this direction the states he takes for mystical are rare, exceptional, open only to an élite, and then only at the price of a severe discipline. But the question does not lie there, for what we want to know is simply this: whether, yes or no, we can admit the possibility of a coincidence, even partial, between the human substance and the Divine substance—whether we can admit it to be then in fact realized. To admit this is to evacuate the conception of mysticism of all its content for a Christian. For the Christian God is Being—*Ego sum qui sum*—and this creative being is radically other than the being of His creatures. The whole drama of Christian mysticism lies in the fact that the creature feels a need for his Creator much more absolute than that of any being for his god in any other metaphysical economy, and in the fact that, for the same reason, a Creator is much less accessible to His creature than is any god to beings less radically dependent on him. The Christian asks, and always asks: How can I rejoin Being, I, who am nothing? If you lower, were it but for an instant and at any point, the barrier set up by the contingence of being between man and God, then you rob the Christian mystic of his God, and you rob him therefore of his mysticism. He can do without any god who is not inaccessible; the sole God Who by nature is inaccessible is also the sole God he can in no wise do without.

The fact is, of course, that no other God exists. St. Bernard puts it clearly enough for those who are willing to listen. No matter how the mystical union may be interpreted in his doctrine, this at least must be laid down before everything else: that it absolutely excludes all confusion, all substantial unification, between the Divine *Being* as such, and the human *being* as such, and conversely. Had we no knowledge of the general tendency of his mysticism, or of the wholehearted Christianity it expresses, we should have, if we needed them, his own explicit declarations to assure us of this. Never, in any event, will the substance of the mystic himself become the substance of God; never, in any event, not even in that of the beatific vision—which otherwise would abolish the thing it is destined to perfect and fulfil—will any part of the human substance coincide with that of God; never, in any event, will that part of the substance of the soul we call the human will, coincide with this substantial Divine attribute: the will of God. *Manebit quidem substantia,*[171] the text is formal. There are others of the same kind, as we shall show farther on; but before coming to this point we must set out in detail a second thesis that flows at once from the foregoing.

Without going so far as to detect pantheist tendencies in St. Bernard, without even dreaming of such absurdities, some historians have credited him with a vague tendency to conceive the mystic union as an annihilation of the human personality, as if this were destined to be wholly dissolved in God. Here again the interpretation does not survive examination of the very texts which suggested it. Everybody thinks in this connection of the famous comparisons proposed by St. Bernard between the soul "deified" by ecstasy and the drop of water diluted in wine, or the air transfigured into light, or the glowing iron that becomes fire. But let us consider these expressions attentively;

for never does his ardour tempt him to lose sight of that careful measure which is the true theologian's golden rule. What happens to the drop of water? "Deficere a se tota *videtur*"; it seems, but we know that even when indefinitely diluted it does not cease to exist. What happens to the glowing iron? "*Igni simillimum* fit"; it becomes as like it as possible, but it *is* not it, nor indeed could it possibly be it if it is to be free to become like it. What happens to the air illuminated by the sun? It is so penetrated with its light, "ut non tam illuminatus, quam ipsum lumen esse *videatur*". Here again we have a mere appearance, a transfiguration of an indestructible substance by the glorious form in which it is henceforth arrayed.[172] St. Bernard therefore never spoke of any abolition of the creature, but of a transformation.

It is true that this transformation may appear at first glance as the equivalent of an abolition: *pene adnullari;* but that, in truth, is mere appearance. To what extent it is illusory, how far it corresponds to a reality, we shall have to consider. For the moment, however, we must particularly note that it can mean neither a destruction of the soul by the ecstatic union, nor even any diminution of its individuality. Quite the contrary. With its face set towards the beatific vision, ecstasy, although essentially distinct from that vision, prefigures and partakes of its characteristics. Now the beatific vision is the crowning of the whole work of creation. It consummates it. It is the establishment of the creature in a divine state of glory, in which it is borne to a supreme point of perfection such as only a God could gratuitously bestow. *Creatio, reformatio, consummatio,*[173] these are the three great stages of the Divine plan; and just as the "reformation" is that of the creation corrupted, so the "consummation" is that of the creation restored. It is already the same in the case of the mystic union, where the soul is borne, for short instants, to a perfection that is more than human, a perfection which, far from annihilating it, only exalts and glorifies.

Thus we are already assured of two closely connected points: the soul does not become the substance of God, neither does it lose its own being in ecstasy. Let us turn now to the positive side of these states and try to explain their nature without falsifying St. Bernard's expressions, retaining them all and weakening none. For observe— he does not hesitate to speak of a "deification": *sic affici, deificare est.*[174] What then are we to make of such a state? Undoubtedly it is a union, and the resultant unity. But of what nature is this union?

The answer can be put in a few lines. The mystical union integrally respects this real distinction between the Divine substance and the human substance, between the will of God and the will of man; it is neither a confusion of the two substances in general, nor a confusion of the substances of the two wills in particular; but it is their perfect accord, the coincidence of two willings. Two distinct spiritual substances—two substances even *infinitely* distinct— two wills no less distinct as far as concerns the existential order, but in which intention and object coincide to such an extent that the one is a perfect image of the other, there we have the mystical union and unity as St. Bernard conceived them. We have only to compare them with the union and unity of the Divine Persons and we shall see at once how far they go and where also they stop short. The unity of God is that of the *consubstantiale*, the unity of man with God is limited to the *consentibile*: "Between man and God, on the contrary, there is no unity of substance or nature, and it cannot be said that they are One, albeit it may be said with certainty and perfect truth that if they are attached to each other and bound together by the tie of love, then they are one spirit. But this unity results rather from a concurrence of wills than from a union of essences. By which is made sufficiently clear, if I do not mistake, not only the difference but the disparity of these unities, the one existing in the same essence, the other between distinct essences. What could be more different than the unity of that which is one, and the unity which is merely the unity of several?

"Thus it is with these two unities. The thing that delimits their respective spheres is, as I have said, the line that separates 'to be one' (*unus*) from 'to be the One' (*unum*). For the word One designates the unity of essence in the Father and the Son, but to be one, when we speak of God and man, designates quite a different kind of unity, a tender consent of affections. Undoubtedly we may very well say that the Father and the Son are one (*unus*) if we add some defining word, as, for example, one God, one Lord, and so forth, for then we speak of Each with respect to Himself and not with respect to the Other. For their Godhead or their Majesty is no more diverse in Each than is their Substance, their Essence, or their Nature; and none of these last, if you consider it with due piety, is a thing diverse in Them, or distinct, but altogether One. I say too little; they are One also with Them. What shall we say of that other unity whereby many hearts may be reputed one, and many souls one? I think it does not deserve the name of unity when compared with this, which instead of being a union of a plurality, marks the singularity of One. That, therefore, is a unity unique and supreme, not brought about by any unifying act but existing from all eternity. . . . Much less can it be considered as due to any sort of conjunction of their essences or consent of their wills, for here there can be no such thing. In Them, as I have said, there is but one Essence and but one Will; and in that which is thus One there cannot be consent, or composition,

or conjunction, or anything of that kind. There must be
at least two wills if there is to be consent, and similarly
there must be two essences if this consent is to produce
conjunction or unification. There is nothing of this kind in
the Father and the Son, since in Them are neither two
essences nor two wills. Each of these things is one with
Them; or rather, as I remember to have said before, these
two things are the One in Them and with Them; whereby
abiding Each in the Other, unchangeably and incom-
prehensibly, they are truly and uniquely One. Yet if anyone
wishes to say that between the Father and the Son there
is accord, I shall not contest it, provided it be understood
that this is not a union of wills but a unity of will. But as
to God and man each subsisting separately in his own
proper substance and his own proper will, if they abide
mutually in each other we understand it quite differently:
they are not one by confusion of two substances but by the
accord of two wills. In that then consists their union, a
communion of wills and their accord in charity. Happy
that union if you experience it; but if you compare it with
this other, nothing."[175]

Words heavily charged with meaning, admirably defining
the position of St. Bernard. The promised deification of
the *De diligendo Deo* is nothing less, but also nothing more,
than a perfect accord between the will of the human
substance and the will of the Divine substance, in a strict
distinction of the substances and the wills. And let it not
be supposed that here we have to do with any minimizing
interpretation of the doctrine of St. Bernard; to refuse to
accept it under the pretext that it wears the air of a *pia
interpretatio* would amount to a refusal to grasp anything
whatever in his thought. Nor let us imagine, that if it
is not to be charged upon the timidity of the interpreter,
it gives us any right to denounce a constraint or embarrass-

ment in St. Bernard's thought itself. Harnack thought so, and would persuade us to the same opinion. Seeing in St. Bernard an ardent mystical piety—the true piety— beating vainly against the obstacles heaped in its path by the rigidity of dogma, he could not but see in his doctrine the concrete expression of that conflict between the interior life of the soul on the one hand and dogma on the other, in which, according to him, the whole history of medieval theology may be summed up.[176] Strange subjective illusion in a scholar whose work, so highly praised for its objectivity, is more deeply involved than any other in the personal faith of its author. For there we have a complete misconception of the facts. St. Bernard is no mystic of love forced against all his real inclinations to stop short of his aim by the dogma of the Divine transcendence; the three points we have touched on in succession are strung upon an unbroken thread which, when followed out, will lead us on to a fourth: the substance of God will never be our substance, the will of God will never be our will, union with God can never be anything but the accord of two distinct wills, and *therefore* this union with God can be effected in no other way than by and through love. Here is no case of a love resigning itself to the transcendence of its object. If its object were not transcendent there would be no basis for the existence of the love.

Here too we are in no need to fall back upon one of those logical reconstructions with which history has perforce at times to content itself. St. Bernard is not only fully capable of grasping his own thought but excels in formulating it: "God, the same God Who has said: *Ego sum qui sum*, in the true sense of the term *is*, because He is Being. What partici- pation, what conjunction can there be between him who is not and Him who is? How can things so different be joined together? *For me*, says the Saint, *to adhere to my God is my good.* Immediately united to Him we cannot be, but this union may be effected perhaps through some intermediary."[177] What is this intermediary, this middle term, between the creature and Being? We might perhaps be tempted to think of cupidity or of fear, but we know already why these must be considered as merely temporary expedients. The sole truly sure and indestructible bond is charity, for the man in whom it dwells *tam suaviter quam secure ligatus, adhaerens Deo, unus spiritus est cum eo.*

Hence we may be well assured that the thought of St. Bernard is all of a piece; it is not in the least in the nature of a compromise between his deepest aspirations and any kind of external pressure or constraint. On the contrary, love is there inserted between Being and beings as called for by the gulf which otherwise would separate the creature from his Creator; it pours itself out in order to fill it. But observe well the way in which it fills it: the man who loves God becomes *unus spiritus cum eo.* Unity of spirit, therefore, is the sole bond of unity conceivable between creature and Creator. What are we to understand by that?

A unity of spirit is a unity, first of all, which is no more than the unity of two spirits, that is to say it is not that identity of substance we have explicitly excluded above, but only the perfect accord of their structures and lives. The true nature of this unity is expressed unequivocally in the word "likeness". The only way in which one spirit can become another without ceasing to be itself, is by way of perfect resemblance to this other. The thing that invests St. Bernard's mysticism with its distinctive character is the manner in which the mystical union is linked up with the nature of the divine image in man,[178] for it is just this that makes all the difficulties with which his mystical theology has been encumbered move towards the solution he provides. Let us go over the objections charged against it and see

what becomes of them when looked at from the true centre
of everything—the fact that man is an image of God.

Cistercian ecstasy, it is said, and precisely in virtue of
its ecstatic character, tends towards a sort of loss of the
individual in God.[179] That love, whose so great vehemence
precipitates the soul towards its divine object, can by no
means attain it save by total self-renunciation—an exigence
at issue with the very foundations of the doctrine, since
love of self is there laid down as primary and indestructible.
The objection is feeble. What is the object of the Cistercian
ascesis? Progressively to eliminate the *proprium* in order to
install charity in its place. What is this *proprium*? Unlikeness—that in virtue of which man wills to be different from
God. But what, on the other hand, is man? A divine likeness. It is therefore perfectly clear that in such a doctrine
there is a coincidence between the loss of "proper will"
and the restoration of our true nature. To eliminate from
self all that stands in the way of being really oneself, that
is not to lose but to find oneself once more. The whole
difficulty in which St. Bernard is here supposed to be
involved is therefore simply due to a misconception. The
soul that forsakes itself, detaches itself from self, far from
renouncing its own being, is merely re-established on the
contrary in its own proper substance under the transforming influence of divine love.

For what in fact is the true meaning of such expressions
as "*deficere a se tota videtur*", "*a semetipsa liquescere*" and others
of the same kind? Always it is two-fold. In the first place
St. Bernard would say that the soul empties itself of this
false ego, this illusory personality of self-will, brought into
it by sin. In so doing, far from annihilating itself, it restores
itself to its own nature. A disfiguring mask falls away,
revealing the true countenance of a soul whose nature it is
to have been made to the image of God.[180] In the second

place, such expressions have always a positive meaning as well, which is indicated by St. Bernard when he adds this commentary; "a semetipsa liquescere, *atque in Dei penitus transfundi voluntatem.*" A commentary, for the rest, with which we might easily find fault on account of its brevity, were it not in turn commented by the entire mystical work of St. Bernard. For this transfusion into the will of God is unity of spirit itself, and it is so moreover in a two-fold sense.

Ontologically, the soul henceforth lives by the spirit of charity, by way of grace, which in us is the gift of the Holy Spirit. The life of the soul has therefore become, in virtue of and by right of this gift, what the life of God is by nature. Unity of spirit, because by this same Spirit by which God lives in Himself, we live now by grace. Impossible to unite more closely two subjects that must needs remain substantially distinct. But unity of spirit once more, because since the soul is a likeness to God, the more it conforms itself in will to God's will so much the more does it become itself. Then the soul knows itself as God knows it, loves itself as God loves it, and loves God as He loves Himself. It subsists, but now it is to be considered as a substance which, although irreducibly distinct from that of God, had no other function than to be the bearer of the Divine likeness. This likeness is its "form"; the more it is enveloped by this form, as it is here below by charity and is destined to be the more so in glory, so much the more does it become indistinguishable from God. And so much the more is it itself. Of man, then, it may be said that he tends in effect, by way of love, to make himself invisible; for this image of God will never be fully itself till nothing is any longer to be seen in it save only God: *et tunc erit omnia in omnibus Deus.*[181]

And now perhaps we may read one of these much-debated texts with some little hope of understanding it more or less as St. Bernard did.

"But flesh and blood, this vessel of clay, this earthen dwelling-place, when shall it attain at last to this [sc. this love by which a man loves not even himself save for the sake of God]? When shall it feel affection like this [*affectum :* i.e., here, love], so that inebriated[182] with divine love, forgetful of self, and become to its own self *like a broken vessel* (*Ps.*, XXX, 13), it may utterly pass over into God, and so adhere to Him as to become one spirit with Him, and say: *My flesh and my heart hath fainted away, thou art the God of my heart, and the God that is my portion for ever?* (*Ps.*, LXXII, 26). Blessed and holy should I call that man to whom it has been granted to experience such a thing in this mortal life, were it only rarely or even but once, and this so to speak in passing and for the space of a moment. For in a certain manner to lose thyself, as though thou wert not, [*quadammodo,* for man does not lose himself], and to be utterly unconscious of thyself and to be emptied of thyself and brought almost to nothing [*pene,* for the substance endures] —that pertains to the life of heaven and not to the life of human affection. And if, indeed, any mortal is occasionally admitted to this, in passing, as I have said, and only for a moment, then straightway the wicked world begins to envy him, the evil of the day disturbs,[183] this body of death becomes a burden,[184] the necessity of flesh provokes,[185] the weakness of corruption does not endure it, and, what is even more insistent than these, fraternal charity recalls.[186]

[182] *Debriatus amore:* metaphor bearing a precise significance. See p. 238, note 164, and p. 139, note 208.

[183] *Malitia diei:* a Scriptural metaphor of technical significance. It means, in St. Bernard, the duties of the active life in so far as they obstruct the free development of the contemplative life. See *In Cant. Cant.*, Sermo III, 7; P.L., CLXXXIII, 796 BC.

[184] *Corpus mortis:* the concupiscence engendered by sin. See p. 99, note 127. Cf. *Sap.* XI, 15, cited in *In Cant. Cant.*, Sermo XVI, 1; P.L., CLXXXIII, 848–849.

[185] *Carnis necessitas:* the natural necessity, the needs of nature, as contrasted with sinful cupidity. See p. 99, note 127.

[186] The duty of spiritual charity for his brethren, and of taking care for their souls, snatches the contemplative from his joys. See *In Cant. Cant.*, Sermo IX, 9; P.L., CLXXXIII, 818–819.

Alas! he is compelled to return into himself, to fall back into his own,[187] and miserably to exclaim: *Lord, I suffer violence, answer thou for me ;* and this: *Unhappy man that I am, who shall deliver me from the body of this death ? (Rom.,* VII, 24).

"Nevertheless, since the Scripture says that God *hath made all things for Himself (Prov.,* XVI, 4), the creature will surely at some time conform itself and bring itself into harmony with its Author. Some day, then, we shall come to love as He loves; so that, even as God willed all things to exist only for Himself, so we too may will to have been and to be, neither ourselves nor aught else save equally for His sake, to serve His will alone and not our pleasure.[188] Truly not the appeasing of our necessity,[189] nor the obtaining of felicity,[190] will delight so much as that His will shall be fulfilled in us and concerning us;[191] which, too, we daily ask in our prayer when we say: *They will be done on earth as it is in heaven.*

"O holy[192] and chaste[193] love! O sweet and tender

[187] To fall back *in sua*, into that whereby it is not one spirit with God and separates itself from the Divine life.

[188] The whole substructure of St. Bernard's mysticism is here revealed. God created all things for Himself; the last end of man is conformity with God; ecstasy brings this conformity to the highest point it can attain in this life; mystical union consists therefore in realizing the closest conformity possible between the created image of God and its Exemplar.

[189] That is, our ceasing to feel the need to which the natural necessity of the body subjects us in this life.

[190] For then we shall have obtained it, but we shall no longer think of it as a reward, any more than God, to whose will shall then be united, considers His eternal beatitude as a reward for His perfection. We shall return again to the question of the disinterestedness of love.

[191] *In nobis,* because henceforth there is perfect accord between His will and ours; *de nobis,* because the realization of this accord is the end for which God created us.

[192] SANCTUS, SANCTE.—Holy love (*amor sanctus, sancte amare*) is spiritual love of God, as contrasted with the concupiscence of the flesh—"Amat sancte, quia non in concupiscentia carnis, sed in puritate spiritus" (ST. BERNARD, *In Cant. Cant.,* Sermo VII, 3; P.L., CLXXXIII, 807).

[193] CASTUS. CASTE.—*Chaste,* in St. Bernard, means always *disinterested.* Here then it means that a love in this state, turns towards its object for the sake of the object itself, to the exclusion of every other consideration and every other affection. For this reason *amor castus* is synonymous with *amor purus.*
"Amat profecto caste, quae ipsum quem amat quaerit; non aliud quidquam ipsius" (ST. BERNARD, *In Cant. Cant.,* Sermo VII, 3; P.L., CLXXXIII, 807).

affection! O pure and perfect intention of the will!—surely so much more perfect and pure as there is in it nothing now mixed of its own,[194] the more sweet and tender, as nought is felt but what is divine. Thus to be affected is to become Godlike (*deificare est*).[195] As a small drop of water mingled in much wine seems to be wholly lost and to take on the colour and taste of the wine; as a kindled and glowing iron becomes most like to fire, having put off its former and natural form;[196] and as the air, when flooded with the light of the sun is transformed into the very brightness of light, so that it seems to be not so much illumined as to be the light itself, so it must needs be that all human affection in the Saints will then, in some ineffable way, melt from itself, and be entirely poured over into the will of God. Otherwise how will *God be all in all*, if in man somewhat remains over of man?[197] The substance indeed will remain but in another form, another glory, and another power."[198]

Let us now consider the problem of love in the light of the foregoing conclusions. We know that man is an indestructible substance, resistant to the fusion of ecstasy or even to that of the beatific vision. But we know also that the end for which this substance was created is to realize a perfect divine likeness. Now if it be true that in virtue of its form it tends to differ from God in ever less and less degree than any given degree, then it is very evident that, at the limit, the famous antinomy between love of self and pure love disappears—at the limit it has neither meaning

[194] That is, of the *proprium:* of the proper will, which constitutes our unlikeness.

[195] This expression, as well as the following comparisons, was taken by St. Bernard from MAXIMUS THE CONFESSOR *Ambigua, loc. cit.*, p. 26.

[196] Remember that in St. Bernard's terminology the form is *never* the substance of which it is the form, so that a change of form implies no change of substance.

[197] Whether natural necessity or the *proprium;* that is, something of that whereby man is unlike God.

[198] *De diligendo Deo*, X, 27–28; P.L., CLXXXII, 990–991 [The present translator is here indebted to the English translation of E. G. GARDNER, London, Dent, but is bound to add that he has not followed it in every detail.]

nor *raison d'être*. God is a Love of Himself for Himself. Man is so much the more himself as he is the more like God. Since he is an image, the less he is distinguishable from the original the more he exists. If then we eliminate from his nature this *proprium* which is no part of his nature but corrupts it, what remains is a perfect image of God, that is to say of an infinite good that loves itself only for itself. What difference is there then, at the limit, between loving God and loving oneself, then, when one is no longer anything but a participation in the love which God bears Himself? In the soul which loves itself no longer save for God's sake, the love it bears itself is englobed in God's love for Himself, since God loves it only as a likeness to Himself and it loves itself only as a likeness to God.[199] Now this is elaborated minutely and at length in another text which by reason of the very closeness of its condensation ought to be read and meditated by everyone who seriously desires to enter into the thought of St. Bernard.

"1. We have been occupied for three days now, as far as the prescribed time permits, in showing the affinity that exists between the soul and the Word. To what end does all this labour tend? To this. We have shown that every soul, burdened as it may be with sins, caught in the net of vice, seduced by pleasures, a captive in exile, imprisoned in this body, fixed fast in this clay, sunk in its mire, close bound to its members, weighed down by cares, absorbed in business, shrunken by fear [the *contractio* being the proper effect of *timor*], afflicted by sorrows, wandering in error, a prey to anxieties and uneasy suspicions like a

---

[199] "Nunc vero, etsi ex parte jam similis, ex parte tamen dissimilis, contenta esto ex parte cognoscere Te ipsam attende et altiora te ne quaesieris . . . Alioquin *si ignoras te, O pulchra inter mulieres* (*Cant.*, I, 7); nam et ego te dico pulchram, sed inter mulieres, hoc est ex parte; cum autem venerit quod perfectum est, tunc evacuabitur quod ex parte est (I *Cor.*, XIII, 10): *si ergo ignoras te;* sed quae sequuntur, dicta sunt, et non opórtet iterum dici" (ST. BERNARD, *In Cant. Cant.*, Sermo XXXVIII, 5; P.L., CLXXXIII, 977 B).

stranger in a hostile land[200] and, as the Prophet says,
(Baruch, III, 11) defiled with the dead and counted with
them that go down to the dead; although a soul I say,
be thus under condemnation, thus despairing, yet have we
shown that it may still find in itself not only reason for
breathing freely in the hope of pardon, in the hope of mercy,
but even for daring to aspire to the nuptials with the Word,
not fearing to enter into bonds of alliance with God and to
bear the sweet yoke of love with Him who is the King of
angels. For why should it not venture confidingly into
the presence of Him by whose image it sees that it is still
honoured [for it is still there, being indestructible] and in
whose noble likeness it knows [though it *sees* it no longer,
having lost it] that all its glory consists? What should it
fear, I ask, from that Majesty, seeing that the very thought
of its origin should be enough to fill it with confidence?
[being an image of God it knows itself still capable of the
Divine majesty: *capax majestatis*]. All it has to do is to
remain true to the nobility of its nature in honesty of life,
or rather to seek to adorn the original honour in which it
was created with the fair colours of virtuous thought and
action.[201]

"2. Why then does it allow its zeal to fall asleep?
[*industria* (*zeal*), a word designating the part that falls to
free-will in the work of the restoration of the lost likeness].
For surely this is the greatest gift of nature; if it fails to
play its part will not all the rest of our nature be frustrated
and covered all over, so to speak, with the rust of old age?
But that would be an outrage on its Author. For if its
Author, Who is God Himself, has willed to preserve always
in the soul this manifest sign of the Divine generosity,

---

[200] Because in exile "in regione dissimilitudinis".
[201] That is to say: All that it has to do is to remain faithful to the original
nobility of a nature created free, to the image of God, and to restore in itself,
by way of the acquisition of virtues, the divine likeness lost by its fault.

[the image] this was that it should always bear in itself a perpetual reminder from the Word [for He is the Image, and the soul is made *ad imaginem*][202] to live always in the company of the Word, and there to return if perchance it should have strayed.

"It does not stray as by any change of place, or steps taken with the feet, but it is moved in the manner of a spiritual substance,[203] that is to say by the degradation of its affections, or rather by its defections or fallings away from itself [for then it loses the *similitudo* which it had], when by the depravity of its life and conduct it renders itself unlike God and becomes degenerate. But that unlikeness abolishes not its nature [which is to be an image], but invades and vitiates it, for in the measure in which it diminishes the goodness of nature, in that measure it defiles it. But this return of the soul is its conversion or turning to the Word [*conversio*, movement of the will from proper to common] to be reformed by Him and rendered conformable [restored to itself, since it was made to His likeness]. In what respect? In charity. For it is written: *Be ye followers of God, as most dear children*, [for charity raises the slave or hireling to the status of son] *and walk in love as Christ also hath loved us* (*Ephes.* V, 1, 2).

"3. Such conformity [of the will now become 'common' by charity] marries the soul to the Word, since, already like the Word by nature [He is *Imago*, the soul is *ad imaginem*], she now shows herself like Him in will, loving as she is loved [she loves herself for God's sake even as God loves her for His own]. If then she loves perfectly she is wedded to the Word. What more full of joy than this conformity?

[202] See on this point, besides the texts already analyzed, ST. BERNARD, *In Cant. Cant.*, Sermo LXXX, 2-5,; P.L., CLXXXIII, 1166-1169. The doctrine of the *imago* and of the *similitudo* is there developed at length.

[203] Relations of "proximity" or "distance" between spiritual substances are really relations of likeness or unlikeness. See ST. AUGUSTINE, *De Trinitate*, Lib. VII, cap. 6, n. 12; P.L., XLII, 946.

What more to be desired than this charity, whereby no more content with human teaching, O soul, thou may'st of thyself draw nigh to the Word in all confidence, attach thyself for ever to the Word, address thyself to Him familiarly consulting Him in all things, as capacious now in intelligence as bold in desire? This is a marriage contract truly spiritual and truly holy.

"But what do I say—a contract? It is an embrace. An embrace in truth, since to will the same and to fly from the same makes of two spirits one.[204] Nor believe that the inequality of persons here renders halting the accord of wills, for love has no respect of persons. It is from loving that love is named, and not from honour. Let him honour, who is struck with awe, with astonishment, with fear, with admiration; all these are nothing to him who loves. Love passes over all the rest; when it comes, it absorbs into itself all other affections [fear, cupidity], and overcomes them. Wherefore the soul that loves, loves, regardless of all else. He whom it would be but just to honour, to reverence, to admire, loves rather to be loved. These twain are Bridegroom and Bride. What other bond would you have between spouse and spouse, save only this: to love and to be loved? This bond outweighs even that which nature most closely binds, the love of parents for their children.[205] And hence it is said: *for this cause shall a man leave father and mother and cleave to his wife* (*Matt.*, XIX, 5). You see that this affection in those that are wedded is not only stronger than all other affections, but stronger even than itself.

"4. Add too that this Bridegroom is not only loving, He is Love. Is He then Honour? Let him maintain it who pleases, I have not read it; I read indeed that *Deus caritas est*

[204] Certainly a reminiscence of CICERO, *De Amicitia*, XXV. See above, p. 12. Cf. SALLUST, *Catalina*, cap. XX.
[205] Very probably a reminiscence of CICERO, *De Amicitia*, V: "namque hoc praestat amicitia propinquitatis. . . ."

(I *John*, IV, 16), but that God is honour or dignity, this I have not read. Not that God would not be held in honour, for does He not say: *If I be a Father, where is mine honour?* But there the Father speaks, for if He spoke as Bridegroom would He not change the word and say: If I be Bridegroom where is my love? Had He not already said: *If I be a Master where is My fear?* (*Mal.*, I, 6). God then requires that He should be feared as Lord, that He should be honoured as Father; but as Bridegroom He would be loved. Which of all these outweighs the rest? Surely love. Without it, fear afflicts [for then it is fear of punishment, not fear of God] and honour hath no attraction. Fear is servile when not set free by love; and as to honour, if it springs not from love, it is not honour, but adulation.

"To God alone, indeed, are due honour and glory; but neither of these will He accept if they be not seasoned with the honey of love. For love alone suffices to itself, it pleases of itself and for its own sake. It is itself its own merit, and its own recompense. It needs no other cause and no other fruit than itself. Its use is its fruit.[206] I love because love, I love that I may love. A great thing is love, provided only that it return to its principle, look to its origin, and flowing back towards its source draw thence the pure waters wherewith it may flow unendingly. Of all the movements, sentiments, and affections of the soul, love is the only one whereby the creature can, though not as an equal, repay to its Author what it has received, or at least give something of like kind in return. For example, should God be displeased with me, am I therefore to be displeased with Him? By no means, but I shall obey, tremble and ask pardon. Or again, should He reprehend me, I shall not do the like to Him, but rather admit that He reprehends me justly.

---

[206] Certainly a reminiscence of CICERO, *De Amicitia*, cap. IX: "omnis ejus fructus in ipso amore inest". See Chap. I, p. 11.

Nor when He judges me shall I judge Him, but adore; and when He saves me, He does not ask to be saved, for He has no need to be freed Who Himself frees all. If He asserts authority, it is my part to serve Him; if He commands I must obey, nor is it for me to demand service in return, or obedience. Now you see how otherwise it is with love. For when God loves, He desires nothing else than to be loved, because He loves only that He may be loved; knowing that those who shall love Him will be blessed in their love.

"5. A great thing is love, but it has its degrees. The Bride stands at the highest. For sons also love, but they think of their heritage, and when they think in any way to lose it, then indeed they have the more respect for him from whom they expect it, but the less love. I hold that love in suspicion which seems to hold out some hope of advantage. It is weak; for if the hope be withdrawn, it is either extinguished or diminished. Impure is that love which desires another thing. Pure love is not mercenary; it draws no strength from hope, nor is it weakened by any mistrust.[207] This is the love that is felt by the Bride, for all that she is, is only love. The very being of the Bride, and her one hope, consists in love. In this she abounds and with this the Bridegroom is content. He seeks nought else of her, and she has nought else to give. It is for this that He is Bridegroom, and she is Bride. This belongs wholly to the wedded pair; none else can attain it, not even a son. For He cries out to His sons: '*Where is mine honour ?*' but not,

---

[207] For it is impossible to separate love from confidence: FIDUCIA.— State of the soul in which the ardour of love and the inebriation that accompanies it, give it confidence enough to dare to hope for the kiss of the mystic union. *Fiducia* is therefore the opposite of *timor*, and goes along with the liberation of the soul by charity. That is why all mistrust is excluded from love as by definition. "O quanta amoris vis! Quanta in spiritu libertatis fiducia! Quid manifestius, quam quod perfecta charitas foras mittit timorem?" (1 *John*, IV, 18). (ST. BERNARD, *In Cant. Cant.*, Sermo VII, 3; P.L., CLXXXIII, 808 A).

'Where is my love?'—for that is the prerogative of the Bride. True it is that man is bidden to honour his father and his mother (*Deut.* V, 16), and no mention is made of love: not because parents should not be loved by their children, but because many children are disposed more to honour them than to love. True, the honour of a king delights in judgment; but the love of the bridegroom, and still more the Bridegroom who Himself is Love, asks nothing in return but love and faithfulness. Let therefore the Bride love well in return. And how could she do otherwise, she who is the Bride, and the Bride of Love? How could Love ever not be loved?

"6. Rightly then does she renounce all other affections, giving herself up wholly to love and to love alone, since it is to Love Itself that she must render love for love. For were she to pour forth all herself in love, what would that be compared to this ever-flowing and inexhaustible spring? Not with equal abundance flows that stream from the lover and from Love, from the soul and from the Word, from the Bride and from the Bridegroom, from the creature and from the Creator; the thirsty wayfarer might then be compared with the spring. What then? Shall the vow of the betrothed, the desire of her heart, her loving ardour [208] and her daring trust, [209] shall all these perish and become of none effect because, forsooth, she cannot contend in swiftness with the Giant who runs his course, or dispute the palm of sweetness with honey, of gentleness with the lamb, of whiteness with the lily, of brilliance with the sun,

---

[208] ARDENS, ARDENTER.—Ardent love (*amor ardens, amare ardenter*) is love at that degree of intensity which brings forgetfulness of the infinite Majesty of God, and a bold desire to enter into union. Bernard frequently compares this ardent love to an inebriation. It is characteristic of the state of the Bride, as contrasted with that of the disciple (obedience) or of the son (honour). "Amat ardenter, quae ita proprio debriatur amore, ut majestatem non cogitet" (ST. BERNARD, *In Cant. Cant.*, Sermo VII, 3; P.L., CLXXXIII, 807.)

[209] See above, p. 138, note FIDUCIA.

F

or of charity with Him who is Charity Itself? No; for although, being a creature she loves less than He by whom she is loved, because indeed she is less, yet if she love with her whole self her love lacks nothing, since all she has is given. Wherefore, as I have said, to love thus is, to enter into marriage.[210] For she cannot love thus and yet be little loved, since in the mutual consent of two parties consists a full and perfect marriage. Unless perhaps someone should doubt whether the soul is not first loved, and with greater love than hers, by the Word? But we know well that in loving she is both anticipated and surpassed. Happy is the soul that merits to be prevented with the benediction of such sweetness. Happy the soul that experiences such sweet embrace, which is none other than a love holy and chaste, a love sweet and delightful, a love as sincere as it is pure, a love mutual, endearing, powerful, which makes of two, not one flesh indeed, but one spirit, as says St. Paul: *He who is joined to the Lord is one spirit* (I Cor. VI, 17).

"And now let us rather listen to her whom God from afar has made our mistress in these matters: the unction that instructs and oft-repeated experience. But perhaps it would be better to reserve this for the beginning of another sermon, so that we may not confine so excellent a matter within the narrow limits of that which now comes to an end. So then, if you approve, I will break off this discourse before reaching the end of the subject, in order that to-morrow, like hungry souls, we may come together to taste those delights which the holy soul merits from the Word, her Bridegroom, Jesus Christ Our Lord, Who is above all God blessed for ever. Amen" (*In Cant, Cant.*, Sermo LXXXIII).

This most remarkable text contains not only an outline

---

[210] Because love is a mutual affection by definition it implies this accord of two wills which constitutes unity of spirit itself. Unity of spirit consists in likeness, which is, for spirits, the equivalent of carnal union in the corporeal order.

of the theological principles governing the question of ecstasy as St. Bernard conceives it, but sets forth also with all desirable precision his conception of love. The formulae that define a pure love have certainly not passed without remark, for we know to what use, not to say abuse, they were to be put by the Quietists. For indeed any number of texts in support of Quietism might be cited from St. Bernard —provided only that care be taken to make them say the opposite of what they mean.

The first characteristic of pure love in the doctrine of St. Bernard lies in the exclusion of every other affection. I put it as St. Bernard puts it, but what he means to say is rather that pure love is *inclusive* of all the other affections. The reason is this. The purity of love is one and the same thing with its intensity; let us say, if we want at any price to maintain a distinction between the two conceptions, that its purity is the first and most immediate effect of its intensity. That is why the reference to *ardent* love recurs so incessantly in his writings. The ardour of love, pushed to the last degree of intensity, has for apparent effect the elimination from the soul of all that is not itself. There is no longer any room left for the rest. But we have to remember on the other hand that love is essentially the very opposite of a destroying force, and that the only thing that it really eliminates is non-being—the rest it transforms and brings to fulfilment. That is what takes place in the case of all the other affections. As regards what is positive in them none is destroyed. Thus cupidity survives in respect of the whole positivity of its essence; it is "ordered", that is to say when everything that would falsify it is eliminated then no more of it remains save that element which was capable of being set in order: love. It is just the same in the case of fear and hope; love consumes all, but only to consummate. [211]

In the second place, since all the other affections are re-absorbed in the ardour of love, it is at once evident that pure love is disinterested. Its very definition itself demands it, but far from excluding the substance of the other affections which the creature owes to his Creator, it absorbs and exalts them by bringing them to their point of perfection.[212] This is especially to be noted as regards the desire of beatitude. Pure love neither desires no hopes for any reward, but it enjoys it; it is essentially fruition of the Divine good. It may be asked perhaps how this character can be added to love without vitiating its purity. But it is not added; it is of the very essence of love, and that is why St. Bernard says that love is itself its own reward.[213] Being by its very nature a participation in the Divine life, which is beatitude, it is a participation in beatitude. To say therefore that love carries with it its own reward is to say simply that its purity is that of the fruition of God.

To historians of spirituality such phrases as "pure love" "disinterested love", almost always seem to carry a suggestion of quietism. The spectre of Mme. Guyon flits around a truth and makes the place uninhabitable. It is true that pure love, as St. Bernard conceives it, is a love that looks for no recompense; but we have just seen why. At the root of the whole question we must put the Scriptural phrase so often cited: love drives out fear. Throughout the course of all St. Bernard's meditations we watch the gradual elimination of the fear of Divine chastisement by certitude of the possession of God in love. In so far as the thought of the contemplative is still busied with consideration of Divine Providence, or of Divine Judgment on our conduct,[214] it has not yet arrived at its term: it has not yet attained to pure love. But suppose, on the contrary, that the intensity of love has invested it with this purity which absorbs all other affections into itself, then, from that very moment, it is married to the Word, it rejoices therefore in God; it achieves this state of *fiducia* which is but the very consciousness of being united with the Divine beatitude. Obviously, from that moment also it can no longer stand in any fear of chastisement. Absorbed as it is in its joy, it can no longer even *think* of a chastisement. And this St. Bernard indicates in the foregoing text where he says that the soul that loves thus no longer looks for reward, *nor does it feel any mistrust*. This is the point that decides all, and it is precisely for lack of taking it into account that the Quietists have raised questions of which the very enunciation is excluded by St. Bernard's doctrine in the most formal manner.

To be assured on the point we have only to resume the key positions of St. Bernard touching the nature and conditions of pure love. If we turn to the fundamental text of the *De diligendo Deo*, VII, 17, we see there first that love of God cannot go unrewarded, and then, next, that pure love of God is nevertheless a love without any thought of reward: *non enim sine praemio diligitur Deus, etsi absque praemii intuitu diligendus est.* Now what does that mean?

It means that pure love, as conceived by St. Bernard, is essentially a mystical experience. What we have to do with here is neither an idea, nor an habitual disposition, but the brief and perpetually interrupted *excessus* of the soul of the mystic, when God unites it with Himself by exceptional graces. This primary difference between St. Bernard and the Quietists is important and should never be lost sight of. The former speaks of a momentary ecstasy—*rara hora, sed parva mora*—in no way of a state; when he deals with the habitual state he calls it, not *amor purus*, but *vicissitudo*.[215] A continual pining desire, interrupted by the fleeting and always unforseeable joys of the divine union—there we have the picture of his life. And he knows moreover that

even his pure love, when it brings its joyous reward, is far
from being absolutely pure. There will never be any love
that is purely pure save in heaven.

This point decides a second. Since pure love is a mystical
experience, it is an affection and nothing else; or nothing
else at any rate for the consciousness of him who experiences
it. By that let us understand that at the moment when he
experiences it the ecstatic is integrally occupied by it, no
room being left in his soul for anything else whatever. In
the forefront of all that love by its very intensity expels
stand the considerations of the reason, and this exclusion
takes effect against two possible orders of rational calculation, the calculations of cupidity and the calculations of
fear.

First those of cupidity; for in fact the soul that rejoices
in God no longer thinks of Him as of a recompense. She
no longer thinks of Him as of a recompense in prospect since
she possesses Him already—that absurdity is at once excluded by the very nature of ecstasy, which is beatifying.
But neither does she think of Him as of a present recompense,
because now she does not represent Him to herself in any
way whatever; she loves Him, and that is all. St. Bernard
says precisely: "absque praemii *intuitu* diligendus." In other
words, the idea of recompense is then no longer in the mind's
eye. The ecstatic no longer says to himself: "I find blessedness in this love, and therefore I must feel it"; or again:
"If God makes me blessed in His love, as He does, then I
must continue in this love so that He may continue to
bestow this blessedness." All that has now fallen away.
Love is not a contract, it is an affection: "Affectus est, non
contractus." It is not a "contractus", but an "amplexus".
That is why, in virtue of its very nature, it can be neither
empty-handed nor mercenary: "Vacua namque vera
charitas esse non potest nec tamen mercenaria est." It

never goes empty-handed because it is an embrace, but neither is it ever mercenary, because it is nothing but an embrace. Either then there is a rational calculation, and then we are no longer in the presence of a simple *affectus*, a love that is nought but love; and then it merits no reward, or rather cannot have it since the reward is precisely the simple embrace of love—and if it is not there, how should the recompense be there? Or else on the other hand there is no longer any rational outlook, any contractual calculation, but only the pure affection of a soul that loves and *knows* nought else; and then the affection merits recompense, or rather it is it, since it is the *amplexus*—which is much less an embrace of God by the soul, than an embrace of the soul by God. "Verus amor seipso contentus est. Habet praemium, sed id quod amatur."[216]

Consider now the relation between pure love and fear. It must of necessity amount to an exclusion of fear, and for the same reasons. Pure love cannot be a love that still keeps fear in view any more than it can be a love that has reward in view, and this simply because it excludes all "views". It is in no wise a contract, neither to obtain joy, nor to avoid pain; it is an affection. St. Bernard's *fiducia* therefore no more expresses a satisfaction at the prospect of avoiding an only too well-merited punishment, than his *amplexus* expresses the joy of holding at last the long-desired reward. The one excludes all thought of punishment, as the other excludes all thought of reward. Literally, according to the word of Scripture, fear has just been turned out of doors, and there it remains as long as the ecstasy endures; but no longer. The spontaneity of love—*sponte afficit, et spontaneum facit*—therefore presupposes a thoroughgoing elimination of any motive other than itself as long as it subsists in its purity, and in proportion to this purity itself. We are just as far from Luther's state of *fiducia* as from the state of pure love imagined by the followers of Fénelon. St. Bernard's *fiducia*, without doubt, is a certitude of salvation, but it would be much better to say that it marks the point where the question of salvation ceases to arise either one way or the other. The Lutheran *fiducia* is a faith in which the sinner feels himself a sinner and nevertheless feels that he is saved by Jesus Christ.[217] St. Bernard's confidence is a charity which, not by any means for a whole lifetime, but for short instants, succeeds in transcending the normal state in which the question of punishment still arises. When a soul thinks of punishment she can think of it in no way if not as deserved; when she no longer sees that she deserves it, that is not because she knows herself guilty but pardoned, but because she no longer thinks of it at all. That is why forgetfulness of the God of power, and justice and judgment can be the work of nothing but pure love. None but pure love has power to lay hold, without shame and without fear, of this subsistant Beatitude, in whose possession the very notions of promise, of hope, of threat, or of punishment become void of meaning.

Hence we may also perceive at the same time how far removed from St. Bernard was even the genius of St. Francis de Sales when he declared himself ready to love hell with the will of God even above heaven without it.[218] There is naturally no question of objecting to him here that heaven is the very will of God itself. St. Francis de Sales was not such a novice as all that; he is perfectly well aware that his hypothesis is "an imagination of an impossible thing"; but what has to be brought out on the other hand, since this is precisely the starting-point of the whole Fénelonian mistake, is that inasmuch as a man is still capable of imagining, whether possible things or impossible, he has not yet arrived at pure love. For pure love imagines nothing, it possesses. St. Francis de Sales is quite well aware that love is not to be divorced from the joy that it gives,[219] but perhaps he never knew the joy of the ecstatic in actual love of God for God's sake; and that is why he still reasons and argues when the time has gone by for anything but love. A doubly-fatal illusion, for it was to lead the Fénelonians to miss the essence of pure love itself; an illusion that was inevitable, however, from the moment the attempt was made to make the language of St. Bernard express the spiritual life of Mme. Guyon or of Fénelon. Pure love may be taken to mean either the Cistercian ecstasy or the Fénelonian state, but it cannot possibly be both at once. Fénelon, of course, was free to adopt the definition he preferred, but when he cites St. Bernard in support of his own thesis we can but choose between two hypotheses either he failed to understand him, or he falsified. I have no doubt at all that he failed to understand. The plain fact is that the definition of pure love for the Quietists is the definition of impure love for St. Bernard. Purify your love still more, he would say to them, and then you will see that the problem that worries you no longer arises. To ask whether we could love God when certain of never possessing Him—that is certainly a question; on condition, however, that love has not yet filled the whole soul. Let it put forth all its power and then it will forget all about chastisements to the point of feeling no fear of them; and all about rewards to the point of renunciation.[220]

Thus, to whatever side we turn, we must always come back to the image of God in man, if the problems involved in the interpretation of the doctrine are to be solved. Move away from this central point, and everything is shifted out of perspective, difficulties and apparent contradictions accumulate; return, and everything falls back into order. It remains to verify this in connection with the famous doctrine of charity as knowledge of God. St. Bernard says

F *

and repeats, appealing moreover expressly to Gregory the Great,[221] that charity is knowledge or even vision of God. What are we to understand by these formulae?

One might be tempted to take them quite literally as meaning that love exerts a cognitive function properly so-called, and is strictly a "sight" That would amount to a formal identification of knowledge and love. On the other hand, this thesis seems at first sight so paradoxical that we might be tempted to take it for no more than a metaphor, without any definite doctrinal content. But St. Bernard's expressions are so formal that this will soon appear a mere shift to evade the difficulty. Doubtless the true solution is equally removed from either extreme; love undoubtedly for St. Bernard is a genuine sight of God, but only in a certain sense.

We may remark in the first place that although he has left us but few indications as to how he understood cognition, we know at least this, that for him it is based entirely on a likeness of the subject knowing to the object known. Where such likeness is wanting, knowledge is impossible. How did St. Bernard picture the assimilation of subject and object in sensible or intellectual cognition? We do not know. His friend, William of Saint-Thierry, has left us some precise indications of the way in which he would answer the question for himself. Perhaps it would not be too bold an hypothesis to imagine that St. Bernard looked at it in very much the same way; but we cannot tell, and after all the point is without importance. It may be that St. Bernard did not think about it at all. But what on the contrary is of the highest importance is to note that, with him, the resemblance of subject and object is the indispensable condition of any knowledge of the one by the other.

Once that has been laid down the thesis in question is forced upon us as an unavoidable conclusion. In whatever way the intellectual cognition of objects be interpreted, it is possible only if some action proceeding from the object has transformed the knowing subject to its likeness. On the other hand, when once the likeness between subject and object has been set up, the knowledge of the object by the subject follows of itself. We may therefore say that the likeness is the knowledge itself, at least in the sense that it is the indispensable and sufficient condition of the knowledge. Now, in the case of knowledge of God, what is it that transforms the soul to the likeness of God? Charity, love, and nothing else. In the precise measure in which love shall have transformed the soul to the likeness of God, Whose name is charity, in that same measure it will be in a position to know Him and will indeed know Him effectively.[111]

But then, it will be said, with what kind of knowledge will it know Him? It will know Him by feeling Him. The affection of love of God for God's sake is, to the soul that loves, if not the equivalent at least the succedaneum, of her vision of bodies. God is neither perceptible to our senses nor conceivable by our intellects, but He is sensible to the heart. To love Him as He loves Himself, to love Him as He loves us, and by the gift of that very love with which He loves Himself and loves us—that truly, as St. Augustine had already said, is to have God in us. To perceive within itself this divine love which circulates in the soul henceforth one in spirit with God, is to perceive God in the sole manner in which this Spirit is perceptible here below to ours: in charity. Thus, for the soul reformed to the Divine likeness by love, the very affection of love is the sole possible substitute here below for the vision of God which we lack, and love therefore in us stands for vision.

And this St. Bernard will explain to us if we allow him to speak for himself once more; and thus we may watch his master-theses as they pass beneath our eyes for the last

time in one of the most highly condensed syntheses he has
left us.

"When the soul discerns in her own nature two things so
opposed [the likeness of the image and the unlikeness of sin]
how should it not cry out between hope and despair: *Lord,
who is like unto Thee?* Drawn towards despair by so great
an evil [unlikeness] it is recalled to hope by this great good
[the persistence of the image ²²³], Thence it is that the more
it is offended by the evil within it the more ardently it aspires
to the good which equally it sees there, and desires to become
what it was meant to be, [not simply an *image*, but a likeness]
that is to say simple, [by absence of cupidity] upright,
[by absence of fear²²⁴] yet fearing God [but not God's
chastisements] and departing from evil. Why should it not
be able to depart from that which it has been able to
approach, or to draw near to that from which it has been
able to withdraw? This it can do, be it noted, if it relies on
grace, not on nature, nor even on its own zeal (*industria*).
For it is wisdom that conquers evil (*Sap.* VII, 30), not
nature, nor zeal. Nor does it count on grace without reason,
for its conversion is to the Word [now the Word is precisely
Wisdom]. This noble kinship of the soul to the Word, of
which for three days we have discoursed, is not barren
[*kinship*, since the Word is *Imago*, and the soul is *ad imaginem*],
nor is the persistent likeness, the witness of this kinship
[the *imago*]. The Spirit [introduced by the Word] will
deign to admit into His fellowship this soul so like to Him
by nature; and that for a natural reason, for like seeks like.
Hear the voice of One who calls: *Return, return, O Sulamitess,
return that we may look upon thee* (*Cant.* VI, 12). He will look
upon her now that she is in His likeness, she whom when she
was unlike He saw not, but He will admit her also to the
vision of Himself. For we know that when He shall appear
[beatific vision] we shall be like Him; for we shall see Him

as He is (I *John* III, 2). Rather hold it then for a thing difficult, not a thing impossible, when thou hearest what is asked: *Lord, who is like unto Thee?* (*Ps.* XXXIV, 10). "Or again, if you will have it so, let us call this a cry of admiration. For surely most wonderful and admirable is that likeness from which there springs the vision of God, or rather which is that vision of God; but this I speak of that vision which is in charity. For charity is that vision, charity is that likeness [for it re-establishes the likeness which determines the vision]. Who does not stand amazed at beholding the charity of a God despised, Who none the less recalls us to Himself? Well therefore did that wicked one of whom I spoke a while ago deserve the reproach addressed to him, in that he would usurp the likeness of God to his own profit, [by willing to give himself his own law, which is God's privilege], since in loving iniquity [his 'proper will'] he could love neither himself [for he is no longer himself now that he is no longer like God], nor God [because he prefers himself to God]. Thus must we understand the word: *He that loveth iniquity hateth his own soul* (*Ps.* X, 6). When then this iniquity shall be taken away, which is the cause of our part in unlikeness, then will there be union of spirit [since union between two spirits is made of their very likeness], then will there be mutual vision [since each may know the other in knowing himself], and mutual dilection [like loving his like]. When that which is perfect is come [charity] then that which is in part [unlikeness] shall be done away; and then between God and the soul shall be nought but a mutual dilection chaste and consummated, a full mutual recognition, a manifest vision, a firm conjunction, a society undivided, and a perfect likeness. Then shall the soul know God even as she is known (I *Cor.* XIII, 10); then shall she love as she is loved; and over his Bride shall rejoice the Bridegroom, knowing and known, loving and beloved, Jesus Christ Our Lord, Who is over all things, God blessed for ever. Amen" (*In Cant. Cant.*, Sermo LXXXII, 7 and 8).

Thus have we tried to pass in review the chief ideas that enter into the composition of the mysticism of St. Bernard, and to suggest the manner in which they are interconnected. Perhaps it would be better to say that we have tried to suggest some of their more frequent interconnections—for nothing can equal the easy mastery with which their author works them into combination. It would be illusory and altogether unjust to St. Bernard to take such analyses—even supposing them to be always exact—for the equivalent of his mystical theology. For they stand to that much as an anatomical specimen would stand to the living organism whence it was taken. To understand it as it truly is we should have to be able to seize in one unique and simple intuition the work of a God who creates man in order to associate him, by way of beatitude, with His own likeness, Who gives man back the lost likeness that he may give back the lost beatitude, and Who, while awaiting the day when the work shall be fully accomplished, gratuitously raises to like felicity souls whom the gift of charity has already made conformable to His nature—*Deus charitas est*—closely enough to enable them to taste even here below of the blessedness of His life. And then it is that there reigns between God and the creature made to His image, this perfect conformity, this unity of spirit, in which the human substance finds at last its full actuality; and in that creature the great work of creation is completed, for he becomes at last that very thing for which he was made—a translucid mirror in which God now sees nought but Himself, and in which the soul now sees nought but God: a created participation of His glory and of His beatitude.

APPENDICES
AROUND ST. BERNARD
MEN AND MOVEMENTS

APPENDIX I

CURIOSITAS

In the introduction to his English translation of the *De gradibus humilitatis et superbiae*, Mr. Barton R. V. Mills points out that St. Bernard allots nearly as much space to the description of the first degree of pride as he does to all the other eleven degrees put together; whence he concludes that St. Bernard accorded it the greatest importance as the starting-point of the degradation of the soul.[225] The remark is very just, and I would merely add a few more precise indications.

To grasp the exact nature of "curiositas" and its importance in St. Bernard's eyes, we must see in it, as he saw, the very negation of Cistercian ascesis. To be convinced of this we have only to peruse the text closely, for it is full of significant indications.

Come back to the starting-point. At the heart of the whole question St. Bernard puts preoccupation with salvation. All that bears upon this is indispensable, all the rest is vain. Now if it be true that a Christian is bound in duty to help others to salvation, it is none the less true that he cannot save others unless they save themselves, and that nobody can save him unless first he saves himself. Each man therefore should aim in the first place at assuring his own salvation (*De consideratione*, I, 5, 6; P.L., CLXXXII, 734).

Set out then from that. Of the quest of souls, as of everything else, it is true to say with St. Matthew (XVI, 26): "Quid enim prodest homini, si mundum universum lucretur, animae vero suae detrimentum patiatur?" A text which St. Bernard somewhat boldly transposes thus: "Alioquin quid tibi prodest, juxta verbum Domini, si *universos* lucreris, te unum perdens?" (*loc. cit.*, 734 B). To exclude oneself from one's own charity, since one is man, is charity ill-understood. To exclude oneself

from the benefit of one's own wisdom, is to want for wisdom:
"Etsi sapiens sis, deest tibi ad sapientiam, si tibi non fueris"
(*op. cit.*, II, 3, 6; 745 C). What then will our wisdom want?
All. "Quantum vero? Ut quidem senserim, totum." Vain,
then, the knowledge of hidden things, of all that is on the face
of the earth and in the height of heaven; if we know not ourselves we shall have built without foundations. All will be but
as a handful of dust that is swept away by the wind.

By this détour then we come back to self-knowledge, to this
Christian *Nosce teipsum*, without which no salvation is to be had:
"A te proinde incipiat tua consideratio, non solum autem, sed
et in te finiatur." In whatever direction our thoughts may
stray it is always of advantage to salvation to bring them back
home. "Tu primus tibi, tu ultimus." As the Word proceeds
from the Father and returns to the Father, so should our word,
which is our "consideratio", proceed from us and remain
inseparable: "Sic progrediatur, ut non egrediatur; sic exeat,
ut non deserat." We must think of nothing that is contrary
to our salvation, nay, of nothing beside it. "In acquisitione
salutis nemo tibi germanior unico matris tuae. Contra salutem
propriam cogites nihil. Minus dixi: *contra; praeter*, dixisse
debueram." And St. Bernard concludes: "Whatever it be
that offers itself to thy consideration, if that does not in
some way advance thy salvation, reject it" (*op. cit.*, II, 3, 6;
745–746).

To be occupied with any kind of knowledge whatever which
has no bearing on oneself from the standpoint of salvation, that
is precisely *curiosity*. If St. Bernard allots to this first degree
of pride as much space as he gives to all the rest, that is precisely
because, just as the *Nosce teipsum* gives birth to all the other
degrees of humility up to the highest, so does curiosity engender
all the remaining degrees of pride, down to the lowest. Here
we stand at the parting of two ways, one leading to salvation
by way of self-knowledge, the other to perdition by way of
curiosity.

This then is the way in which St. Bernard's description of
curiosity is to be understood. What ails the soul of the *curious*

monk? The malady that makes him: "dum a sui circumspectione torpescit incuria sui, curiosam in alios" (*De gradibus humilitatis*, II, 10, 28; P.L., CLXXXII, 957 C). Then it goes with him as it says in the Canticle (I, 7): "Quia enim seipsam ignorat, foras mittitur, ut haedos pascat." He goes about to pasture his kids—his eyes and ears—on everything that catches their fancy from without: "In his ergo pascendis se occupat curiosus, dum scire non curat qualem se reliquerit intus" (957 C). All he needs to know is himself: "Whither then, O inquisitive one, will you retire from your own presence? To whom in the meantime will you entrust yourself? How dare you lift up your eyes to heaven who have sinned against heaven? Look down to the earth if you would know yourself again. It will show you what you are, for earth thou art and to earth shalt thou go" (957D). Here then St. Bernard takes up his stand upon the *Nosce teipsum* of the Ancients. Like the Roman mosaic found on the Appian Way, reproduced at the beginning of this book to recall the close connection between Christian and Ancient thought, the ascesis of St. Bernard requires of mortals that they shall remember that they are mortal. But for pendant to the first we should need to find another mosaic, Christian this time, in which to behold, rising above the *Nosce teipsum*, above the terrestrial man, the heavenly man renewed in the image of God.

APPENDIX II

ABELARD

WHEN we look for the source of the courtly conception of love, we must not forget to reserve an important place for Peter Abelard. The times in which he lived (1079–1142) bring us sufficiently close to those that were marked by the birth of courtly poetry. We know from his own account that he composed and sang a large number of songs in honour of Heloïse. It is difficult to say from the text whether they were in Latin or the vernacular; but evidently these love-songs were very like those of the Troubadours or Trouvères which have survived (ABELARD, *Historia calamitatum*, P.L., CLXXVIII, 128 BC). Abelard adds that most of these verses were still well known and sung at the time when he was writing. The testimony of Abelard is fully confirmed by that of Heloïse: *Epist*. II, P.L., CLXXVIII, 185 D—186 A. Cf. 188 A. It is most unfortunate that all these songs should have perished; had they been still extant they would have constituted our earliest witnesses to the courtly poetry of the north of France. Until they are recovered, if ever they are, we shall not be able to tell whether Abelard put anything else into them besides sentiment—that is to say any conception of the nature of love. That would not be surprising, since we are dealing with a philosopher; but we know from the passage above referred to that he was not then in a speculative humour. In default of documents it is useless to discuss it. On the other hand we know for certain, since we possess his theological works, that he formed a certain conception of love, and we know what it was.

We do not know at what precise period of his life it was formed. This is the more to be regretted inasmuch as the Abelardian doctrine of love is an exaltation without reserve, and, as far as I know, without parallel at that time, of disinterested love.

His two sources of inspiration on the point were Cicero and Heloïse.

It is Abelard himself who refers us to Cicero. He cites the definition of friendship contained in the *De inventione rhetorica*, II, 55, at the opening of his *Introductio ad theologiam*, lib. I, P.L., CLXXVIII, 982. But he returned to the question in another text, the most important of all, where it is difficult not to suspect an influence other than Cicero's. The text occurs in his *Expositio in Epist. Pauli ad Romanos*, lib. III, P.L., CLXXVIII, 891A—893C). Let us first resume the text, and then we shall see why it is by no means absurd to suspect the influence of Heloïse.[226]

The starting-point of his train of thought is a text of St. Paul, which must have strongly attracted the partisans of pure love: "Non quaerit quae sua sunt, omnia suffert, omnia credit, omnia sperat, omnia sustinet" (I *Cor.*, XIII, 5—7). Doubtless the text was not a perfect one for the purpose, for it still envisaged the question of hope; but the opening offered an excellent starting-point. This Abelard seized upon, and out of it drew the most daring consequences.

Suppose, with him, that the model of *dilectio* is Christ's love for humanity. Then we must say:

1. That true love goes out directly and solely to the person loved, excluding all consideration of recompense to the person loving (891 B).

2. Doubtless he who thus loves is certain of reward, but it is not with reward in view that he ought to love; for this would be but a mercenary love, albeit in the spiritual order (891 B).

3. Hence we ought to love God for Himself and in no wise for the sake of the beatitude we may hope to obtain of Him. "Nec jam est caritas dicenda si propter nos eum, id est pro nostra utilitate, et pro regni ejus felicitate, quam ab eo speramus, diligeremus potius quam propter ipsum, in nobis videlicet nostrae intentionis finem non in Christo statuentes. Tales profecto homines, fortunae potius dicendi sunt amici quam hominis, et per avaritiam magis quam per gratiam subjecti" (891 C).

4. Let us go further: we must not even love God because He loves us (we are far from the *De diligendo Deo* and the *Ipse dilexit*

nos). Even if God did not love us, we should still have to love Him; in any event, if God loves us, it is not on that account that we have to love Him: "Denique si Deum quia me diligit diligam, et non potius quia quidquid mihi faciat, talis ipse est qui super omnia diligendus est, dicitur in me illa Veritatis sententia: *Si enim eos diligitis qui vos diligunt, quam mercedem habebitis* (*Matt.* V, 46)" (892 A). We should have to love God just the same whether He punished or rewarded us, for His punishments can never be anything but just (892 B).

5. Here Abelard notices an objection, which moreover arises of itself. Up to this point his whole reasoning has amounted to saying that since a man does not sincerely love another man if he looks for a recompense, neither does he sincerely love God if he looks for God to reward him. Now the two cases are not comparable, for God is the sovereign good and beatitude itself. Therefore one cannot love God without loving beatitude. Abelard puts the objection with extreme forcefulness: "at fortasse dicis, quoniam Deus seipso nos, non alia re est remuneraturus, et seipsum, quo nihil majus est, ut beatus quoque meminit Augustinus, nobis est daturus" (892 C). And indeed, in an important text of which Abelard cites a long fragment, St. Augustine teaches that God is not to be loved for anything except Himself; but evidently he does not dream of a love of God which would disclaim all interest in divine beatitude. On the contrary, by a "gratuitous" love St. Augustine clearly understands a love of God desiring nothing other than God, but nevertheless desiring God: "Quid est gratuitum? Ipse propter se, non propter aliud. Si enim laudas Deum ut det tibi aliquid aliud, jam non gratis amas Deum" (ST. AUGUSTINE, *Enar. in Ps. LIII,* 10; P.L., XXXVI, 626). But Abelard will not admit that to love God for the beatitude He has promised would be to love God sincerely. God must be loved because He is good, that is, perfect, and because, no matter what He may do in respect of ourselves or others, He is worthy of love because what He does is good: "At tunc profecto Deum pure ac sincere propter se diligeremus, si pro se id tantummodo, non pro nostra utilitate, faceremus; nec qualia nobis donat, sed in se qualis

ipse sit attenderemus. Si autem eum tantum in causa dilectionis
poneremus, profecto quidquid ageret vel in nos vel in alios,
quoniam non nisi id optime faceret, eum, ut dictum est, aeque
diligeremus, quia semper in eo nostrae dilectionis integrae
causam inveniremus, qui integrae semper et eodem modo
bonus in se et amore dignus perseverat" (P.L., CLXXVIII,
892—893). Cf. *op. cit.*, 893 B.

Such then is the position of Peter Abelard. It may be summed
up by saying that he defines pure love of God as being a love of
God for His own perfection even to the point of eventual
renunciation of the beatitude He has promised us. The *Introductio
ad theologiam* was condemned in 1121 at the Council of Soissons;
now it contains in germ, with the reference to Cicero, the doctrine
of pure love. We are therefore sure that this doctrine, in Abelard,
antedates that of St. Bernard, the earliest expression of which
dates about 1125. Thus one might draw the strange conclusion
that the dialectician provided the mystic with his conception of
love. That, let us hasten to add, would be a wholly unjustified
illusion, for, first, Abelard's thought did not come to full
expression on the point until towards 1136, in his Commentary
on the Epistle to the Romans, and then, especially, his position
is very much rather the negation of St. Bernard's than its source.

Abelard gives us a dialectical definition of love; St. Bernard
speaks of pure love as of an exceptional state, and one moreover
never fully accessible in this life. Furthermore, Abelard, precisely
because he remains on the plane of rational knowledge, defines
pure love as a love motivated only by the Divine perfection,
and as a love that remains intact even if never to be rewarded.
St. Bernard, as we have seen, would never have accepted such
an hypothesis, which in fact is more like Mme. Guyon's than his
own. In Cistercian mysticism, as soon as a love is pure, *fiducia*
is set up in the soul, and there cannot even be a question of going
unrewarded. The dialectical exercises of Abelard, who accepts
in pure love the eventual severity of a just God, would be in
St. Bernard's eyes an irrefutable proof that he has not yet attained
to pure love. Here, then, we have a doctrine specifically different
from St. Bernard's. The only love that Abelard regards as

sincere is a love that renounces and makes sacrifice of itself, in short, a love that is ready to waive beatitude.

What could have suggested an ideal of this kind to Abelard? We may think of himself in the first place—if not of his heart at least of his dialectical intelligence. For evidently he speaks of these things as a pure theorist. He executed a brilliant dialectical exercise on the idea of pure love, without troubling himself about the realities of mystical experience to which he remained a stranger, nor about the theological conditions of the problem which he approaches like a novice in theology. That is why he finally arrived at this doctrine in which the most absolute of pure loves may seem to triumph, but which the first theologian who came along was able to deflate with one prick of the needle: *"Quod autem est absurdius uniri Deo amore et non beatitudine?"* (WILLIAM OF SAINT-THIERRY, *De contemplando Deo*, VIII, 16; P.L., CLXXXIV, 375 D).

However, it seems difficult to suppose that dialectic alone was concerned in the case, for it fails to explain how Abelard first came to conceive this ideal of a love prepared to sacrifice its object. Dialectic lays bare the way in which the operation may be executed, but does not explain how the dialectician came to dream of attempting it. Evidently the error is due to the assumption that the pure love of a human being for God could be described in the same terms as the pure love of a human being for another human being. It is only when man is concerned that a sincere love has to envisage the case of the frustration of its joy in its object. One might show, if this were the place for it, that the theological reasonings of Abelard are vitiated by the constant neglect of this principle—that the love of God is a unique case, because God is a unique case. What could have put him in the mood for this ideal of a human love attached to its object, without caring to know whether it will receive punishment or reward, ready to accept any treatment that its object may accord it on the ground that this is demanded by the very essence of a disinterested love? When the question is put in this way the answer can hardly be in doubt. It was Heloïse. The description of disinterested love that Abelard, turned theologian, proposes, is that very same with which Heloïse bitterly reproached him with never having understood when he pretended to love her. The Abelardian doctrine of Divine love amounts to this, that God is not to be loved as Abelard loved Heloïse, but as Heloïse loved Abelard.

For Abelard tells us that God is not to be loved for the sake of anything but God, not even for the happiness of possessing Him. Let us translate: I never loved Heloïse; what I loved in her was my own pleasure. If Abelard had harboured the least doubt on the matter Heloïse would not long have left him to his illusion. "Concupiscentia te mihi potius quam amicitia sociavit, libidinis ardor potius quam amor. Ubi igitur quod desiderabas cessavit, quidquid propter hoc exhibebas pariter evanuit" (*Epist.*, II; P.L., CLXXVIII, 186 B). That is the exact opposite of true love, of which Heloïse herself, if we may believe her, was the perfect image: "Dum tecum carnali fruerer voluptate, utrum id amore, vel libidine agerem, incertum pluribus habebatur. Nunc autem finis indicat quo id inchoaverim principio" (*Epist.*, II, 187 A).

Like every other human being, especially in such circumstances, Heloïse somewhat flatters herself,[227] but undeniably her words have a large basis of truth. The whole history of her love for Abelard is here in question, and Abelard's own *Historia calamitatum*, is an implacable witness against himself. He recounts some of the reasons (*plerisque tacitis*, as Heloïse was to observe, 185 A) for which she had earlier refused to marry him. This is not the place to attempt an analysis of these reasons, which would show up, very naturally, we may say, their composite character, but it is evident that her principal motive was to avoid ruining the career and genius of such a man and compromising him for ever in what, on his part, was a mere adventure. A man like that belongs not to a woman but to the world (130 B); if he married Heloïse, his philosophic genius would founder, entangled in the daily routine of domestic life (131 A); transposing with astonishing intrepidity the remarks of Cicero on friendship, she applies his principles in a way that would have filled him with amazement. Cicero taught, in *De Amicitia*, that

the bond of friendship outweighs in dignity the bond of kinship
(*op. cit.*, V); Heloïse declares that friendship, taking the word
in a sense that is not to be misunderstood, outweighs the con-
jugal bond, for it is free of all bond but itself: "mihique honestius
amicam dici quam uxorem, ut me ei sola gratia conservaret,
non vis aliqua vinculi nuptialis constringeret" (*op. cit.*, 132 C).
To these motives, which Abelard mentions, and which Heloïse
never disavowed, let us add some of those of which she herself
has thought proper to inform us. Two at least are worth repeat-
ing: first, when she refused the marriage Abelard offered her,
that was the proof that what she had been seeking was not her
own pleasure but Abelard's. Such a word goes far; at the command of Abelard, without a sign of revolt, she altered the whole
current of her thoughts and life, entering religion to make it
plain to everyone that she was the absolute mistress of her own
heart and body: "Cum ad tuam statim jussionem tam habitum
ipsa quam animum immutarem, ut te tam corporis mei quam
animi unicum possessorem ostenderem. Nihil unquam (Deus
scit) in te nisi te requisivi; te pure, non tua concupiscens. Non
matrimonii federa, non dotes aliquas expectavi, non denique
meas voluptates aut voluntates, sed tuas (sicut nosti) adimplere
studui" (184 D). A love, consequently, which is a pure love,
because renouncing the joys normally implied in possession of
its object.

Heloïse's second remark confirms the foregoing and forbids
all hesitation about its meaning. Love, as she conceives it, is
not content with renunciation of its normal joys, but aspires to
humiliation, contempt, provided that would redound to the
greater honour of the beloved: "Et si uxoris nomen sanctius ac
validius videtur, dulcius mihi semper exstitit amicae vocabulum;
aut, si non indigneris, concubinae vel scorti. Ut quo me videlicet
pro te amplius humiliarem, ampliorem apud te consequerer
gratiam, et sic etiam excellentiae tuae gloriam minus laederem"
(184 D—185 A).

Compare now this attitude, so rare in the Middle Ages apart
from romances, with the truly unique doctrine of Abelard, and it
seems difficult not to perceive that the second is a mere abstract

transposition of the first. In both cases—and the two cases, each virtually unique, are connected in the way we know—we stand in the presence of a conception of love which regards that love only as pure which not only renounces joy in the possession of the object, but accepts humiliation and dissolution to assure the joy and honour of the beloved. A conception of human love that nothing could have surpassed, if Heloïse, who knew her Cicero so well, had not forgotten this other precept of the Pagan moralist: "in iis perniciosus est error, qui existimant, libidinum peccatòrumque omnium patere in amicitia licentiam; virtutum amicitia adjutrix a natura data est, non vitiorum comes" (*De Amicitia*, XXII). But nevertheless a conception of human love which, even when rectified by ancient wisdom in default of Christian Wisdom, loses all its meaning when transformed into a doctrine of divine love. For in that case the purity of the love is the indispensable condition, but also the sufficient condition, of the beatifying glorification of the lover. A bold transposition, but fatal to both loves. Here Heloïse triumphs over Abelard more completely, though none the less deplorably, than ever she could have hoped. At last she made him understand something. Do you wish to love God? he asks us. Then do not love Him as I loved Heloïse, but as Heloïse loved me.

Let us sum up the conclusions to be drawn from these facts. Abelard was the author of love-songs, now lost, in which he celebrated his love for Heloïse. They had a considerable success and, towards 1130, they were sung more or less everywhere. Some of these poems would seem to have been in Latin distichs in the manner of Ovid, meant for recitation (*amatorio metro . . . tam dictaminis. . . .*); others were songs properly so-called, whether in Latin rhythm or in French rhyme, but more probably in Latin (*vel rhythmo composita . . . quam cantus saepius frequentata;* see *Epist.*, II; P.L., CLXXVIII, 185 D). Furthermore, Abelard had elaborated before 1121 a doctrine of pure love in which are recognizable the influences of Cicero and Heloïse. This doctrine owes nothing to Cistercian mysticism because it antedates it; but Cistercian mysticism on the other hand, owes nothing to it because it traverses its conclusions. The two doctrines, however, in spite of their differences, and even fundamental opposition, are both outlined on a common humanist background; behind both we feel the presence of Cicero's *De Amicitia*. Finally, even considering the twelfth century only from the standpoint of the year 1125, we may say that it offers us, from the outset, an efflorescence of highly original doctrines of love, apparently springing up simultaneously in diverse surroundings. The order of their appearance will be somewhat as follows:

First. Abelard, in the *Introductio ad theologiam*, a little before 1121, and later in the *Commentary on the Epistle to the Romans*, between 1136 and 1140.

Second. William of Saint-Thierry, still a Benedictine, who seems to have composed the *De contemplando Deo* and the *De natura et dignitate amoris* between 1118 and 1135.

About this date, then, we arrive at the beginnings of the Benedictine mysticism of the twelfth century, which, in the case of William, was soon to coalesce with the Cistercian mysticism properly so-called.

Third. St. Bernard joined the group, almost about the same date, perhaps one or two years later, but with an originality of so striking a character that it is impossible not to regard him as an independent starting-point. If we put the *De gradibus humilitatis* about 1125, at the latest, and the *De diligendo Deo* in 1127 or a little later—which dates are generally accepted— we arrive at the conclusion that three great doctrines of love appeared almost simultaneously at the beginning of the twelfth century, and that they are virtually independent of each other, at least as regards their fundamental inspiration. In any event, if there is any interdependence between Abelard and St. Bernard, then, since Abelard's doctrine appears in complete form only after 1136, it must be admitted that it was Abelard who wished to attach the note of egoism to the doctrine of love proposed by St. Bernard about 1125-1127. It is curious that St. Bernard never replied. Perhaps he considered that the exposition of his own doctrine was all that was needed to make an end of Abelard's.

APPENDIX III

BERENGER THE SCHOLASTIC

AMONG the personages who move in the background of this scene we must find a place for an obscure polemic, whose work is of no importance in itself, but reveals the true character of some of the opposition raised against St. Bernard at this period. His name was Peter Berenger, of Poitiers, or Peter Berenger the Scholastic. The notice in the *Histoire littéraire de la France* which deals with him (t. XII, p. 251) is reproduced in Migne, P.L., CLXXVIII, 1854–1856.

This Berenger is known more especially for his *Apologeticus*, directed against St. Bernard after the condemnation of Abelard at the Council of Sens, in 1140. The text of this plea may be found in Migne, P.L., CLXXVIII, 1857–1870. Written in the heat of his resentment at the announcement of the condemnation, the *Apologeticus* would be little posterior to the event that occasioned it.

Berenger's pamphlet is of no philosophical interest, but it is rich in historical sidelights on the state of mind that prevailed in Abelard's entourage. It is addressed to St. Bernard himself. Its tone is violent, passionate, insulting throughout, and at times extremely gross. To understand and excuse it we have to take this production for what it is: an expression of the pain felt by the disciples of Abelard at the persecutions directed against a master whom they dearly loved. Abelard, in fact, was beloved by his pupils; St. Bernard was responsible for his condemnation; and the blame must be laid at his door. Let us add that the opposition of the two men was above all an opposition between two modes of thought and feeling. Let us say finally, and this time clearly in exoneration of Berenger, that their resentment may in a measure be justified. He insists on the point that even if Abelard was in the wrong, which he does not deny, he ought not to be treated with all this severity. Possibly not. His disciples, in any event, could hardly think otherwise, and if that does not excuse Berenger's unjust violence against St. Bernard, we may understand to some extent the motives that provoked it.

The most interesting passage in the work, as far as we are concerned, is that relating to St. Bernard's sermons on the Canticle of Canticles. One might have hoped to find there some discussion of the problem of love, comparing and opposing the two standpoints; but nothing of the kind appears. The work is incomplete, lacking for a second part which seems never to have been written and which possibly might have contained the missing dogmatic discussion. Berenger's criticism, in fact, is purely external; it is that of a humanist, a professor of literature, criticising an ill-written composition. His chief grievances are as follows:

1. Why make a commentary on the Canticle? That has been done often enough before. If Bernard had unveiled mysteries revealed to him, but escaping his predecessors, that would have been quite in order. But he has nothing new to say. He merely disguises under new formulae what four of these predecessors had already said in their own commentaries: "Supervacua igitur explanatio tua esse videtur. Ac ne quis me putet improbabilia prolocuturum, proferam super hunc librum quadrigam expositorum, Originem scilicet Graecum, Ambrosium Mediolanensem, Retium Augustodunensem, Bedam Angligenam" (P.L., CLXXVIII, 1863 C).

2. The attempt might pass if it had been a genuine commentary, but Bernard apparently set out to write a tragedy. After beginning his explanation of the text he suddenly stops short and dedicates "duos pene quadernos" to a funeral oration on his brother. Why should that trouble our critic? Well, there precisely we get to the root of the matter. St. Bernard's unpardonable crime consisted in perpetrating a *mixture of literary genres*. Don't laugh. The objection is poor enough in all conscience but highly instructive, especially when propounded in this period, and with so serious an air. There were people then in the twelfth century so much wrapped up in rhetoric, so full of the *Ars Poetica*, that in the face of the mysticism of St. Bernard they can put no better question than this: are these sermons composed according to the rules? For this is what the objection comes to: The Canticle is a nuptial song, a song of joy; and so a funeral oration ought not to be mixed up with it.

"Tu vero terminos transgrediens, quos posuerunt patres tui, Cantica in elegos, carmina in threnos sorte miserabili convertisti" (*op. cit.*, 1864 C). Then Horace comes to the rescue: "Humano capiti cervicem pictor equinam Jungere si velit . . ." Here is the important point: "non recte lamenta epithalmio, conjugasti" (1865 B). Berenger draws attention moreover, and rightly enough, to a literal reminiscence of St. Ambrose *De excessu Satyri*, in St. Bernard's text, but this will surprise no one who knows how deeply he was penetrated with sacred and profane literature, and how freely he turned it all to account (1865 C).

3. To these formal objections Berenger adds only a single doctrinal one on the problem of the soul, and one other, more revealing as to the spirit of the Abelardians, on the opening of the *De diligendo Deo*.[228] Recollect St. Bernard's formula: the *modus* of loving God is to love Him *sine modo*. It is easy enough to see what that means provided that one is not a dialectician. God is such that we cannot love Him in the measure that is His due. But, objects our dialectician, "quomodo sine modo diligemus quem cum modo diligere non valemus" (1867 A). In short, how love beyond all measure Whom we cannot even love in due measure? Bernard falls back upon rhetoric and presents us with an *impossibile*.

Berenger's fury over these trifles is explicable, as we have said. He wants to show that Bernard has perceived the mote in Abelard's eye, and missed the beam in his own. St. Bernard is no more infallible than anyone else and ought to moderate his tone. The thesis would have sufficed, one might have thought, without all this torrent of abuse. Berenger's intervention has at least this interest: it shows us that behind the moral and literary humanism of St. Bernard there lay another, purely literary, that if the literary pedagogues, whose whole intellectual equipment would seem to have amounted to a certain acquaintance with the ancient authors and a veneer of dialectic. Such men were well below Abelard's level, how much more beneath St. Bernard's! They represent the caricature of the genuine humanism of the twelfth century, and thus help to make up the picture. The schools would be charming places if they were peopled exclusively by masters, but there are plenty of smaller fry as well.

APPENDIX IV

ST. BERNARD AND COURTLY LOVE

It is difficult to study St. Bernard without raising some at least of the numerous problems bearing on his literary influence. Here we shall deal with only one: did his *mysticism* have any influence on courtly love? Chronologically, the two movements are virtually contemporary. Diez puts the beginnings of the art of the Troubadours as far back as 1090, and J. Anglade admits that its most flourishing period was towards the end of the twelfth century. It may therefore be said that the work of St. Bernard belongs to the opening of its most brilliant period, but somewhat after its beginnings. As tô the poetry of the Trouvères, it gives its definitive expression to courtly love only in the second half of the twelfth century and during the course of the thirteenth. It cannot then be admitted that St. Bernard contributed anything to the birth of courtly poetry, but he might have influenced its development. The question then is simply whether this possibility was realized in fact.[229] We are not competent to treat of the matter *ex professo*, being particularly lacking in a sufficiently thorough knowledge of the courtly literature. The following pages will contain merely the remarks of a reader familiar with the work of St. Bernard, and his reactions on contact with those of the courtly poets he has had occasion to read. Specialists, no doubt, will have every right to contest them in the name of other witnesses whom their author has not taken into consideration.

Perhaps, however, it will be allowable for the *indoctus* who ventures on this slippery ground to take some defensive precautions at the outset. Discussions bearing on courtly love are often conducted by very dubious methods. It might almost be supposed that authors and texts, from the first Troubadours to Dante, are interchangeable. That is by no means the case.

Dante, who was to choose St. Bernard as his supreme guide towards ecstasy, was evidently under the influence of his doctrine. If you show that, all well and good; but the fact that Dante's art was the final culmination of that of the Troubadours, is no good ground for maintaining that his ideas were the final culmination of their ideas. To go back from his texts towards theirs, to suppose that because he is in their succession poetically he is therefore also in their succession doctrinally, is an altogether unjustifiable *petitio principii*. I shall therefore leave Dante entirely outside the discussion and confine myself to the Troubadours and to the Trouvères properly so called. I shall accept, on the other hand, the testimony of André-le-Chapelain, for if this theorist put a great deal more scholasticism and mysticism into his treatise than did the poets themselves, it was nevertheless their conception of love that he set out to codify.

A second ambiguity, almost inevitable after the first, must nevertheless be recognized as such. In speaking of Cistercian mysticism we know what we mean: St. Bernard has but one doctrine of love, that of divine love. But what then is "courtly love"? Strictly speaking, it is love as this was conceived in the courts, just as scholastic philosophy is the philosophy elaborated in the schools. This conception of love was by no means one: it varies from poet to poet and, according to his mood, in the same poet. All that these poets wrote for the courts ought, as a matter of right, to enter into the definition of courtly love; historians as a matter of fact make cuts, eliminate the over-crude grossnesses of certain poets or certain pieces, and thus elaborate, by way of selection, the ideal type of a chivalric courtesy of which all the elements are taken from the historical reality, but which appears in their books in quite another guise than it did in history. The method has its dangers; it runs the risk of falsifying the meaning of those elements it takes into consideration by treating them in isolation from the rest.

This very well appears from the controversies between the historians themselves. One proves the "disinterestedness" of the Troubadours; against that another cites a Troubadour with very positive appetites; the reply is that *this* particular Trouba-

G

dour is not a witness to courtly love. If, in the works of a poet who passes for a singer of courtly love, we point to lines of excessive crudity, they are challenged in the same way; on that particular day the poet was not singing of courtly love. But suppose it happens in the same piece? Well, of course, a change of mood—the doctrine of ideality is safe in any event. It will always be safe by these methods.[230]

True; but it is thus reduced to the state of an abstraction. The proper procedure would be by way of a series of monographs on schools, even on individual poets, to seize the ideas of each of them and so arrive finally at a definition of courtly love, instead of starting off with a ready-made one and then selecting historical texts to justify it. But we have not got so far as that yet. It is perhaps allowable, in the meanwhile, to examine the texts in the light of *all* the contexts. Then, perhaps, we shall no longer be in danger of seeing the effusions of an ascetic in the writings of *bons vivants* like Thibaut de Champagne, whose obesity was the chief obstacle he had to overcome in order to attain to perfect love.

I

CISTERCIAN MYSTICISM AND COURTLY LOVE HYPOTHESIS OF FILIATION

1. *The Object of Love*

There can be no hesitation about the object and nature of mystical love as conceived by St. Bernard. It was a spiritual love, in sharp opposition to every kind of carnal love. His doctrine is too uncompromising on the point to leave any room for doubt. In a sense it was the whole of his doctrine. Carnal love, wherever it springs from concupiscence, is something that has to be extirpated, and even when it occurs in the spiritual order it is something to be surpassed.

There exists a widespread illusion which attributes an attitude of the same kind to the Troubadours and Trouvères; and it has suggested the hypothesis that mystical love had an influence upon courtly love. But in fact, to start with an obvious point, this courtly love is a "worldly" conception of love. It is addressed to creatures, and if it were true that it amounted to a divinization of woman it would be a caricature of divine love in Cistercian eyes, a horrible deformation of sacred love, in short, a sacrilege. Thibaut de Champagne seems not far short of it if you take some of his expressions literally:

> Si me vaudroit melz un ris
> De vous qu'autre paradis.
> (Wallensköld, p. 71, 53–54.)
>
> More worth your smile to me
> Than any heaven—

St. Bernard, I imagine, would have had nothing to do with fooleries of that kind; even if we make all due allowances for poetic licence it is clear that here we are at the antipodes of Cistercian love.[231]

But might not this divinization of woman represent at least an influence in rebound, a sort of inversion of mystical love, thrown back from the Creator on to the creature? Well, perhaps it might have been so—but then think how very differently Cistercians and courtly poets love the respective objects of their desires!

Courtly love, it seems, is sometimes taken for a love that is purely spiritual, and, in the vulgar sense of the word, Platonic. If the thing could be proved it would be of the first importance. We might then have the right to suppose that these poets, prompted by mystic love, came to love their ladies only for their souls, that is, for their intelligence and virtue; that if indeed they praised her beauty this was only as Plato would have it loved, as a sign or symbol of a beauty purely intelligible, moral, spiritual. The fact is that this popular view of courtly love has never been unreservedly accepted by those who have studied its expression in the texts; but since it still flourishes vigorously it seems desirable to say as clearly as possible that it is altogether without justification. The matter is a somewhat unpleasant one, and I regret to have to insist on it.

In the fourth chapter of his book on *Les Troubadours*, where he considers *La doctrine de l'amour courtois*, J. Anglade introduces us to some extremely discreet poets. "They were certainly not exigent in the matter of love; they contented themselves with very little, so at least they assure us. Most of them ask their lady to give them countenance as her servitors, nothing more, to accept their poetical homage" (p. 82). No doubt it fell out thus when the lady was absolutely inaccessible by reason of her rank or anything else, but the courtly poet, like the poets of all ages, contented himself with that only in default of better. He loved without recompense when there was nothing else to be done. These amorists expressed a cycle of feeling common to all poets. The lady is virtuous, rightly then does she hold herself dear; but if she keeps the loving heart waiting too long, then she becomes a cruel one, incapable of feeling any love at all; at last she yields; for a time she is encompassed about with an infinity of worship expressed in lyric praises that know no reserve; but she loses all her virtues on the day when the disillusioned poet perceives that she accords without scruple to "a hundred others" that for which she made him languish so long as the rarest of favours. All that is simply human and supposes no particular effort at spiritualization of the object of love. The lady is a real being, of flesh and blood, and the most that can be said in favour of the courtly poets on this score is that they had the art, so useful to poor mortals, of making a virtue of necessity.

If we must come to a final point on this delicate matter I would first of all draw attention to the coarseness of some of these poems. Speaking of Marcabrun, Anglade writes that his satires against love contain things of "untranslatable crudity" (p. 103). Let us note in passing and before we return to it, that there is no such thing as satire against divine love among the Cistercians; and as for the crudity, it never ceased to appear in this sort of poetry. Contemporary with the Comte de Poitiers, it persists well into the thirteenth century. The Troubadour Jausbert de Puycibot expresses himself in such terms that his translator is forced to resort to artifice on several points. But the text itself is only too clear.[232] In this matter many of the Trouvères followed the lead of these Troubadours.

Among the works of Thibaut de Champagne, [233] there occur verses that are neither to be cited nor translated (*ed.* Wallensköld, p. 149, vv. 23–28), but if you want to know what he thinks at certain moments about courtesy and its worth, just meditate such lines as these:

> Baudoÿn, assez treuve l'en
> Vieilles plus laides que nuns chiens
> Qui ont cortoisie et gran sen
> Mais au touchier ne valent riens.
>
> (p. 125, 33–36).

Baudouin, there be many old ladies, more ugly than any dog, with good wit forsooth, and courtesy; to touch worth nought at all.

Here it is Thibaut himself who speaks, and we see that when it comes to choosing between courtesy on the one hand and the palpable realities of love on the other, he does not hesitate for an instant. Admire in passing the influence of received ideas on paleography. Faced with this text M. Jeanroy reads without a flutter "Mais au couchier ne valent riens".[234] Hesitating at this word which seems to be "gross" and "here somewhat out of place", M. Wallensköld points out that the difference between a *c* and a *t* is so slight in manuscript that his own reading may well be preferred. So said, so done; but if it is necessary to raise these paleographic discussions it will have to be admitted that, from St. Bernard's standpoint of spiritual love, the difference between *touchier* and *couchier* is not appreciably more considerable than that between a *c* and a *t* for the practised eyes of a paleographer. Morals, like paleography, have their subtleties, but there is no need to see them where they do not exist.

Let us leave the chapter of crudities. They would offer no interest if they did not help us to a more precise understanding of certain passages which the literary historians would seem to read in oblivion of permanent traits of human nature. It is all to their honour, be it said, but none the less it marks one of those little professional weaknesses to which we are all exposed. It is difficult to believe that so many passages in which the poets declare that the mere sight of their lady, or at most a kiss, will suffice them, ought not to be often read in the light of the mediaeval rule: *minus dicens et plus volens intelligi*.[235]

The "disinterested" character of courtly love has been very much exaggerated. True, love does not always receive its "guerdon", but Thibaut would have it do so rather more often:

> S'amor vosist guerredoner autant
> Come elle puet, mult fust ses nons a droit,
> Mès el ne veut, dont j'ai le cuer dolent.
>   (92; 16–18).

Would but my love grant all guerdon it could, then in high honour would I hold its name; but alas, 'twill not, whereof my heart is sad.

> Nule paine, qui guerredon atent
> C'est aese, qui bien le set entendre.
>   (46; 17–18.)

No grief has he who waits reward,—
Take but that word aright, 'tis pleasure.

How then are we to understand him? Any misconception will certainly demand some good-will:

> S'a ce je puis venir
> Qu'aie, sanz repentir
> Ma joie et mon plesir
> De li, qu'ai tant amee,
> Lors diront, sanz mentir,
> Qu'avrai tout mon desir
> Et ma queste achevee
>   (50; 38–44.)

Could I, without let, have my joy and pleasure of her whom so much I have loved, then could I truly say that all my desire were fulfilled, my quest at end.

Would we have something more precise? Mythology and legend will help us out:

> Pleüst a Dieu, pour ma dolor garir,
> Qu'el fu Tisbé, car je sui Piramus;
> Mes je voi bien ce ne puet avenir;
> Ensi morrai que ja n'en avrai plus.
>   (69; 11–14.)

Would to God to heal my sorrow that she were Thisbe, for Pyramus
am I; but that I know can never be, so shall I die and never have
her more.

> Douce dame, s'il vos plesoit un soir
> M'avriez vos plus de joie doné
> C'onques Tristans, qui en fist son pouoir
> N'en pust avoir nul jor de son aé.
>
> (80; 32–35.)

Sweet lady, should it please you one night, more joy could you
give me than ever had Tristan, who joyed at his will, on any one day
of his life.

Unless we seriously modify our conception of the loves of
Yseult and Tristan, we can have but little doubt about the
true nature of Thibaut's feelings. He speaks so clearly, moreover,
on other occasions that no hesitation can remain:

> Par maintes foiz l'ai sentie
> En dormant tout a loisir,
> Mès quant pechiez et envie
> M'esveilloit et que tenir
> La cuidoie à mon plesir
> Et ele n'i estoit mie,
> Lors ploroie durement
> Et melz vousisse en dormant
> Li tenir toute ma vie.
>
> (118; 28–36.)

Full oft have I felt her in quiet sleep, but when by sin and lust
awakened I thought to hold her at my pleasure and there by my side
I found her not—then wept I bitterly, and rather had I held her all
my life in sleep.

The invocations to God, when they occur, are in no wise
directed to attract the "visitations" of the Word, but to something rather more prosaic that would certainly not have edified
Bernard:

> Mais je l'aim plus que nule riens vivant,
> Si me doint Deus son gent cors embracier.
>
> (10; 19–20.)

But more I love her than all living things—so would God grant her
sweet body to my arms.

The situation is clear enough; for poetry of this type Bernard
could have felt nothing but horror. The cult of sensuality, the
apotheosis of cupidity, that is precisely the thing against which

he waged a pitiless warfare, and if you want a testimony to his success you will not find it in this courtly poetry.[236]

2. *The Nature of Love*

We may still ask ourselves however whether the courtly conception of love, although oriented in the opposite direction to the Cistercian, was not a kind of reversed copy of it, at least in some respects. A parody is an imitation, and attests the success of the original. Does courtly love thus attest the success of the Cistercian mysticism?

In considering a question of this kind we must beware of apparent resemblances and come down in the end to the necessary degree of detail. M. E. Anitchkof, in his book on *Joachim de Flore* (Rome, 1931) does not hesitate to speak of the "filiation of ideas and sentiments connecting St. Bernard's mystical love with courtly love" (p. 105). That is a very bold formula unless accompanied with solid proof. To point out, along with St. Bernard, that in the case of a being born of concupiscence love begins by being carnal, is to prove nothing at all for courtly love is the poetic expression of concupiscence, whereas this is the very thing that Bernard proposes to eliminate. Filiation is not to be proved by pointing to a fundamental opposition. As to the fact that in both doctrines love has its degrees—which M. Anitchkof considers the essential point—it would seem to be hardly more decisive.

Guiraut de Calanson admitted three degrees in love, and nobody, so we are told, pays any attention to it. What a scandal! But first, as we have seen, Bernard admits that love has four degrees, [237] and there your proof is upset. For finally, if the fact that they agree on three degrees proves a filiation of one from the other, then the fact that one has three and the other four should prove the contrary. But let it pass, let us assume agreement on the number of degrees—what in fact are these degrees? In the one case they are degrees of sacred love, in the other of profane love, of which the former is a radical negation. But perhaps the degrees of the one correspond to the degrees of the other? Not in the least: these degrees are not merely degrees of opposed tendencies; they are not even the same degrees; nowhere, up to the present, has anyone found in a courtly poet a classification of the degrees of love into servile, mercenary, filial and nuptial. This however, or something sufficiently like it, will have to be found if the parallelism of degrees is to support the hypothesis of a doctrinal filiation of the kind affirmed.

M. Anitchkof is not without some sense of the difficulty. To the objection that St. Bernard spoke exclusively of love towards God, he replies with magnificent assurance: "Thus the Troubadours transformed certain theological conceptions into literary ideas" (p. 107). The thing is not impossible in itself, and we believe indeed that St. Bernard's doctrine was turned to account by some profane authors, but what we want to know is whether it was turned to account by the Troubadours. To prove this, it has to be established that the courtly conception of love is a sensual interpretation of the mystical conception of love developed by St. Bernard. Sophistries you may have ready to your heart's content for the justification of the thesis and in spite of all it will remain a sophism, and that for a very simple reason: since mystical love is the negation of carnal love one cannot borrow the description of the one in order to describe the other. It is by no means sufficient to say that they have not the same object; we are bound to add that precisely because they have not the same object they cannot have the same nature.

We stand in no need here of torturing the texts in order to make them say what we want them to say, all we have to do is to hold to a few very simple ideas that rule their interpretation. What has contributed more than anything else to a certain ambiguity about the nature of courtly love, is the fact that the Troubadours and Trouvères protest that they prefer rather to love without reward and to suffer than to be rid of their suffering along with their love. True, but what does that prove? Listen once more to Thibaut de Champagne:

De tous maus n'est nus plesanz
Fors seulement cil d'amer.

(4; 1–2.)

G*

> In no evil lies delight
> Save but in this of love.

> Qui plus aime plus endure,
> Plus a mestier de confort,
> Qu'Amors est de tel nature
> Que son ami maine a mort;
> Puis en a joie et deport,
> S'il est de bonne aventure.
>
> (117; 1–6.)

Who loves the more, the more endures, so much the more is com-
fortless; for Love in the end his lover slays. Then has he joy, when
fortune smiles on love.

What mean these complaints? That love is an evil that is
worth enduring, especially if there is some chance of its finding
its due reward; but, finally, it is an evil. The most pleasing of
evils, of all evils the most beneficent, an evil that makes the sufferer
superior to those who never feel it, but still an evil; it is the well-
known "*mal d'amour*" dear to the sentimental romances of all
times. It is an evil because it makes one suffer, and one suffers
because it is not always rewarded. Therefore, it is said, since it
is still cherished, it must needs be disinterested. Perhaps; but
first of all it is so only up to a certain point. When hope vanishes
for good and all, then Thibaut begins to cast about to rid himself
of this so beneficent evil:

> Si je de li me poisse partir
> Melz me venist qu'estre sires de France.
>
> (65; 11–12.)

Could I be quit of it, 'twere more to me than to be King of France.

Never do we find St. Bernard seeking to disembarrass himself
of the love of God. Nor is this merely a matter of chance but
touches the root of the whole question, for here we may clearly
perceive that the two loves are of opposed natures. Courtly love,
let us say, is an evil because it may well have to go without its
reward.[238] Take this in its most immediate sense, and understand that even in a purely sentimental way it may very possibly
not be returned—for sentiment can exist without the rest and
the rest without sentiment—then that is enough to set up a radical

distinction between courtly and mystical love, to set them in
opposition to each other as human love to divine. Here we have
precisely the suffering that Bernard would avoid, and from which
he would help us to free ourselves. Men suffer because they love
and are not loved in return; love therefore God and you will
never know what it is to feel an unrequited love: for—let us
never forget it—God has loved us first: *ipse prior dilexit nos*!
Such is the true love, not the desolate plaint of a soul that
languishes in solitude, but the joy of two wills knowing themselves united in intention and desire. For that love indeed is
never disappointed, and Thibaut knew it well when he wrote
in a weary moment:

> Or me gart Deus et d'amor et d'amer
> Fors de Celi, cui on doit aourer,
> Ou on ne puet faillir a grant soudee.
>
> (29; 41–43.)
>
> Now keep me, God, from love and loving
> Save only There where man must needs adore
> And cannot want for great reward.

In these three lines are contained the principles of Cistercian
love, but they are also a denial of courtly love and an affirmation of its fundamental vanity. If there is filiation from St.
Bernard in the poetry of the Trouvères it amounts to no more
than that: he inspired them perhaps with a few fleeting impulses
to renounce it.

But let us go further: we should still be but skimming the
surface of the problem were we content to say no more than that
divine love always brings with it its "*grant soudee*", its great
reward. The very nature of love is here involved. Is an unrequited love even conceivable? St. Bernard and all the Christian
mystics answer, no. Love belongs to the order of friendship,
and friendship essentially implies mutual good-will; we are not
friends with anyone who is not our friend, we can only desire
his friendship, and that is not the same thing as possessing it.
Love is in the same case. What the courtly poets call by this
name is merely desire in the eyes of the Christian mystics. To
transpose what the poets say into mystical terms we should have

to express ourselves thus: I desire with a desire that goes unrequited, therefore not only am I not loved, but I myself do not love, for all love is mutual as by definition. We see then how far we are out when we set up facile equivalences between formulas having a certain external resemblance but remaining inwardly contradictory. Even the dryness of the mystic is not to be compared with the forlorn state of the courtly poet. For the mystic too desires, but he realizes that if then he suffers from his love as from a wound, it is not because he is not loved, nor because he loves, but because he does not yet give enough love for love. The problem for Christians is never to make themselves loved by a God Who created them out of love and redeemed them in His blood, but for themselves to love in measure sufficient to attain to union with Him who is Beatitude: *Quidni ametur Amor ?*

This fundamental opposition appears in a striking trait that has not been sufficiently noticed. Courtly love, being never sure of requital, is often a prey to fear. Fear is a word well known to Thibaut de Champagne, and well he knows its meaning:

> Et la poors est dedenz moi entree.
> (64; 37.)

> And into my heart hath entered fear.

That is a certain sign that we are moving on paths that are wholly alien to the Cistercian mysticism, for there love never leads to fear, least of all to fear of going unrequited; on the contrary, it drives out all fear according to the promise of St. John which St. Bernard meditated so often and at such length: *Caritas mittit foras timorem.* Charity, that is to say the true love, but not the desire of what is not God. That is always haunted by fear because such desire is orientated towards false goods, which cannot fail to disappoint us.[239]

To pin this opposition down to its essential point we may say that the word "love" has not the same meaning in the two systems. Courtly love, since it amounts to desire, may imagine itself disinterested on the ground that it has sufficient strength to last until reward or weariness make an end of it. Even if we suppose—a thing that seldom happens save in verse—that it fixes upon a single object and lasts a whole lifetime, it will still be nothing but a hopeless or resigned desire. The Christian is never in this situation. God has forestalled us; He loves us, and would have our love only for our own beatitude; to desire Him is therefore to give Him love for love, it is truly to love, and it is to love beatitude. It is a love, as St. Bernard says, at once both disinterested and rewarded. That is why the Cistercian can read Thibaut's songs with a tranquil heart; they prove only one thing that he knew already: as between the poet and himself it is he alone who knows how to love. He has chosen the better part.

Thus courtly love, to retain its traditional name, has perforce to content itself with less than mystical love; it lives and endures without attaining its end, whereas charity, by definition, is the embrace of its object: *vacua esse non potest*. A sole point remains on which the two conceptions might be compared, and this perhaps is what is meant when both, albeit in different senses, are qualified as disinterested. Courtly love, even when rewarded, is a thing distinct from its reward, it is other than the joy that crowns it; gathering this up like a fruit of love, it does not confuse it with the love itself. So also Bernard when he affirms that to love the Father for the expected inheritance, legitimate as this may be, is still only to love the inheritance and not the Father Himself. That is true, but we always have to return to certain fundamental considerations. For the Christian the problem does not really arise. What could be more absurd than to think of being united by love to Beatitude and not to be happy? Now we are united to Him by the very fact that we love Him; a disciple of St. Bernard cannot ask himself whether it is possible to will Beatitude without willing to be happy. He cannot even ask whether he can will this without the happiness it gives— since it is that happiness. The question might have a meaning in any other case, but not in this.

To bring out the difference still more clearly let us look once more at each of these loves from the standpoint of the other. As seen by a courtly poet, it is the Cistercian love which is strongly suspect of not being disinterested; for, finally, if it is so, how does it know it? Its perseverences, even in the midst of all its drynesses, prove nothing; what merit is there in perseveringly pursuing an end when one is sure to attain it? But if we turn to courtly love, and look at it from the Cistercian standpoint, its position does not appear any more satisfactory. What would you, St. Bernard would say to the poet—a love which is to be deprived of its recompense in order to be assured of its disinterestedness? That is a contradiction in terms, since love is itself its own recompense. The thing that leads you astray is the inveterate habit of desiring creatures; for, taking that to be love which in fact is only concupiscence, you lend your desire the name of love, and since it is inevitably frustrated you conclude that it can do without reward. But, if it were really love, it could in no wise do without it, for then it would be its own reward. To twit love for not being able to do without recompense is to twit it for not being concupiscence, but love.

The dialogue might go on for ever, for the two interlocutors do not speak the same language. They could reach agreement only if one of them tempted the other to the point of leading him to be satisfied with human desire, or of wholly abjuring it in order to give himself up to the pursuit of divine love. It seems quite clear in any event that the two systems are mutually exclusive, and that any communication between them is conceivable only with difficulty. There cannot be filiation between two conceptions of love in which the very name of love bears contradictory meanings. There is no passage from Cistercian love to courtly love save by apostasy, nor from courtly love to Cistercian love save by abjuration: think of Lancelot, Galahad.

When all is said, what common residue is to be found in the two doctrines? This only, that in both the beatifying love goes to the beatifying object itself and for itself, rather than to the joy that it gives. If it does not give it, as sometimes happens in the case of courtly love, then the love persists; if it gives it, as always happens in the long run in the case of mystical love, then pure love still goes to it and for its sake, and not *propter aliquid ipsius*. That is all, and that indeed is something—but which doctrine is in debt for it to the other? The fact that two systems of ideas so opposed have this element in common, suggests that both received it from a third. And that in fact seems to have been the case. Classical Antiquity may perhaps have been a more important source of the courtly poetry, and even of the Cistercian mysticism, than it has hitherto been supposed.

Turn then once more to the *De Amicitia* of Cicero, a text and an author we certainly know to have been read in the twelfth century. The idea that friendship produces benefits but is not born of them, is there expressed with all desirable force: "Atque etiam mihi videntur, qui utilitatis causa fingunt amicitias, amabilissimum nodum amicitiae tollere: non enim tam utilitas parta per amicum, quam amici amor ipse, delectat . . . Non igitur utilitatem amicitia, sed utilitas amicitiam, consecuta est" (*De Amicitia* XIV). Do we want a formula that might have come from St. Bernard himself? Here we are: "Sic, amicitiam, non spe mercedis adducti, sed quod omnis ejus fructus in ipso amore inest, excolendam putamus" (*De Amicitia* IX). Recollect the many equivalent formulas of St. Bernard, already cited: "Verus amor seipso contentus est." "Amor praeter se non requirit causam, non fructum. Fructus ejus, usus ejus. Amo quia amo, amo ut amem." Neither the sound of the words nor the accent are the same, but the same fundamental notion of love is indeed affirmed by the Latin moralist and the Christian mystic. Something analogous may be found at times in the representatives of courtly love. Both have turned to their own account and utilized for ends which for the rest are very different or even opposed, a doctrinal element which was offered them by the classical culture of their time. It would be easy to find others, but none that played such a part in the constitution of these two doctrines, and its presence in both suffices to account for the analogy that may be held to exist between them, without any need for an hypothesis of filiation.

II

COURTLY LOVE AND CHRISTIAN MYSTICISM
HYPOTHESIS OF INFLUENCE

We have tried to bring out the fundamental opposition that exists between Cistercian mysticism and courtly love. But we have still to ask whether, in default of filiation, there might have been an influence passing from Christianity to the courtly poetry. Yet how shall we put the question? If all we want to know is whether the terminology of the Troubadours and the Trouvères betrays the fact that they lived in Christian surroundings the answer seems obvious. Many signs show them to have been Christians, even when the sentiments they express are anything but Christian. It might also be said that the influence of Christianity in general had something to do with the appearance of a form of love which, sensual as it was, marked a progress nevertheless on the licentious love of Ovid. That is evident at once, nor do I dream of disputing it.[240] Courtly love in fact is inconceivable save in a Christian atmosphere. But when we come to ask whether certain *mystical* ideas were introduced into this poetry and are there incorporated, then we enter the field of disputable hypotheses—that is to say of hypotheses that need to be demonstrated and are open to refutation. In this field we propose to remain.

If we are to attempt to do so it will need to be delimited; and that is a matter that has been insufficiently attended to. How can we discuss the question of this supposed influence unless we agree on the marks by which it is to be recognized? The first rule, which should never be forgotten, seems to me to be this: *we cannot prove that one doctrine depends on another by the mere fact that the same idea appears in both, when the idea in question is one that is easily discoverable in itself, or easily discovered elsewhere.* A rule of simple good sense but rather too often forgotten. Thus M. E. Wechssler thinks that courtly love begins, just as Christian love does, with a kind of vague nostalgia, the *Sehnsucht*. We do not dispute it, but was it worth the trouble of collecting so many texts in which the poets speak of their "desire", to prove so obvious a thing? It is easy to cite passages in which the mystic declares himself unable to think of God without desiring Him, just as the poet affirms that he cannot think of his lady without desiring her, but no proof can be drawn from that because no one needs to be taught that desire is the beginning of love. What is desire? asks St. Augustine; and replies: "*Desiderium est rerum absentium concupiscientia.*"[241] There is nothing mysterious about that, nothing that calls for special-research; everyone who puts the question will see the answer without needing to consult any books. Filiations are not to be established on the basis of general analogies of this sort.

The case is the same with another common trait brought forward by the same historian: violent love is a passion which absorbs and renders insensible those of whom it takes possession.[242] The proper question to put here is not whether the mystics affirm this of charity as the poets of love, for we know they do; but whether we are sure that the poets would have failed to say it if the mystics had not said it first. That is the whole question. Is it a case of agreement or a case of influence? No amorous poet had any need to read a description of ecstasy in order to put himself in the way to describe an amorous transport.

Other precautions are also needed. It is all to the good that historians of literature should have recently manifested some interest in the history of ideas. The two domains cannot be separated. However, we cannot pass from one to the other without taking certain precautions, of which the first is to learn to treat ideas with some of that precision which is commonly brought to bear upon texts. That is very far from being always observed, one of the commonest errors being to treat ideas as comparable merely on account of certain analogies in expression, although the meaning may be altogether different. Let us therefore propose a second rule: *The influence of one work on another is not to be proved from the fact that they contain formulas that are literally similar, but of different meaning.* That kind of proof is often offered, and it has not been omitted in the case of the relations between Cistercian mysticism and courtly love.

The procedure is particularly tempting when ecstasy is in question, and particularly dangerous. After citing mystical texts descriptive of ecstasy, M. Wechssler accumulates poetical texts where the lover becomes lost in contemplation of his lady. To both phenomena we may very well give the name of ecstasy; and St. Thomas himself would readily agree, because he considers all love to be ecstatic as by definition. That is not the question. What we want to know is whether the idea that love is ecstatic came to the poets from the theologians. One might put it just as easily the other way round and be equally unable to prove it, for these two ecstasies are opposed not merely in the sense that one excludes the other, but also because the nature of the one is contrary to that of the other. The same problem therefore arises again. That love naturally carries the lover outside himself, makes him pass, so to speak, into the object loved, is something easily divined by anyone with any experience of love. If anyone felt absolutely bound to verify the fact in a book, an author so little mystical as Cicero would have sufficed. For did he not write in his *De Amicitia* : "*est enim (verus amicus) tanquam alter idem*" ? Now this identification of two "selves"— is it not developed spontaneously and independently in two different directions in courtly and mystical love? That is much the most tenable hypothesis if we bear in mind the radical difference we have noted between the two conceptions.

From the window of a tower Lancelot sees Queen Guinevere carried off by an enemy. When she passes beneath his eyes and his gaze meets hers, he falls into a trance, and would have fallen from the tower had not his friend Gawain held him back. Accumulate as much of this sort of thing as you like, add the *cœur éperdu* of Jaufré Rudel and the *oublis* into which the courtly poets fall at the sight of their beloved,[243] never in all that they say will you discover the slightest reminiscence of mystical ecstasies. To doubt it we should have to forget what these last are.

M. Wechssler, however, has very well defined them: "The soul's effort to emerge from the finite, and its passage into the infinite by the power of ecstatic love."[244] Now what is here called the "ecstasy" of the courtly lover is, contrariwise, an effort of the soul to become absorbed in the finite by force of human love. Note that we are certainly concerned once more with the intimate structure of the sentiments in question; save only this ecstatic element common to all love, recognized by St. Thomas even in insanity—*alienation* from self—nothing of all that enters into the definition of one of these affections is to be found in the other. We may then well ask: how can historians who admit it picture the influence of the one on the other?

Do they even try to picture it at all? By what conceivable interchange of ideas can they represent the supposed passage? We are reduced to conjectures. However, what is true of animal forms is true also of ideas: you cannot pass indifferently from any one of them to any other. Can we pass from the *raptus* of the mystic to the *ravissements* of the poet, or from the *excessus mentis* of the mystic to the *ecstasies* of courtly love? That is the whole question.

We shall put aside the question of terminology. Supposing— a point I have not verified—that the word ecstasy had been used by a poet of the twelfth or thirteenth century, we should still have to ask what he meant to express by it. I must ask pardon for insisting, but it goes to the bottom of the question. Having passed these various aspects of the matter in review, M. Wechssler adds honestly: "Only a small number of these motifs are specificially mystical. We can assert it categorically only of the notions of rapture or ecstasy."[245] There lies the ambiguity; are the poet's rapture or ecstasy really mystical states, or did they not rather cease to be so when they passed from mysticism into poetry? Let us not call that a subtlety of merely theological interest. To admit that Christian mysticism exerted a demonstrable influence on courtly poetry is to under- take to prove that something of the rapture or ecstasy of the mystic is recognizable in those of the poet. If nothing of this kind is recognizable, the question is no longer one of "Vorstel- lungen" but merely one of words. The simplest way to settle it is once more to compare the two conceptions of love in question: "Höfliche Frauenminne und chrisstliche *charitas*."

M. Wechssler himself puts the question, and he is too well acquainted with the problem not to feel what is paradoxical about it. "The courtly love of women and the Christian *charitas*— what have they to do with each other?"[246] None the less he sets out to discover it. The thing that especially strikes him is that love, as the mystics themselves conceive it, is substantially one; whether there is question of carnal love or love of God, we have always the same *affectus*, modified by the different forms it takes. The remark is perfectly just, and we have seen to what extent it is verified in the doctrine of St. Bernard. M. Wechssler therefore is quite right on this important point;[247] but its consequences demand careful consideration.

To simplify the question, let us return to the point that decides everything: *when a courtly poet speaks of pure love, what he has in mind is exactly the contrary of what a Cistercian mystic designates by that name.* Leave aside all those cases, and they are by far the most numerous, where the disinterestedness of courtly love is merely a last resource, and consider only those in which it voluntarily surrenders possession of the object loved in order to assure itself of its own disinterestedness. Then the poet finds himself in the situation described with bald crudity by André-le-Chapelain: "Amor quidam est purus et quidam dicitur esse mixtus. Et purus quidem amor est, qui omnimoda dilectionis affectione duorum amantium corda conjungit. Hic autem in mentis contemplatione cordisque consistit affectu; procedit autem usque ad oris osculum lacertique amplexum et verecundum amantis nudae contactum, extremo praetermisso solatio."[248] These are the words of a cleric, and of one who borrows the words *amor purus* from mystical authors; but then, what concept does he borrow along with them? None at all. It would be easy to insist on the equivocal side of this extraordinary conception of purity, but let us rather, on the contrary, emphasize the fact that the very thing that here constitutes the proof of the purity of love for the poet or the theorist of courtly love, would be the proof of its impurity in the eyes of the mystic. The fundamental opposition of the two systems of ideas here appears in all its force. The carnal character of courtly love is such that the love itself has to be divorced from its fulfilment in the joy of the object; the joy in question, being fundamentally impure, cannot coexist with the love without contaminating it, or at least without rendering it suspect even in the eyes of the lover himself. And so courtly love here follows out its logic to the bitter end, and disallows the union of lover and beloved; and that is why some of its theorists consider it to be incompatible with marriage, in which legitimacy and security of possession make every illusion of disinterestedness impossible.[249] But mystical love, too, no less intrepidly follows out its logic in the affirmation that the mark of spiritual love, brought to its point of perfection, consists precisely in that real .union which courtly love denies itself. This last is not pure unless it has all except that: "extremo praetermisso solatio"; mystical love has no other ambition than to receive this final favour, and it is not sure of its purity until it obtains it. That is why the mystical symbolism of the Canticle of Canticles is always interpreted by our authors as that of Bridegroom and Bride. The pure love of the mystic is essentially the marriage of the soul to God: the Spiritual Nuptials, the Mystical Marriage, all such expressions are the direct negation, if not of courtly love, at least of its timidities or resignations. For, properly speaking it does not merely lead to the marriage of the soul to God, it is that marriage itself: *sic amare, nupsisse est ;* for it, no intermediate position exists between "mixed love" and the mystic marriage of pure love: "*aspirare ad nuptias Verbi,*" that is its supreme aim, and nothing will hold it back, neither reverence nor shame, until it shall have attained it.

How then shall we not perceive herein the sign of a profound difference between the two loves? A parallelism between them may persistently be sought by maintaining that courtly love, by its very exclusion of carnal union—when indeed it excludes it—succeeds in imitating the spirituality of mystical love, or attempts to do so at any rate. Grant the attempt, in the sense that it here borrows the language of pure love, never for an instant does it get farther than the phrase "pure love", it is excluded for ever from participation in the idea. A "pure carnal love" is a manifest absurdity for any one who considers the exclusion of the carnal element in love as the first condition of its purity. Grant to le Chapelain that in his awkward position he does what he can, the heart of the difficulty is none the less that the two systems are necessarily "non-communicating", hermetically sealed against each other, because they make use of the same word "love" in opposite senses. Placing himself on the plane of the spiritual life the mystic is in a position to ask of supernatural love what, as man, he would ask of carnal love. Now on this point there is no room left for doubt: human love is never fully realized save in that union of man and woman which makes them one flesh. Man is a carnal being; therefore the union of two human beings, if it is to be complete, cannot be limited to a union of thought or affection, or even, to adopt the language of André-le-Chapelain, of contemplation, but must be a union of the whole being. No other relation of human being to human is to be compared with that, not even that of parents to children, as moreover it is written: "Thou shalt leave father and mother . . .," no bond can prevail against this bond, at once natural and holy. The mystic can have no thought of union with God by way of his body (albeit this body is hereafter to participate in beatitude) for God is spirit; but in the order at least of spiritual life which is his, he will never conceive a union of love which is not, in its own way, total: *Sponsus et Sponsa sunt ;* love will have that, or it will be frustrated of what it is impossible for it not to desire without ceasing to be itself. The impure love of which the mystic speaks is a love that desires something else: "*Impurus est qui aliud cupit*", but pure love, on the contrary, is a love which desires precisely that, for this is the love of the Bride, and she is Bride because she is this love itself: "*Sponsae hic est, quia hoc Sponsa est quaecumque est.*" In short, pure courtly love is defined by exclusion of that precisely which constitutes the pure love of the mystics: the real union of lover and beloved. Nothing can efface or extenuate this opposition.

What was it then that really happened? This: the theorists of courtly love (for the poets themselves furnish only rare and vague texts on these questions), by dint of attempting to appropriate the language of the mystics, elaborated a conception of love not opposed only to that of the mystics but even opposed to that of the Christian moralists. Their pure love, in the eyes of the mystics, would be the very height of impurity because it is carnal; but it is not even the supreme form of carnal human love, because it excludes the very mark and pledge of its perfection, the final joy it gives, the *extremum solatium*. We must not allow ourselves to be seduced by the facility of a deceptive exterior parallelism. The mystic and the courtly poet, although both renounce, the one all and the other certain of the joys of the body the better to assure the spiritual purity of their love, move none the less in opposite directions; for the mystic, putting the problem of love between his spirit and the Spirit, can resolve it integrally while sacrificing nothing of the exigencies of love: he aspires therefore to the delights of the divine union, and there it is that love finds its purity. The courtly poet, putting the problem of love between two beings of flesh and blood, can conceive of purity only in the exclusion of all real union between these beings; so that the purity of courtly love keeps the lovers apart, while that of mystical love unites them.

It is therefore altogether chimerical to seek out an influence of mystical on courtly love, beyond a few verbal borrowings. Of all that which defines the one nothing passed into the definition of the other because no passage from the one to the other was possible at all. Analogies of expression that some may be pleased to produce must therefore always be read transparently over the underlying opposition. When that is done we rapidly become sceptical about the alleged connections that certain historians believe themselves to have discovered.

They are prepared to go a long way, however, in the affirmation of their thesis. "The thing that sustains and carries forward this lyricism is not to be found in any particularities of thought or even in the current conceptions of the age, but in a rooted disposition towards a certain mystical mode of feeling."[250] This *Grundbestimmung mystischer Gefühlsart* is very evident in Dante, but although his poetry is allied with that of the Troubadours the situation in his case is altogether different. To say it of him would be true and not very useful, but when it is said of the courtly poets we may seek in vain in such a case for some acceptable sense of the word "mystical". It would seem, to judge from M. Wechssler's commentary on it in this place, that we are here concerned with what he calls an element common to all mystical experience, whether poetic or religious; but if the poetic experience is not mystical its aesthetic element is not more so. To say that "every mysticism may be an aesthetic act as well as a religious one" is to prove nothing at all, since we have just seen that pure love of the courtly type has nothing mystical about it; its aesthetic element is not a religious aesthetic element, and neither is it therefore a mystical aesthetic element in the Cistercian sense of the word mystical.

Who can number the confusions into which the history of the question has been plunged by the neglect of these fundamental distinctions? "The Church was always unanimous in systematic condemnation of all *amor carnalis.*"[261] Never did St. Bernard condemn it, for carnal love may be blessed and hallowed by the Church; it is too often forgotten that marriage is a sacrament, and the very text of Hugh of Saint-Victor appealed to in this connection ought to make it clear what he has in mind, since it condemns carnal desire: "*supra modum vel contra rationem effervens.*" It is a long way from that to a systematic condemnation of all carnal love. It is the theorist of courtly love, not the theologian, who condemns it. To add therefore: "Thus no doubt is possible on this, that the love of the singer of woman falls under the heading of *fornicatio*", is to go a great deal further than need be. Courtly love might be and often was a fornication, but it was never so of necessity, and was not always so in fact. Say what you will of it, a love-song, even a human love-song, is not necessarily a *peccatum criminale,* nor was it so even in the Middle Ages; it all depends on the love it sings or sang, and we may very well ask whether the much despised *amor mixtus* of André-le-Chapelain was not in reality more sane and inoffensive in this respect than his *amor purus.* If the fact of singing of carnal love sufficed to exclude the Troubadours from mysticism it did not on that account suffice to make rebels of them. That, however, is what is alleged in the end, and it is hardly surprising.

If it be admitted that courtly love drew inspiration from mystical love, then, since the two loves are of contrary tendency, it must necessarily be concluded that the first drew inspiration from the second only to withstand it the better. Are we then to believe with M. Wechssler that the Troubadours wanted to effect a "*Umwertung der Werte*", to announce a new conception of the world in open opposition to that of the Church?[252] That is a dramatization of the facts for which there is no justification at all. The love they sang is often culpable in the eyes of the Church; nor was there any need to wait for the appearance of the Troubadours to discover it, for confessors had been busy for centuries in giving absolution in such matters. In default of nature, Ovid would have been there to remind men of its basest forms. The *popular* French poetry, which antedates that of the Troubadours, did not, moreover, omit to mention carnal love and to sing of it after its own fashion.[253] If we allow ourselves to be carried away by simplifications of this sort we arrive at last at one of these schematic pictures of history in which the Middle Ages are now made out to be a period of pure asceticism and now, as in this case, the witness of this revolt of the flesh against the spirit which already prepares and heralds the Renaissance. "In place of asceticism the joy of life now became not merely the right but the principal duty of cultivated men and women."[254] But the real spectacle offered us by the twelfth century is one of a magnificent vitality, human and mystical at once; the Troubadour poetry sounded no knell for an expiring asceticism, for the asceticism of St. Bernard appeared in the world at the same moment: if there was a "Renaissance of the twelfth century" here is the place to remember that "St. Bernard and his mule" were just as much a part of it as the Troubadours. Courtly love presents itself in no wise as a utilization of mysticism, nor as a reaction directed against asceticism in the name of human love. Standing apart from both it much rather expresses the effort of a society, polished and refined by centuries of Christianity, to elaborate a code of human love which should be neither mystical nor even specifically Christian, but more refined than the broad licence of Ovid, and one in which sentiment should take precedence of sensuality. There, it would seem, lies its true historical significance. Sensuality in the service of sentiment, sometimes the most exquisite sentiment as in Jaufré Rudel, or even in the service of reason as in Chrétien de Troyes[255]—this in itself was something worth discovering; and if we attributed nothing more to the Troubadours and Trouvères we should not seem to despise them.

Courtly love therefore is to be taken neither as a revolt against an asceticism which was in course of development at the same time, nor yet as an attempt to imitate it. To speak of "courtly asceticism",[256] as if this phrase had any meaning at all, is to fall into this second mistake. Every text cited in its support shows that the amorists of the Middle Ages knew how to wait when circumstances compelled them to do so, to be content with what was accorded them, and to introduce a certain decent moderation into their desires; but asceticism is something more than a healthy management of carnal love, it is an inexpiable warfare against concupiscence in all its forms; in the way of renunciation of the flesh it would not be content with this "*verecundum amantis nudae contactum*" celebrated by André-le-Chapelain. "*Höfliche Askese*" is a phrase that it would be preferable to drop. "Courtly chastity" is very little better if this chastity amounts to the very simple idea that a true love is hardly compatible with a multiplicity of other loves all going on at the same time. A limited chastity, as we may perceive, and of which André-le-Chapelain says, and very justly this time, that love "reddit hominem castitatis *quasi* virtute decoratum". This *quasi* is good theology;[257] it would be prudent to attach it to every one of these expressions.

In what floods of erudition are we overwhelmed which a little reflection might have avoided! Why compare the courtly poet's "eye of the heart" with that of the mystics? The first is merely the eye of imagination, often of the most sensual kind, while the latter is defined by the exclusion of every sensible image, of those which it is precisely the function of the first to supply in the absence of the objects. What relation is there between the mystical eye which opens only when all images are extinct, and the eye of the heart which retains these images in presence for the nourishment of carnal love?[258] The poets declare that they *believe* in their lady, or *hope* in her, but there is no more sign of Faith or Hope in that than there was of Charity in the previous case. They fear; but we have already noted that Christian love precisely drives out all fear; and as for comparing the Troubadour who asks his lady for *favours* to the Christian who asks his God for *grace*, that is an equivocation hardly less grave than that which consists in comparing the Christian virtue of patience with this other patience with which the Troubadours are obliged to arm themselves.[259] To revert to a classical comparison, there is no more connection between these notions than there is between the Sign of the Dog in the heavens and a dog that barks in the night.

Courtly love, and the Cistercian conception of mystical love, are therefore two independent products of the civilization of the twelfth century. They express the different surroundings in which they were respectively born; the one codifying life as led in a princely court, and the other expressing what men make of it in a Cistercian monastery. Undoubtedly the vocabulary of the one might be helped out with terms borrowed from the other, but since it is necessary to renounce the one of these loves before embracing the other it is not to be wondered at that no definite concept exists that is common to both. When Cistercian love would enter into profane literature it could do so only by driving out courtly love and taking its place. The *Quête du saint Graal*, the cry of a heavenly chivalry, does not merely ask of the earthly chivalry that it should moderate and refine its desires but that it should renounce them. St. Bernard may have largely contributed to the decadence of the courtly ideal, but never in him could it have found its inspiration.

APPENDIX V

WILLIAM OF SAINT-THIERRY deserves a doctrinal study no less elaborate than those which have been bestowed on the works of St. Bernard. He is a very great theologian, in whom firmness of thought goes hand in hand with a remarkable power of just expression. Intimately connected with St. Bernard, in full accord with him on the principles of the mystical life and the solution of its problems, he knew how, in the midst of his unreserved admiration for the Abbot of Clairvaux, to preserve an absolute independence of thought. The following notes are not intended as any equivalent for the work which we should like to see undertaken, but for an invitation to undertake it. They merely indicate the ruling ideas and sketch out, so to speak, the plan of the doctrine. Anyone who will try to set it out for us in all its life and beauty will be surprised at the wealth of material at his disposal and the embarrassment that awaits him when he finds himself forced to choose. For William of Saint-Thierry has everything: power of thought, the orator's eloquence, the poet's lyricism, and all the attractiveness of the most ardent and tender piety.

To find our way through the questions surrounding his writings we shall find a sure guide in Dom A. WILMART, *La série et la date des ouvrages de Guillaume de Saint-Thierry*, in *Revue Mabillon*, t. XIV (1925), pp. 157–167.

—— On his life: A. ADAM, *Guillaume de Saint-Thierry, sa vie et ses œuvres*, Bourg-en-Bresse, 1923. A useful work, unfortunately not to be found on sale, but the *Bibliothèque Nationale* has a copy.

—— On his doctrine, besides H. KUTTER, *Wilhelm von St. Thierry, ein Repräsentant der mittelalterlichen Frömmigkeit*, Giessen, 1898 (which is useless), consult:

L. MALEVEZ, *La doctrine de l'image et de la connaissance mystique chez Guillaume de Saint-Thierry*, in *Recherches de science religieuse*, t. XXII (1923), pp. 178-205, and pp. 257-279. Solid articles, very thorough and penetrating.

M.-M DAVY, *Les trois étapes de la vie spirituelle, d'après Guillaume de Saint-Thierry*, in *Recherches de science religieuse*, t. XXIII (1933), pp. 569-588. Analysis of the *Epistola aurea*.

Writings of William of Saint-Thierry

1. *Epistola ad Fratres de Monte Dei* (called *Epistola aurea*), P.L., CLXXXIV, 307-354 (excluding Book III).

2. *Meditativae orationes*, CLXXX, 205-248. New edition, with French translation by M.-M DAVY, Paris, J. Vrin, 1934.

3. *De contemplando Deo*, CLXXXIV, 365-380.

4. *De natura et dignitate amoris*, CLXXXIV, 379-407.

5. *Disputatio adversus Abaelardum*, CLXXX, 249-282.

6. *Disputatio catholicorum patrum adversus dogmata Petri Abaelardi*, CLXXX, 283-340 (not his, but "cujusdam abbatis nigrorum monachorum": Geoffroy d'Auxerre, P.L., CLXXXV, 596).

7. *De sacramento altaris*, CLXXX, 341-366.

8. *Speculum fidei*, CLXXX, 365-398.

9. *Aenigma fidei*, CLXXX, 397-440.

10. *Brevis commentatio in priora duo capita Cantici Canticorum*. P.L., CLXXXIV, 407 (apocryphal).

11. *Commentarius in Cantica Canticorum e scriptis S. Ambrosii collectus*, P.L., XV, 1947-2060.

12. *Excerpta ex libris S. Gregorii Papae super Cantica Canticorum*, P.L., CLXXX, 441-474.

13. *Expositio altera super Cantica Canticorum*, P.L., CLXXX, 473-546 (interrupted, by the polemic against Abelard and the Life of St. Bernard, at III, 3).

14. *Expositio in Epistolam ad Romanos*, CLXXX, 547-694, (a compilation the sources of which it would be important to discover).

15. *De natura corporis et animae libri duo*, P.L., CLXXX, 695-726.

SKETCH OF HIS MYSTICAL THEOLOGY

William constructed a very carefully adjusted mystical theology, and it is necessary to understand its structure if we are to grasp the exact meaning of any one of its parts. Because some amongst these have been isolated from the whole to which they belong they have been given a meaning that is alien to his thought, and even deformed in a manner apt to make them extremely dangerous. We are not here concerned with making any kind of *pia interpretatio* of his doctrine but simply with setting it out as it really is; and that, we think, will show it at the same time to be beyond reach of attack.

I. THE SCHOOLS OF CHARITY

William's mystical doctrine comes to birth and lives entirely within the framework of the cenobitic life, whether it be that of a Benedictine monastery, or a Cistercian, or Carthusian. The Cloister is considered as a school,[260] in opposition to those other schools, already so numerous in the twelfth century, in which profane letters were taught along with the various disciplines of the *Trivium* and the *Quadrivium*. The profane schools taught a doctrine of profane love, with Ovid for chief master and his *De arte amatoria* as the classic book. The monasteries were equally schools of love but schools that would teach charity. The whole position was long ago summed up in a perfect formula: William of Saint-Thierry would write an *Anti-Naso*.[261] What then will this teaching be?

The art of loving is the art of arts, but Ovid is not the man to teach it, but rather nature, and God the Author of nature. For love was infused into the soul by its Creator, but its natural nobility has been corrupted by guilty affections so that now, to-day, it has to be taught.[262] These points must always be borne in mind if we would maintain the doctrine of William on its true basis. Let us consider them in turn.

1. Love, in us, is an innate natural affection. Created by God, it ought still to-day to be what it was at the moment

of creation. If this were the case it would not now need to be taught; if our nature remained as God created it we should merely have to consult it in order to know what and how we ought to love. To learn from nature would be, in effect, to learn from God the Author of nature. In right, therefore, love should not need to be taught.

2. That this is no longer the case is due to a deviation our affections have undergone. As St. Augustine teaches, every natural being is drawn by its *"pondus"* towards its proper place.[263] Thus it is with the soul of man, but with this difference, that being free it was able to deviate from its path. That is what happened as a consequence of original sin. Since then it tends always to its natural place, which is beatitude, its natural *"pondus"* draws it on irresistibly; but it has missed the way and is unable to find it again unless it be re-taught. That is why every man is henceforth in need of another man to instruct him on what he can no longer read in his own nature: what beatitude is, where it is, and how it is to be attained.[264]

3. What then will be the function of this human master? Not to teach love as if it did not already exist in the heart of man, but to rectify it. The professor of love must proceed to a re-education of love. He teaches therefore how love may be purified, how made to grow, how consolidated.[265] His function is confined to that, nor should he aspire to any other; all that he can do is to teach souls how to yield themselves to charity.

4. These professors are the Novice Master, the Prior and the Abbot; the school is the monastery; there one learns otherwise than by verbal arguments and answers, for the doctrine to be taught is a life, and disputes are concluded by acts. A monastery where such teaching is given, and where it is received in this spirit, is the only genuine school of philosophy there is. Not souls alone, but even bodies, reflect the charity with which all its members are animated, so that the monastic community becomes a social life, as like as is possible on earth to that of the blessed in heaven.[266]

What has to be underlined more heavily than all the rest in this doctrine, is the special sense of the word *naturalis*. Perhaps its nearest English equivalent would be the word *normal*. A thing is natural, in William's eyes, not as being non-supernatural, but as being what it ought to be because it was thus that God willed it. Doubtless this terminology lends itself to confusion, because the natural thus conceived must be distinguished into the natural properly so-called and the supernatural, that is to say into what belongs to pure nature and what belongs to grace. Like St. Augustine, William is quite ready to make this distinction, but for the most part he moves on another plane. The distinction between pure nature and grace, however well founded, however indispensable in itself, is too abstract, too theoretical, to retain his attention. He is chiefly interested in the moral and religious problem raised by the present state of man. Now this state is no longer what it should be since it is no longer the state in which God created the nature, and hence it is no longer a natural state. Thus, given what God wished to do and did in creating man, the loss of the supernatural gifts that man received from his Creator leaves him in a state which is not his natural state; if nature is to be restored it must regain these supernatural gifts, for they are a part of it. That is why William sees no difficulty in writing that charity is the visual organ, the natural faculty of seeing, the *natural* light of the soul, created in it by the Author of nature.[267] It is therefore also always in this sense that we should understand these formulas, which otherwise might very well lead us astray about his true thought: *amor ergo, ut dictum est, ab auctore naturae, naturaliter est animae inditus.*[268]

Suppose therefore the novice entered into one of these schools of charity, what method should he follow to put himself in the way to receive from God the lost charity?

II. NOSCE TEIPSUM

The first precept of the method is: Know thyself! William of Saint-Thierry, like St. Bernard, strongly insisted on this primary necessity. Both, in this respect, were inspired by St. Ambrose and St. Gregory the Great; but the fact is especially certain in William's case, for he has taken care to collect in the two commentaries on the Canticle of Canticles which he extracted, the one from Ambrose and the other from Gregory, their chief declarations touching the necessity for self-knowledge.[269] Compared with the *bloc* formed by these texts the passing allusions of St. Augustine to the *Nosce teipsum* have but little weight. We may therefore take it for certain that on this point his inspiration came from Ambrose and Gregory.

Following the example of these two masters William at once interprets the precept to know ourselves as an injunction to man to recognize that he is made to the image of God. But here their influence is in a manner supplemented by that of St. Augustine. For St. Bernard, the man who seeks to know himself recognizes simultaneously both his misery and his greatness; his misery, inasmuch as of himself he is nothing; his greatness, inasmuch as he is made to the image of God in respect of his freedom. William of Saint-Thierry is here distinguishable from St. Bernard by the greater fidelity with which he follows St. Augustine. For the soul, to know itself is to know its greatness, which is to have been made to the image of God; but this image, for him, resides chiefly *in mente*, in the mind. [270] Therefore the soul will know itself as a divine image by exploring the content of the mind, and by that very fact will also know the God whose image it is.

In what does this image consist? Still following St. Augustine, William finds it in a sort of created trinity recalling in structure the creative Trinity. Fundamentally the likeness of man to God is found in the bosom of the mind, in reason, but reason itself plays this part only inasmuch as it is linked up with the memory understood in the Augustinian sense, that is to say with the memory of God.[271] In creating man God breathed into him a breath of life: *spiraculum vitae*. The word *spiraculum* suggests the "spiritual" nature of this breathing; spiritual, therefore also intellectual. The word *vitae* on the other hand indicates that this breath was at the same time an animating power. It may be said then that God created man as a living and animated being endowed with an intellectual faculty of knowing. Now at the summit, so to speak, of this being, God placed the memory,

H

that is to say, according to St. Augustine's sense of the term, the faculty of recognizing in itself at every moment the latent presence of God, particularly His power and goodness. This memory is not to be confused with any actual recollection of God which might be supposed alone to enable us to know Him; it simply expresses the fact, to speak once more in Augustine's terms, that God is always with us even if we are not always with Him. At the summit of the mind therefore there is a secret point where resides the latent remembrance of His goodness and His power; and there also lies the most deeply graven trait of His image, that which evokes all the others and enables us to make ourselves like Him. In God, the Father generates the Son, and from the Father and the Son proceeds the Holy Spirit. In us in the same way, immediately and without any interval of time, memory generates reason and from memory and reason proceeds the will. The memory possesses and contains in itself the term to which man should tend; reason at once knows that we ought so to tend; the will tends; and these three faculties make up a kind of unity but three efficacies, just as in the Divine Trinity there is only one substance but three Persons.[272]

It is hardly necessary to insist on the importance of this genesis of the faculties of the soul. It determines once and for all the conditions of their legitimate exercise. A reason that is no more than an offshoot of a memory of the goodness of God can have no other object but God. Born of that which contains the *quo tendendum*, it has no other *raison d'être* than to testify to the *quod tendendum*; its function is written in its essence: it is an apprehension of the fact that we must tend to God, and that all the rest is vain curiosity. Similarly for the will. As the issue of memory and reason it can be nothing other than a *tendit*, that is to say the tendency towards the term which the memory contains, and to which reason knows that we must tend. Here then we have the thing that God created; here also therefore we see what is man's "natural" state: that of a reason that knows naught but God, of a will that tends to naught but God, because the memory whence they proceed is filled with nothing but the remembrance of God. Such also was the divine image in man when it shone out in all its splendour, before it had been tarnished by sin; this is the likeness we have lost and which the apprentice-ship of divine love should put us on the way to recover. To know oneself is to know oneself for a tarnished image of God, in which the soul, shorn of its first glory, no longer recognizes its Creator.

III. THE REDEMPTION

The restoration of the effaced likeness is not to be effected without man's own effort, but would have been impossible without the Redemption. Seeing that man had lost his likeness, and could not recover it by his own powers alone, the Divine Trinity took counsel how this disorder might be remedied. Man, by his own fault, had strayed away into the Land of Unlikeness ("*abisse in regionem dissimilitudinis*"). The fallen Angel had wished to be like God; fallen man allowed himself to be persuaded by the tempter that it was open to him to become "*sicut dii*". God could by no means admit that His Son, the splendour of His glory, should have so many equals— and such equals. Angel and man were therefore hurried to ruin. That was but just; but God's work was none the less thereby destroyed. Since justice had nothing to say against it, why not restore the work by mercy?

That is what God determined to do. The Son of God there-fore made Himself the Mediator between His Father and ourselves. That there should be mediation required that man should do something on his side, wherefore God demanded of him faith and hope and fear. As to the Son of God Himself, He, being innocent, decided to die to save the guilty, and by the chastisement of His innocence to buy off that of human disobedience. To be put to death He must needs evade the vigilance of the Devil, and this the Son of God did by hiding His glory under the appearance of human weakness. By means of His humanity He concealed from the devil His divinity; by His miracles He excited his envy, but at the same time conciliated the faith of man whom He would save. The Son of God was therefore put to death. By this unjust death He purchased a new justice based on His sacrifice, and guilty man was absolved. If God henceforth would chastise the sin of man, man can offer Him in expiation the blood of His own Son, spilt by love to save him.

This sacrifice, moreover, is not yet at an end. By means of the institution of the Eucharist it is perpetuated among us. Man can eat the body of Christ, that is to say become the Body of Christ, and, in consequence, the temple of the Holy Spirit. This temple, if adorned with the prescribed virtues, is consecrated to God, and God alone dwells in it. Man, thus transformed by his union with God in the Eucharist, rejoices only in God, and merely makes use of all the rest; he has therefore attained to wisdom, which is nothing other than the love of God in charity. In the face of that wisdom the false wisdom of this world and its philosophers appears only as malice or folly; to the knowledge that puffs up it opposes itself as the charity that edifies. The whole life of the novice, all his effort, will then consist in availing himself of the sacrifice of Christ and the grace of the Eucharist, so to build up again his perverse love into charity.[273]

IV. THE APPRENTICESHIP OF CHARITY

The ruin is consummated, but we must not despair; it would be an insult to the work of God to believe that those who corrupt it must always prevail against the efforts of those who, with the aid of grace, set themselves to restore it. That is why, calling on God from the depth of the abyss into which he is plunged,[274] man should fearlessly propose to himself the highest end conceivable here below: a love of God so ardent that it amounts to a kind of sacred folly. The life of the Benedictine novice is the apprenticeship to this love. Hard on himself, he surrenders himself wholly into the hands of his superiors, and altogether renounces himself so to make free room for the coming of divine love.

The very possibility of this apprenticeship would be incomprehensible if the image of God, indestructible in man, did not always subsist in this memory forgetful of itself, but able still to return to itself with God's help. Human love has become blind, but even a blind man can still use his hands. Thus we have to begin by groping, so to speak, and bending heart and body to think and act as if we really loved God. Thus gradually we gain a "custom" of good will. The service of God which the novice at first takes up as a painful task, becomes little by little more easy. The soul passes to the state of voluntary service and the body spontaneously yields to the discipline which the soul exacts of it. The face of the interior man renews itself from day to day; the soul begins to be rewarded by frequent and unexpected "theophanies";[275] the splendours in which the blessed rejoice in heaven begin to enkindle and light it up. Then begins the life of union with God, with its alternations of joys and desolations, of forlorn awaitings at times indeed fulfilled, which is the very life of charity itself.[276]

That love may allow of these divine revelations, what ought it to be? A love precisely such as that which God created in us, and recreates in us by grace. God is love's birthplace, in Him it was born, in Him it was nurtured and grew. "There it is a citizen; no stranger, but native. For by God alone is love given, and in Him also it comes to rest, for we owe it to none but Him and for Himself."[277] If it be so, to say that God created love in us is to say that He breathes into us the desire to love Him as He loves Himself. In loving us God does not feel an affection that tends towards us; nor does He gain anything from our affection; for in truth God loves us only for Himself, and since our love is but that which He creates in us, this too should be a love by which we love ourselves as He loves us, that is simply for Himself. This perfect union of wills between man and God is possible only by a great grace, but possible it is, and when it is effected then also is effected the restoration of the divine likeness in which man was originally created. He no longer loves God for his own sake, nor himself for his own sake, but loves both God and himself only for God.[278] Let us rather say, since then our love for God is that by which He loves Himself, that it is He who loves Himself in us: *sic nos efficiens tui amatores, imo sic te ipsum in nobis amans.*[279] Christ's prayer in St. John is henceforth granted: "Volo ut sicut ego et tu unum sumus, ita et in nobis ipsi unum sint" (*John*, XVII, 21); the goal of love is then attained: peace, joy in the Holy Spirit, the *silentium in coelo*,[280] that is to say in the soul of the righteous; yet is that but for too short a time—*sed hora est dimidia vel quasi dimidia*—joy in this life is but a fledgling, it will receive its full perfection in beatitude.

The nature of these spiritual consolations is very difficult to define in William's doctrine. As far as can be judged, this union of will with God which crowns the apprenticeship of charity is accompanied by a sensible emotion as sign. William often suggests that he *felt* grace, and the interior consolation thence received is for him the surest index that the goal of effort has been attained.[281] He would seem to regard this tranquil joy as no more than the effect and mark of the transformation of the soul by grace and the restoration of the divine image. It is true, if we follow the letter of the texts, that the joy would be accompanied also by knowledge; it would not be simply a union of wills with the joy that it brings with it, but a contemplation, a sight of God. What are we to think of these expressions?

V. CHARITY AS KNOWLEDGE

Man is now reformed to the image of his Creator; how can we say that by that very fact he knows God? Consider first in what a cognitive process consists, and take for example the case of sensitive knowledge. That there may be perception of a sensible object, there must be a certain image of this object in the mind. Of this object the mind then forms to itself as it were a copy, conformable at once to the nature of the perceiving sense and to that of the thing perceived; and then it is said to know it. The essential condition of knowing is therefore this "similitudo", this phantasm, the presence of which in the mind, enabling it to transform itself to the likeness of the object, enables it by that very fact to know it.

To this cognitive processus there is added always an affective one completing it. As St. Augustine had already explained in the *De Trinitate*, there is neither sensation nor knowledge without a movement of love applying the sense and the mind to their object. Without this desire to perceive and to know that animates us, the object may lie before us but would always elude our grasp, nor should we even see it.

In the case of the love of God attaining its perfection in us, what then takes place? Here, evidently, neither images nor phantasms can play any part; but love replaces them. Since it transforms the soul to the image of God, it effects in it, in a manner incomparably more complex and more profound than can any sensible image, the assimilation of the mind to the object which is the first condition of all knowledge. On the other hand, since it is love alone which here effects this transformation, it is obvious that the affective element required for knowledge will not be lacking; it is not confined to accompanying and facilitating the assimilation of mind to object, as happens in the case of sensible knowledge, but it produces it. It is not surprising then that the soul *feels* God, when it loves God; it feels Him by that very love it has for Him, and by the joy it finds in it; therefore it knows God.[282]

To this, it would seem, is to be reduced the famous doctrine of charity as vision of God which has so excited the curiosity of certain commentators. It means therefore in the first place that in this life no sight of God is accessible to man, not even in ecstasy. The soul seizes God, but: *amatum plus quam cogitatum, gustatum, quam intellectum.*[283] In other words, if love makes us to know God inasmuch as it makes us like to God, the knowledge of God that it brings amounts to the divine likeness it confers and to the joy we feel in it. To be like God is to see Him? No doubt, but to see Him is to be like Him,[284] and to experience the joy of the likeness at last recovered. That is no small thing, but it is that and no more.

Useless therefore to scan William's metaphorical expressions for a mysterious meaning they do not possess.[285] No matter what image he uses, never does he mean to say that charity gives us that knowledge, sight, or vision of God which here below is refused to every intelligence. What intelligence does not know charity knows much less—in any intellectual sense of the term "knows". All that William would say is that in default of a knowledge which is and remains impossible, love, in us, replaces it; which is not to say that they are one. There exist neither species nor phantasms which, transforming the mind to the likeness of God, would enable us in this life to know Him; charity has power neither to create nor to supply for them. But charity produces, by love, in the will, this assimilation of the soul to God which remains in this life impossible for the reason. This union of wills is therefore, in the order of love, the equivalent of the union of mind and object in the similitude of the phantasm. And just as knowledge results from a similitude of the mind to its object, so joy results from the conformity of the will to the will of its object. In us therefore this joy is a certain way of *feeling* God, an affective perception of His presence. Charity then does not know God by any sight properly so-called, but it feels Him, through the joy in Him that it gives, and since this is the sole contact with God that is possible to man in this life, it is not wholly improper to say that our only way of knowing Him is to feel Him.

VI. UNION WITH GOD BY THE HOLY SPIRIT

We have said and repeated, as if the thing were obvious, that union of will with God, realized by charity, is accompanied with joy, and that this joy is even the sign of the union. Why is this necessarily so? Because union with God is effected by the Holy Spirit Who is Himself the internal bond of the Divine Trinity, Its love, Its beatitude.

William's position on this point is characterized by his insistent emphasis on the identity of the Holy Spirit, the Giver of the unifying grace, and the grace, which is the gift of the Holy Spirit. The distinction between the Giver and the gift is implied in each of his texts: it is implied in the very antithesis of *donans* and *donum*, two terms there constantly opposed. However, the distinction is not the thing that interests him, but, on the contrary, the root identity between the Giver and the gift, which persists in the very bosom of their distinction. It is to be regretted that William wrote no theological treatise dealing with this matter, and did not define *ex professo* the created grace, the increated grace, their differences and their relations; but that was not his object. Like a true mystic he fixes, in grace, on that which unites rather than on that which divides, and that is why, even while distinguishing the *donans* from the *donum*, he constantly puts the accent on the fact that they are *idem*.

For it is this basic identity of charity, the gift of God, and the Holy Spirit its Giver, which makes possible the mystical marriage. The Holy Spirit is the love common to the Father and the Son, their Kiss, their Embrace. If then He be present in the soul under the form of Gift, He unites it to God by the same kiss, by the same embrace, and this constitutes the mystical marriage itself; but it does so only because He is *idem donans*, *idem donum*.[286] But a human love thus transfigured by the gift of the Holy Spirit is no longer simply human; it is the Divine love that henceforth breathes in it, and therefore, in a way, it is divinized.[287] This transforming union respects the inevitable distance separating man from God, since being brought about in man, it remains the work of God. That which in God is a con-substantial unity of nature, in man is but the gift of a grace; in God it is a prerogative, in man the Divine condescension. However, it is the same, absolutely the same Spirit.[288]

By this then is effected in the soul of man a profound renovation, restoring it to the divine likeness. Then reigns a true unity between creature and Creator, but a unity of likeness: *unitas similitudinis*, which can never in any event become a unity of nature. It suffices, nevertheless, to carry with it this other unity of likeness which is that of beatitude.[289] For God finds His beatitude in the love of His own perfection; to be united to Him by the gift He makes us of His own love for Himself is therefore to be united to Him by the gift of His own beatitude: *Quid autem est absurdius uniri Deo amore, et non beatitudine?*[290] That is why the restoration of the divine likeness is accompanied even in this life with the joys of the spiritual marriage, while awaiting that perfect beatitude which will go along with perfect likeness hereafter.

H*

VII. THE TRIPLE LIKENESS

Thus the whole of William's doctrine is the story of the divine likeness, given by God, defaced by sin, restored by grace. For in his likeness to God consists man's perfection: *et haec hominis est perfectio, similitudo Dei*. Created to the image of God, to be like God is therefore also our unique end: *propter hoc enim solum creati sumus et vivimus, ut Deo similes simus, cum ad Dei imaginem creati sumus.*[291] This is our perfection, and to this it is our duty to tend, for it is a fault not to wish to be perfect. Every man then is to attain successively to all the degrees of divine likeness, even the highest, and the programme is but one and the same with the one we have already outlined: to attain to all the degrees of love, even the highest. For God is charity, and therefore we shall be like Him only in loving.

The restoration of the divine likeness would be impossible if original sin had totally destroyed it. But that did not happen. For there is a primary likeness to God that no man can lose as long as he lives, remaining in him as testimony to the higher likeness he has lost. It consists in this, that the soul is everywhere and at one and the same time present in its body, even as God, whole and entire, is everywhere and at once present in all His creation. And just as God, without ceasing to be simple, works different effects in nature, so also the soul, without ceasing to be simple, produces the movement and life of the body, its sensations, and its knowledge. A likeness indestructible because written in the nature of man, but one which presupposes no effort on our part and obtains therefore no merit.

Higher than this first likeness is a second, nearer to God because it depends on our will. It consists in virtue. The acquisition of virtue makes us resemble the perfection of God; perseverance in virtue makes us resemble His eternity.

Above this second is a third, by far the highest: "in tantum proprie propria, ut non jam similitudo, sed unitas spiritus nominetur." Of this William says that it makes a man one with God: "cum fit homo unum cum Deo"—to the very great scandal of certain theologians, but we know that here we have to do with a *unitas similitudinis*. It sets up, he adds, a "unitas spiritus"; for the *idem spiritus*, Who is *donans* and *donum*, is at once both God's own love for Himself and our love for Him. Let us go further, to the even greater scandal of these same theologians: not only does it make us will what God wills, but it makes it impossible for us to will anything else. And indeed, *in the measure in which this likeness reigns in us*, how could we possibly will evil, since charity, by which we will, is in us as the gift of the love by which Goodness loves Itself? The Holy Spirit does not here affect our will merely from without; by grace it is indeed Charity itself, that is the Holy Spirit Himself, Who is in us under the form of gift; and He therefore indeed it is Who *is* in us this *unitas spiritus*, and is unity between us and God as He is unity between the Father and the Son. In virtue of this gift, in short, the man who has become a man of God, does not merit to become God, but, in a manner which we can neither conceive nor express, what God is by nature that he becomes by grace: *quod Deus est ex natura, homo ex gratia.*[292]

These texts must be interpreted in the light of the fundamental distinction between Charity uncreated and the gift of charity. Even had William never set out the distinction in express terms, he could be credited with it without fear of mistake. A theologian of his calibre does not write for children in the catechism class, nor does he feel obliged to be constantly recalling the most elementary principles of the Christian faith. But it happens, to be precise, that he makes the distinction repeatedly: it is indeed the *idem spiritus* Who is God and Who is in man, but in God He is the Giver, in man He is but gift.

We should remember furthermore in criticizing these texts, that the third divine likeness corresponds to an ecstatic state. It is disturbing, perhaps, to hear William saying that such a likeness makes a man incapable of sin.[293] It would be very much more strange to say that in the mystical union man could will anything but God. That, however, is what we should have to venture to say in order to contradict William on the point. For the supreme likeness of man to God is effected only when the beatified consciousness is, so to speak, caught up into that kiss, that close embrace, of the Father and the Son which is the Holy Spirit: *cum in amplexu et osculo Patris et Filii, mediam quodam modo se invenit beata conscientia*.[294] William's critics, therefore, have here taken fright at their own hesitations. Having failed to understand that the perfect likeness he describes is the very likeness of the beatific vision, or of the brief ecstasy which carries the human soul above its simply human condition, they do not see that what they take for pantheism is nothing but a description of a mystical and beatifying union of the soul with God.

While awaiting the day of full divine vision the more the soul tries to discover what God is the better she sees what she lacks, and the more also she strives to approach, by way of likeness, to Him from Whom she had withdrawn by unlikeness. Sight of God and likeness to God go hand in hand, because the sight of God is this very likeness, in charity: *et sic expressiorem visionem expressior semper similitudo comitatur*.[295] And the divine likeness goes hand in hand with beatitude, since at the summit of its perfection it makes us to be, not God, but what God is; and He is our beatitude: *Quibus enim potestas datur est filios Dei fieri, data est potestas, non quidem ut sint Deus, sed sint tamen quod Deus est; sint sancti, futuri plane beati, quod Deus est, nec aliunde hic sancti, nec ibi futuri beati, quam ex Deo, qui eorum et sanctitas et beatitudo est*.[296]

NOTES

[1] On the life of St. Bernard, consult among many others, the classical work of d'E. VACANDARD, *Vie de saint Bernard, abbé de Clairvaux*, 2 vol., Paris, Gabalda, 1927 (8th thousand)—or the shorter work of G. GOYAU, *Saint Bernard*, Paris, Flammarion, 1907.

[2] C. H. HASKINS, *The Renaissance of the Twelfth Century*, Cambridge, Harvard University Press, 1927, pp. VIII–IX.—see also G. PARÉ, A. BRUNET, P. TREMBLAY, *La Renaissance du XIIᵉ siècle. Les écoles et l'enseignment*, Paris, J. Vrin, 1933.—M. BLOCH, *Les caractères originaux de l'histoire rurale française*, Paris, Les Belles-Lettres, 1931, p. 17.

[3] This conclusion becomes inevitable if the *De contemplando Deo* and the *De natura et dignitate amoris* are to be considered as William's first spiritual treatises and dated between 1119 and 1135. That is what is proposed by Dom A. WILMART, *La série et la date des ouvrages de Guillaume de Saint-Thierry*, Revue Mabillon, Vol. XIV (1924), pp. 157–167; see p. 166. Such study as I have been able to make of William's doctrine suggests nothing against this hypothesis, quite the contrary.—On the relations between St. Bernard and William some judicious remarks will be found in the excellent work of P. L. MALEVEZ, S.J., *La doctrine de l'image et de la connaissance mystique chez Guillaume de Saint-Thierry*, Recherches de science religieuse, t. XXII, p. 181, note 6, and in A. ADAM, *Guillaume de Saint-Thierry, sa vie et ses œuvres*, Bourg, 1923, chap. II and IX.

[4] As far as this point is concerned the influence of Cicero had never wholly ceased to be operative. We may find traces of it in various authors assiduously perused by St. Bernard, William of Saint-Thierry, and Aelred of Rievaulx. See, for example, CASSIAN, *Liber de amicitia*, P.L., XLIX, 1011–1044, but above all ST. AMBROSE, *De officiis ministrorum*, Lib. II, cap. 22; P.L., XVI, 190–194. The notes to this edition will suffice to show how far St. Ambrose was inspired by Cicero, particularly by the Cicero of the *De Officiis* and the *De Amicitia*. The theme of disinterested friendship, indicated briefly but clearly, is met with again, col. 192 C. We might bring forward other texts of the same kind, but there is nothing in them which would enable us to foresee the passionate interest in the *De Amicitia* displayed by the ascetical and mystical writers of the twelfth century.

[5] *The Holy Rule of St. Benedict*, trans. by Dom B. HAYES, p. 346. London, R. & T. Washbourne Ltd.

[6] The technical term "ecstasy" (*extasis*) would seem to have made its entrance into Christian terminology with Tertullian; he himself says that he borrowed it from the Greeks. He makes use of it in his *Adversus Marcionem*, lib. IV, c. 22. There it means that a man finds himself momentarily placed, by a divine grace, outside his own reason. "In spiritu enim homo constitutus, praesertim cum gloriam Dei conspicit, vel cum per ipsum Deus loquitur, necesse est excidat sensu, obumbratus scilicet virtute divina." (In ROUËT DE JOURNEL, *Ench. ascet.*, text 65, pp. 29–30. Migne, *Pat. Lat.*, II, 413).

In the second text Tertullian does not hesitate to return to the same idea; ecstasy is an *amentia*, a flight of the mind. He would explain, in the *De Anima*, the Christian view of dreams. Among the characteristics of dream he stresses the illusion whereby we think we see realities. How explain it? In sleep the soul is no longer able to avail itself of its corporeal members, and so makes use of its own ("et si caret opera membrorum corporalium, suis utitur", col. 725 B).—Then things which do not really happen have all the air of

215

happening: "actu enim fiunt, effectu non fiunt" (*ibid.*); in other words they are acted out without anything resulting. That is precisely ecstasy: "Hanc vim ecstasin dicimus, excessum sensus, et amentiae instar. Sic et in primordio, somnus cum ecstasi dedicatus (Gen. II): *Et misit Deus ecstasin in Adam et obdormivit.* Somnus enim corpori provenit in quietem; ecstasis animae accessit adversus quietem; et inde jam forma, somnum ecstasi miscens, et natura de forma" (*De Anima*, cap. 45; P.L., II, 726 C. Cf. in the same chapter 726 B). Here then we have a particular case of his materialist psychology; we are well below the plane of St. John and St. Paul, we are even at the opposite pole. For we know that Tertullian, having left the Church and passed over to Montanism, had written a treatise in six books *De Extasi* (P.L., II, 1131-1134). This last treatise is lost; but it seems that it set out to prove the inspiration of Montanus against the Catholics (the *psychicos*). The doctrine was substantially the same as that of the *De Anima*. The Fathers (Epiphanius, Jerome) were to make a lively protest against this assimilation of ecstasy to an *amentia*. The ecstatic, the prophet, said Jerome, "liber est visionis *intelligentis* universa quae loquitur" (P.L., II, 1194 C).

⁷ ST. BERNARD, *De diversis*, Sermo XXXIV, P.L., CLXXXIII, 630-634, commented on a homily of Origen's, *In Levit.*, X, 9. The auditorium protested: "Quidnam sibi vult insolitus iste grunnitus? Aut quis inter vos nescio quid submurmurat?" See J. RIES, *Das geistliche Leben, in seinen Entwicklungsstufen nach der Lehre des hl. Bernhard*, Freib. i. Br., Herder, 1906, p. 16. On the Hellenic elements in Christian mysticism, see R. ARNOU, *Le désir de Dieu dans la philosophie de Plotin*, Paris, Alcan, 1931, chap. VI, pp. 231-282.—On Philo the Jew and his mysticism, see J. MARTIN, *Philon*, Paris, Alcan, 1907, pp. 142-154; on his ecstasies, p. 151, and E. BRÉHIER, *Les idées philosophiques et religieuses de Philo d'Alexandrie*, Paris, J. Vrin, 1925, pp. 196-205.

The two texts of Origen which Bernard certainly had at his disposal are: *Origenis homiliae in Cant. Cant.*, trad. by Saint Jerome; in W. A. BAEHRENS, *Origenes Werke*, Vol. VIII, Leipzig, 1925, pp. 26-60.—*Origenis commentarium in Cant. Cant.*, translated by Rufin; *op. cit.*, pp. 61-241.—The two homilies give a simple, and in some ways popular, exposition of the meaning of this text; the commentary goes much deeper. *Sponsa* represents, in the commentary, first of all the Church, weary now of angels and prophets, and awaiting the coming of the Christ himself (*In C.C.*, I, p. 90, l. 4.); then next the soul, praying for the visitation of the illuminating Word (p. 91, l. 4-15). This visitation is symbolized by the kiss: *osculum*. The image suggests an immediate contact between the soul and the Word. This contact is the divine illumination lighting up the symbolic significance of Scripture in a perfect soul (*op. cit.*, Lib. I, Vol. VIII, pp. 91-92). The multiplicity of "*oscula*", which for St. Bernard stands for that of affective experiences, signifies in Origen that of the meanings of Scripture thus revealed. The effect of this union therefore lies in the spiritual and mystical understanding of Scripture: "spiritalis scilicet intelligentia et mystica" (*In C.C.*, Lib. I, p. 100, l. 28-29). It is given to the soul by divine love (p. 91, l. 29) and received in joy; nevertheless Origen seems to consider it as essentially cognitive (see the commentary on the *Introduxit me Rex*, *op. cit.*, pp. 108-109). Love is indispensable, but as the source of intellection (p. 220, l. 7-16; p. 223, l. 26-29; p. 233, l. 9-13); that is why the divine illumination rewards prayer (ROUËT DE JOURNEL, *Ench. ascet.*, pp. 53-54), which moreover is not to be separated from meditation of the sacred text. The mystical life is especially the life of the illuminative Holy Spirit in the soul of the theologian who seeks the truth in Scripture, with its alternations of light and obscurity corresponding to the presences or absences of the Bridegroom (*In C.C.*, Hom. I, p. 39, l. 15-23). It is the mysticism of an exegete. There is therefore a noticeable difference in spirit; but it is possible that Bernard occasionally made use of Origen while transposing him into a key of more strongly marked affectivity. Compare the last text of Origen cited: "Saepe, Deus testis est, sponsum mihi adventare conspexi. . . .", with St. Bernard's: "Fateor et mihi adventasse Verbum, in insipientia dico, et pluries . . . " (*In C.C.*, Sermo LXXIV, 5; P.L. CLXXXIII, 1141 A).

⁸ GREGORY OF NYSSA, *Comment. in Cant. Cant.*, Pat. Gr.-Lat., XLIV, 755-1120. The work is composed of fifteen Homilies. The Prologue defines the purpose of the commentary: to disengage from the text the "philosophy" concealed beneath it (756 A). Like Origen, whom he apologizes for following (763 B), he employs the allegorical method. The C.C. is a mystery; it can be unveiled only to those whose hearts are already purified (purgative way). It signifies the spiritual and immaterial union of the soul, which is the Bride, with Christ, who is the Bridegroom. This text thus clothes the soul, so to speak, with a nuptial robe, for its mystical marriage with God (*Hom.* I, 765 B); it is an epithalamium celebrating the intimate conjunction (ἀνάχρασις) of the human soul with the divine (769 D-772 A).—On the Canticle as transmitter of the divine influx, see GREGORY OF NYSSA, *op. cit.*, col. 765 BC.—According to Gregory of Nyssa the C.C. contains a philosophy, that of the Saint of Saints; it indicates the way to God (765 D) and corresponds to the perfect age of the spiritual life (768 AB). Its whole secret is summed up in a word: "Love." Love leads to the ἀνάχρασις of the soul with God, a goal to which St. Paul invites us to press on (*Ephes.*, IV, 4); that there may be but one body and one spirit (772 A and D).—It is difficult, in this life, to go very far on this path by way of knowledge since God is ineffable (*Hom.* III, 820 C-821 B); St. John says so (I, 8); St. Paul confirms it (I *Tim.*, VI, 16); and Moses had said it before them (*Exod.*, XXXIII, 20); and that is why all our knowledge of Him here below is more especially negative (*De beatitudinibus*, orat. VI; Pat. Gr.-Lat., XLIV, 1267 C); that is one of the principal ideas developed by Gregory, before Dionysius, in his *De vita Moysis*, *ibid.*, col. 328; 375 D-378 C; 386 D. But we may know Him indirectly by His likeness manifested in creatures (379 A). That is especially true of the soul. Created in the image and likeness of God (*Hom.* XV, c. 1091 *et seq.*; *De hominis opificio* and *In script. verba: Faciamus hominem* . . .), it has allowed this likeness to become effaced by sin. Man no longer sees God mirrored in himself because his heart is no longer pure; if we purify it God will reappear in it: it is therefore always possible to see God in ourselves, for if purity reigns in thee God is there also (*De beat.*, orat. VI; P.L., XLIV, 1270-1271 and 1272 C).—This knowledge remains obscure; it is therefore more important to remember that God is charity (*In C.C.*, *Hom.* IV; P.L., XLIV, 846 CD) and that St. Paul himself, although caught up into heaven, was still face to face with mystery (*op. cit.*, *Hom.* V, c. 858 D and 859 B). The C.C. shows us the way which leads nearest to Him: purification of heart, meditation on the C.C., anagogic contemplation; prayer, which unites the soul with God by illuminating it with understanding of the Prophets and the Law; by this two-fold understanding there finally enters the soul the vision of the true light, the desire to behold the sun, and this desire is finally consummated. God remains incomprehensible (*Hom.* V, 875 CD); from the starting-point of faith there are indefinite ascensions (*Hom.* V, 876 A; VIII, 944 C); however, at each degree of this illumination the soul is truly united to God, "they mutually pass within each other, God descending into the soul, and the soul ascending into God " (*Hom.* VI, 889 D). The two dominant characteristics of this experience are its sublimity and its incompletion, for there is always more there than we can grasp (*Hom.* VIII, 941 C; XI, 1000 A-1001 A). This doctrine (well summarized in *Hom.* XII, 1033 D-1037 A) assigns an important rôle to free-will in the ascetical and mystical life (*Hom.* XII, 1025 D-1028 A), and may be compared with that of Gregory of Nazianzen (cf. ROUËT DE JOURNEL, *Ench. ascet.*, text 307, pp. 175-176, and 309, pp.176-177).

On the part played by the idea of image in Gregory of Nyssa, see DIEKAMP, *Die Gotteslehre des hl. Gregor von Nyssa*, 1896, pp. 67-73; on the recognition of God in the mirror of the soul, pp. 73-90; on the mystical vision and ecstasy, pp. 90-101. H. KOCH, *Das mystische Schauen beim hl. Gregor von Nyssa* (Theol. Quartalschrift, 1898, pp. 397 *et seq.*), insists on the influence exerted by Philo on Gregory, thus also on Dionysius.

On this point all historians of Benedictine mysticism agree. D. Ursmer BERLIÈRE, *L'ascèse bénédictine*, Desclée, 1930, p. 62. D. Cuthbert BUTLER, *Benedictine Monachism*, Longmans, London, 1924, p. 78 *et seq.*; and especially the same author's *Western Mysticism. The teaching of SS. Augustine, Gregory and Bernard on Contemplation and the Contemplative Life. Neglected chapters in the history of Religion.* London, Constable, 1922. These works are of fundamental importance; they say all that is essential on the mystical elements in the doctrines of Augustine, Gregory the Great and Cassian, without which the Cistercian mysticism would never have existed.

I ought to mention, so as not to affect ignorance of its existence, the work of G. G. COULTON, *Five Centuries of Religion*, Vol. I, *St. Bernard, his Predecessors and Successors*, Cambridge University Press, 1929. To judge such a work fairly is no easy matter. Nothing could equal the wide variety of the author's documentation, save perhaps his inability to understand what he is writing about. He would react, and with good reason, against the imaginary medieval Golden Age, which never in point of fact existed. He does it with a passion which takes on all the air of scientific reasoning, but which can delude only those of his readers who have no other means of knowing the Middle Ages. It is a curious work. Its avowed object is to describe, were it only summarily, "the life and work of the myriads of nameless cloisterers who were so naturally dominant in the Middle Ages" (p. XXXVIII). That is a fine subject, poised between the *histoire scandaleuse* which Prof. Coulton has always avoided and the hagiography or apologetic he detests. A very difficult subject too, for these myriads of average monks wrote very little and have hardly any history; but he ought at least to have kept to it. What are St. Benedict and St. Bernard doing in this picture? Are *they* nameless cloisterers? But if they were to be brought forward at all, they should have been brought forward in their integrity. The trouble about studying St. Bernard in connection with a crowd of mediocrities is that the author deems it proper to devote only a single page (out of more than five hundred) to the doctrine his chief figure developed, by which he lived, and many nameless ones along with him. Will Prof. Coulton plead guilty to *ignoring essential evidence?* I doubt it; but there it is.

[10] St. BENEDICT, *Regula monasteriorum*, Prolog., ed. B. Linderbauer, p. 12. 1. 6-8.—E. C. BUTLER, *The Lausiac History of Palladius*, Cambridge, Vol. I, 1898; Vol. II, 1904.—STEPHEN GASELEE, *The psychology of the Monks of the Egyptian Desert*, in *The Philosopher*, July-Sept. 1932 (Vol. X, n. 3), pp. 73-81.—For St. Basil we may conveniently consult W. K. L. CLARKE, *The Ascetic Works of St. Basil*, S.P.C.K., 1925. Cf. D. Ursmer BERLIÈRE, *L'ascéticisme Bénédictine*, p. 63 and note 2.—Dom BESSE, *Les mystiques bénédictins*, pp. 63-64.

[11] ROUËT DE JOURNEL, *Ench. ascet.*, pp. 111-112—St. Gregory the Great described St. Benedict as an ecstatic (P.L., LXVI, 137 BC).

[12] D. Cuthbert BUTLER, *Benedictine Monachism*, Chap. V, p. 46 (London, 1924).

[13] CASSIAN, *Collat.*, XIV, 9; P.L., XLIX, 955 B. Cf. *Collat.*, I, 8; XLIX, 492 AB: "theoria", "contemplatio", "Dei solius intuitum".

[14] CASSIAN, *Collat.*, XIX, 5; P.L., XLIX, 1132 A.—Cf. Dom C. BUTLER, *Benedictine Monachism*, pp. 78-82 (London, 1924).—On Gregory the Great, *ibid.*, pp. 82-86; and also: "It should be noticed that this mysticism of SS. Gregory and Bernard is, in all its characteristic features, in full accord with that of Abbot Isaac of Scete as recorded in Cassian's ninth Conference . . ." (p. 91.)—On Gregory the Great, *op. cit.*, p. 96.

In a general way Dom. C. Butler has very well described the mysticism of St. Bernard, but I should not go so far as he does as to the purely objective, empirical and descriptive character of this doctrine (p. 90). It is not philosophical, but it is a theology, and I believe on the contrary that its speculative character is strongly marked.

[15] S. GREGORIUS MAGNUS, *Mor.*, XXII, 20, 46; P.L., LXXVI, 241 A.

[16] *Op. cit.*, XXII, 20, 50; LXXVI, 243-244.

17 "Unde necesse est ut quisquis ad contemplationis studia properat, semetipsum prius subtiliter interroget, quantum amat. Machina quippe mentis est vis amoris, quae hanc dum a mundo extrahit, in alta sustollit" (S. GREGORIUS MAGNUS, *Moral.*, VI, 37, 58; P.L., LXXV, 762-763). —Cf. *op. cit.*, VII, 15, 18; P.L., LXXV, 775.

18 *Op. cit.*, XXII, 20, 51; P.L., LXVI, 244.

19 "Nobis praesentibus spiritus transit, quando invisibilia cognoscimus, et tamen haec non solide sed raptim videmus. Neque enim in suavitate contemplationis intimae diu mens figitur, quia ad semetipsam ipsa immensitate luminis reverberata revocatur. Cumque internam dulcedinem degustat, amore aestuat, ire super semetipsam nititur, sed ad infirmitatis suae tenebras fracta relabitur; et magna virtute proficiens, videt quia videri non possit hoc quod ardenter diligit, nec tamen ardenter diligeret, nisi aliquatenus videret. Non ergo stat, sed transit spiritus, quia supernam lucem nostra nobis contemplatio et inhiantibus aperit, et mox infirmantibus abscondit" (S. GREGORIUS MAGNUS, *Moral.*, V, 33, 58; P.L., LXXV, 711).—(Cf. a clearly Augustinian method of mystical meditation, *op. cit.*, V, 34, 62; P.L., LXXV, 713).— "sapor intimae contemplationis . . ." (VIII, 30, 49; col. 832).—"Unde aliquando ad quamdam inusitatam dulcedinem interni saporis admittitur . . ." (XXIII, 21, 43; P.L., LXXVI, 277-278).—"Dum enim audita supercoelestia amamus, amata jam novimus, quia amor ipse notitia est" (*In Ezech.*, lib. II, *Hom.* XXVII, n. 4; P.L., LXXVI, 1207 A).

Other texts on mystical contemplation: *op cit.*, XXXVI, 65-66; P.L., LXXV, 715-716.—Breadth, length and depth of God; IX, 14; P.L., LXXV, 930 AC.

20 *Op. cit.*, XXIX, 22, 43; P.L., LXXVI, 500-501.

21 "Saepe autem ita mens accenditur, ut quamvis in carne sit posita, in Deum tamen omni subjugata carnali cogitatione rapiatur; nec tamen Deum sicut est conspicit, quia hanc nimirum, sicut dictum est, in carne corruptibili pondus primae damnationis premit. Saepe, ita ut est, absorberi desiderat, ut aeternam vitam, si possit fieri, sine interventu corporeae mortis attingat . . . Sancti igitur [i.e. Paulus] viri videre verum mane appetunt, et, si concedatur, etiam cum corpore illud attingere lucis intimae secretum volunt. Sed quantolibet ardore intentionis exsiliant, adhuc antiqua nox gravat, et corruptibilis hujus carnis oculos, quos hostis callidus ad concupiscientiam aperuit, judex justus a contuitu interni sui fulgoris premit" (S. GREGORIUS MAGNUS, *Moral.*, IV, 24, 45; P.L., LXXV, 659).—We see God as in a "vision of the night" (*op. cit.*, V, 30, 53; col. 707-708. Cf. XXIII, 20, 39; P.L., LXXVI, 274-275).—This vision is partial and temporary; the soul is "ultra se rapta"; "in quadam novitate aliquo modo recreatur"; "Ibi mens ex immenso fontis infusione superni roris aspergitur" (XXIV, 6, 11; P.L., LXXVI, 292).—The soul is soon "reverberata" (*ibid.*, 12, col. 292-293).— That is why we read in the *Apocalypse*, VIII, 1: "Factum est silentium in coelo, quasi media hora"; since the exercise of contemplation cannot be perfect in this life, "nequaquam hora integra factum in coelo silentium dicitur, sed quasi media hora, ut neque ipsa media hora plene sentiatur, cum praemittitur *quasi* . . ." (*In Ezech.*, Lib. II, *Hom.* II, 14; P.L., LXXVI, 957).

22 Cf. "jam frequentes et improvisae theophaniae . . ." (WILLIAM OF SAINT-THIERRY, *Liber de natura et dignitate amoris*, IV, 10; P.L., CLXXXIV, 386 C). I believe it altogether false to say, as has been said (P. POURRAT, *La spiritualité chrétienne*, Paris, 1921, II, pp. 194-195), that there are any traces in William of the so-called pantheism of Erigena; but it is not impossible that the Abbot of Saint-Thierry had read Erigena. Compare, notably, JOHN SCOT ERIGENA, *De divisione naturae*, I, 12; P.L., CXXII, 452 CD, and WILLIAM OF SAINT-THIERRY, *In Cant. Cant.*, cap. II; P.L., CLXXX, 528 CD. Here we might easily suspect a common source, Isidore of Seville, for example (I have explored him without success), but William's language indubitably recalls at times the Dionysian "chant", so easily recognizable to accustomed ears ("Et sicut semper sibi indissimilis Deus indissimiliter dissimilia in creatura operatur . . .", *Epist. ad Fratres de Monte Dei*, II, 3, 16;

220 NOTES

P.L., CLXXXIV, 348 D); and that is a thing that, so to speak, never occurs in reading St. Bernard.

[23] This will become even more evident if we push the analysis beyond St. Bernard's sources to his doctrinal antecedents. For there is at least a fourth "bloc" that entered into his patiently constructed edifice. This is the doctrine of liberty contained in the *Epistle to the Romans*, whence Bernard drew his *De gratia et libero arbitrio*. Further on we shall see how the "libertas a miseria" coincides in the end with ecstasy. There we have a real stroke of genius which invests the whole doctrine with an admirable profundity: the identification effected between ascesis and mysticism brings about the complete unification of the Cistercian life. Every effort at freedom from sin contributes something to freedom from misery, and a practically complete liberation from this is ecstasy, the prelude to beatitude. When doctrines, however well known they may be in themselves, are united by so deep an intuition, the synthesis becomes something more than the sum of the elements.

[24] We shall have occasion later on to note the profound influence of St. Ambrose on certain important aspects of the Cistercian mysticism. As regards St. Augustine it is not to be doubted that his influence was equally profound; at the time when I was beginning this work I had even supposed it to have been preponderant, and nothing but a patient examination of facts has forced me to abandon this hypothesis, or rather this unreasoned opinion—to my great surprise, let me add. St. Bernard knew his St. Augustine admirably, and often drew suggestions from his *Enarrationes in Psalmos*, especially in connection with the doctrine concerning charity. Many articulations of his thought are Augustinian, but one may say that his doctrine is not the same in fibre as that of Augustine. To be convinced of this we have only to compare the Augustinian ecstasy at Ostia, so thoroughly metaphysical in character, with the affective ecstasy of St. Bernard. The ecstatic experience of Augustine, achieved by way of progressive transcendence of sensations, of images and of judgements, seems almost neo-platonic in comparison (see the important study of P. J. MARÉCHAL, S.J., *La vision de Dieu au sommet de la contemplation d'après saint Augustin*, in *Nouvelle revue théologique*, Feb. 1930). But we may equally be convinced of it on comparing St. Bernard with his friends and successors. It is quite impossible to read William of Saint-Thierry without falling in with a whole handful of Augustinian formulas—such as love as "pondus animae"—or even Augustinian doctrines, like that of the "memoria", which lies at the heart of his mysticism, but plays only a very minor part in St. Bernard. The fact is evident; M. A. Adam (*op. cit.*, pp. 104–105) can write that if William did not wholly disappear in the wake of St. Bernard, but retained his persónality, it was because "in becoming St. Bernard's intimate friend he knew how to remain St. Augustine's disciple". If St. Bernard had been so in the same degree as William he and his friend would no longer be distinguishable. We may try the same experiment by reading the *De spirituale amicitia* of Aelred of Rievaulx, incontestably a disciple of St. Bernard, but one who shows himself from the outset of his treatise as capable of writing "in the style of the *Confessions*".—There is the fact, but I admit that it surprises me. If, as I believe, it really is a fact, I can account for it only by going back to the Rule of St. Benedict. This, doubtless, in no wise excludes St. Augustine, but it expressly referred Bernard towards the First Epistle of St. John, towards Cassian and towards Gregory the Great; he meditated them, and, finding there the elements of the doctrine he sought, had no longer anything essential to ask of Augustine. I give the explanation for what it is worth; perhaps, and precisely on account of its diffuse character, the true nature of this influence has evaded all my efforts to seize it.

The influence of Augustine on St. Bernard is especially apparent in the doctrine of love. St. Bernard gathered up, systematized, and explored a quantity of indications scattered through the works of St. Augustine. For example: in contemplation it is better for the soul to forget herself for love of the immutable God, or despise herself *penitus* with respect to Him (*De lib. arbitrio*, III, 25, 76; P.L., XXXII, 1308). St. Bernard says more, but St.

Augustine invites him to do so.—The chief cause of the Incarnation was that God wished to manifest His love and thus to incite us to love Him (*De catechiz. rudibus*, cap. IV, 7; P.L., XL, 314). We shall see St. Bernard dramatizing this idea in a sermon.—As regards the very nature of love: "Quod non propter se amatur, non amatur" (*Soliloq.*, cap. XIII, 22; P.L., XXXII, 881). This love should be gratuitous: "Quid est gratuitum? Ipse propter se, non propter aliud" (*Enarr. in Ps.* 53, 10; P.L., XXXVI, 626). It is thus a chaste love because disinterested: "Non est castum cor, si Deum ad mercedem colit. Quid ergo? mercedem de Dei cultu non habebimus? Habebimus plane, sed ipsum Deum quem colimus" (*Enarr. in Ps.* 55, 17; P.L., XXXVI, 658). "Praemium Dei, ipse Deus est" (*Enarr. in Ps.* 72, 32: col. 928). It is in this sense that the love of God is "gratuitus" (*Enarr in Ps.* 104, 40; P.L., XXXVI, 1404). Chaste love generates chaste fear (*Enarr. in Ps.* 127, 8-9; P.L., XXXVI, 1681-1683).—As regards the cause and order of love Augustine of course teaches that God creates it and that it is universally diffused: "Deus quem amat omne quod potest amare, sive sciens, sive nesciens" (*Soliloq.*, I, 1. 2; P.L., XXXII, 869). That love is, of itself, spontaneous: "ut se quisque diligat, praecepto non opus est" (*De doctr. christ.*, I, 35, 39; P.L., XXXIV, 34). That we have to begin with love of self; H. M. Delsart, in the introduction to his translation of the *De diligendo Deo* (p. 5, note 1), cites a text altogether decisive in this sense: "Ergo dilectio unicuique a se incipit et non potest nisi a se incipere, ut nemo monetur ut se diligat" (*Serm.* 368, 4, 4; P.L., XXXIV, 1654). It is not certain that this sermon is authentic (in my opinion, indeed, it is not), but St. Bernard might have read it as Augustine's. H. M. Delsart wrongly indicates *Sermo* 268. I owe the correction to Père F. Cayré.

²⁵ "Vultis ergo a me audire, quare et quomodo diligendus sit Deus? Et ego: causa diligendi Deum, Deus est; modus, sine modo diligere" (ST. BERNARD, *De diligendo Deo*, cap. I, 1; P.L., CLXXXII, 974).—St. Bernard is thus inspired, as Mabillon remarks, by Severus de Milevis in St. Augustine (*Epist.* 109, 2; P.L., XXXIII, 419). Cf. JOHN OF SALISBURY, *Polycraticus*, Lib. VII, cap. II; P.L., CXCIX, 661 B.

²⁶ See on this point, E. GILSON, *L'esprit de la philosophie médiévale*, Paris, J. Vrin, 1932, II, Chap. I (English translation, Sheed & Ward, Chap. XI). The Abbe COMBES has just written an important chapter of the history of this doctrine, *Un témoin du socratism chrétien au XV siècle; Robert Ciboule*, in *Arch. d'Hist. doct. et litt. du moyen âge*, t. VIII (1933), pp. 93-258. The study of the sources of Cistercian mysticism has taught me that the theme was already familiar to St. Ambrose, and that William of Saint-Thierry gathered up its various expressions in his Commentary on the Canticle of Canticles drawn from St. Ambrose. See also GREGORY OF NYSSA (?), *De eo quid sit . . .*, P. Gr.-Lat., XLIV, 1332 AB.

²⁷ *De diligendo Deo*, II, 4; P.L., CLXXXII, 976.—The text of this treatise, and also that of the *De gradibus humilitatis*, will be cited from Mabillon's edition, reproduced in Migne's Latin Patrology. This will avoid the necessity of sending the reader to several different editions. Nevertheless, for these two treatises it will be of interest to refer to the recent edition: *Select treatises of St. Bernard of Clairvaux. De diligendo Deo*, ed. by Watkin W. Williams; *De gradibus humilitatis et superbiae*, ed. by Barton R. V. Mills, Cambridge University Press, 1926. The text differs in many places from Mabillon's (without, however, involving the doctrine itself), because the new editors have followed the two MSS. 426 and 799 of the Bibliothèques de Troyes, which belong to another family than those of which Mabillon made use. It is a valuable experiment, and we owe the authors all possible thanks for making it. They recognize themselves, however, that Mabillon's text often has its advantages. Their own is occasionally open to question; for example, p. 13, line 12, "ne aut omnino glorieris" appears to be an error for "ne aut omnino *non* glorieris", which seems to be demanded by the context. The notes, often very useful, are far from being always doctrinally unexceptionable. It is indispensable, however, to notice this edition, the only one that adds any

thing to Mabillon's. Had it done no more than reopen the question of St. Bernard's text and shown the necessity of a new critical edition, its authors would have every right to our gratitude.

[28] ST. BERNARD, *De diligendo Deo*, II, 4; P.L., CLXXXII, 976.

[29] ST. BERNARD, *De diligendo Deo*, II, 6; P.L., CLXXXII, 977–978. Note especially: "Clamat nempe intus ei innata, et non ignorata rationi justitia, quia ex toto se illum diligere debeat, cui se totum debere non ignorat" (978 A). Reason declares the existence of God the Creator, we know therefore naturally that we ought, in strict justice, to love Him above all things.

[30] The passage from the truth of right to the state of fact is strongly marked in St. Bernard himself at the end of the long development just analyzed: "Verum difficile, imo impossibile est, suis scilicet quempiam, liberive arbitrii viribus semel accepta a Deo, ad Dei ex toto convertere voluntatem; et non magis ad propriam retorquere, eaque sibi tanquam propria ordinare" (*De diligendo Deo*, II, 6; P.L., CLXXXII, 978). St. Bernard, then, takes up exactly the same position as St. Thomas Aquinas was to do later on: in right, the natural love of God above all things comes first; in fact, on account of original sin, man at first prefers himself to God. (ST. THOMAS AQUINAS, *Sum. theol.*, I, II, qu. 109, art. 3, Resp. Cf. I, qu. 60, art. 5, Resp.).

[31] "Et est amor carnalis, quo ante omnia homo diligit seipsum propter seipsum" (*De diligendo Deo*, VIII, 23; P.L., CLXXXII, 988).

[32] E. GILSON, *Les idées et les lettres*, Paris, J. Vrin, 1932, p. 156.

[33] ST. PAUL, *I Cor.*, XV, 46–50.—William of Saint-Thierry has a lengthy development of the same idea, but with a different technique. He distinguishes three states of the religious life: *animalis, rationalis, spiritualis*, corresponding to *incipientes, proficientes, perfecti* (WILLIAM OF SAINT-THIERRY, *Epist. aurea*, lib. I, cap. 5. n. 12; P.L., CLXXXIV, 315).—The *status animalis* is analyzed (with very precise reminiscences of St. Augustine) in cap. 5, n. 13; 316–317. On William's analysis of these distinctions see M. M. DAVY, *Les trois étapes de la vie spirituelle, d'après Guillaume de Saint-Thierry*, in *Rech. de science religieuse*, XXIII (dec. 1933), pp. 569–588.

[34] "Viae igitur filiorum Adam in necessitate et cupiditate versantur. Ab utraque siquidem ducimur, et ab utraque trahimur; nisi quod videmur magis urgeri necessitate, trahi cupiditate. Et necessitas quidem specialiter corpori tribuenda videtur. . . . Siquidem e duobus malis longe melius est in necessitate gradi, quam in cupiditate" (ST. BERNARD, *In Ps. Qui habitat*, Sermo XI, n. 3; P.L., CLXXXIII, 226).—The distinction and appropriation of these terms, without being absolutely strict, is usual in St. Bernard. Cf. "Sed quoniam natura fragilior atque infirmior est, ipsi primum imperante *necessitate*, compellitur inservire" (*De dilig. Deo*, VIII, 23; P.L., CLXXXII, 988 A). The comment in W. W. Williams' edition (p. 42, n. 3): "*necessitate:* not, of course, external compulsion, but the binding force of the commandment", is therefore a misapprehension arising from neglect of the technical sense of *necessitas:* it concerns a necessity which is neither external, nor of precept, but internal and natural, although aggravated in punishment of sin. The error is the more strange inasmuch as Bernard himself, a few lines further on, puts it precisely: "nec precepto indicitur, sed naturae inseritur". It is simply a case of what we should call the instinct of self-preservation.

[35] St. Bernard, moreover, here follows in the wake of St. Augustine; this passage of the *De diligendo Deo* seems to have been suggested by the following text, which is its best commentary: "Est quaedam vita hominibus carnalibus sensibus implicata, gaudiis carnalibus dedita, carnalem fugitans offensionem, voluptatemque consecutans. Hujus vitae felicitas temporalis est; ab hac vita incipere necessitatis est, in ea persistere voluntatis. In hac quippe ex utero matris infans funditur, hujus offensiones quantum potest refugit, hujus appetit voluptates; nihil amplius valet. Sed posteaquam venerit in aetatem qua in eo rationis usus evigilet, poterit adjuta divinitus voluntate eligere alteram vitam, cujus in mente gaudium est, cujus interna atque aeterna felicitas" (ST. AUGUSTINE, *Epist.* 150, 2, 3; P.L., XXXIII, 535).—It is not perhaps useless to observe, for greater precision, that St. Bernard's exegesis of the

text of St. Paul is here only partial and that he is well aware of it. The *prius quod animale* may be explained thus, but it means more: *animale* in fact may point now to natural animality alone (as it is taken here), now to the cupidity of concupiscence which cannot be regarded as natural, and, again, to both (see, for example, ST. BERNARD, *De diversis*, Sermo VIII, 2; P.L., CLXXXIII, 562). The extension of the meaning of the text is, therefore, in each passage, a function of the problem into which it is introduced.—William of Saint-Thierry, more rigorous than St. Bernard, merely gives his thought a more precise expression when he says: "Sed nullum vitium naturale est, virtus vero omnis homini naturalis est"; but the habit of sin or neglect often makes vices take on the character of a second nature and become "quasi naturalia" (*Epist. aurea*, II, 2, 7; P.L., CLXXXIV, 343 A).

[36] ST. BERNARD, *De diligendo Deo*, VII, 18; P.L., CLXXXII, 285; *De diversis*, Sermo XLII, 3; P.L., CLXXXIII, 662. Note that this latter text is a description, at once of the ravages of cupidity and of what Bernard calls: *regio dissimilitudinis*. As we shall see more clearly later on, it is by his cupidity that man has become a creature "disfigured". These ideas are resumed in two lines of the *De diligendo Deo*: "at vero si coeperit amor idem (*scil.* naturae insertus), ut assolet, esse proclivior sive profusior, et necessitatis alveo minime contentus, campos etiam voluptatis exundans latius, visus fuerit occupare . . ." (VIII, 23; P.L., CLXXXII, 988).

[37] "Quia carnales sumus et de carnis concupiscentia nascimur, necesse est ut cupiditas vel amor noster a carne incipiat; quae si recto ordine dirigitur, quibusdam suis gradibus duce gratia proficiens, spiritu tandem consummabitur: quia *non prius quod spirituale, sed quod animale, deinde quod spirituale*" (ST. BERNARD, *De diligendo Deo*, XV, 39; P.L., CLXXXII, 998). This text calls for two observations:

First. There is no room for doubting, as W. W. Williams does (*ed. cit.*, p. 65, n. 13), that *carnalis* is here to be taken at once in the emphatic sense of "fleshly" and in the weak sense of *carneus*. The hesitation is the less allowable inasmuch as *carnales sumus* is recognized in this commentary as a reference to *Rom.*, VII, 14. Now if we restore the complete text here alluded to by St. Bernard we find an express mention of sin: "Scimus enim quia lex spiritualis est, ego autem carnalis sum venumdatus sub peccato." Here, then, we are certainly concerned with the flesh infected by sin, and with concupiscence as punishment and source of sin.

Second. The *carnal* character of man in his present state is invoked in this text to explain that human love turns first towards the flesh, whether as a consequence of sin (*carnalis, cupiditas*) or by natural necessity (*carneus, amor noster*). The two kinds of necessity are here covered by the same text of St. Paul. Man's earthly animal nature makes him perforce take care for his own preservation; he is not to be blamed for that. Corruption by sin necessarily makes him subject to concupiscence and to cupidity. We might say that in the first sense he is *carneus*, in the second *carnalis*, and that there are therefore two reasons (one being natural and the other not) why he loves himself before all the rest.—If we feel surprised that Bernard should have made these two important remarks in two chapters so far apart as VIII and XV, we must recollect that these texts belong in reality to two different works. The *De diligendo Deo* extends from chapters I to IX inclusively; chapters XII–XV are an addition and reproduce the principal part of a letter written to Guigo I. the Carthusian, in response to his admirable *Meditationes* (printed in P.L., CLIII, 601–632) which had so aroused St. Bernard's enthusiasm. The end of the treatise is thus prior to the beginning; it is found in its first form in *Epist. XI*, apparently dated in 1125. The *De diligendo Deo*, written somewhat later, is not therefore to be treated as a unity. Chapter VIII contains an exposition distinct from that of Chapter XV, and the respective texts should be co-ordinated, not run together.

[38] The language of St. Thomas marks a decisive progress in this respect when compared with that of St. Bernard. He cannot admit that for any reason whatsoever man *naturally* loves himself more than God: "Alioquin, si natural-

iter plus seipsum diligeret quam Deum, sequeretur quod naturalis dilectio esset perversa, et quod non perficeretur per caritatem, sed destrueretur" (ST. THOMAS AQUINAS, *Sum. theol.*, Pt. I, qu. 60, art. 5). St. Bernard, of course, thought the same, and William, as we have seen (p. 223, note 35), says it. It is therefore *natural* to love God more than all things, but *psychologically necessary* to begin by loving oneself, and, for a fallen nature, deprived of grace, *morally necessary* to prefer self to God. St. Bernard's terminology is thus less perfectly formed on this point than that of St. Thomas, but—and here I reply to an objection I once heard put by a theologian—it is at the very antipodes of that of Luther. The thing that prefers itself to God in St. Bernard is human nature defaced by sin, but grace has power to rectify its deformities, and as soon as man has recovered his likeness to God, the genuine human nature, the normal nature, once more begins to love God naturally above all things. The mystical theology of St. Bernard is but the history of this restoration, and that is precisely the thing that Luther always declared impossible: "Diligere Deum super omnia naturaliter est terminus fictus, sicut Chimaera" (M. LUTHER, *Disputatio contra scholasticam theologiam* (1517), Weimar edn., t. I, pp. 221–228; thesis 18). One may prefer another doctrinal economy to that of St. Bernard, but one must be blind indeed not to see that Cistercian mysticism and Lutheranism are as opposite as fire and water.

⁸⁹ *Amor* is a natural affection which, when duly ordered towards its end, is *caritas*, and when turned away from its end, *cupiditas*. Charity includes in itself all well-ordered love, but it excludes cupidity, which ceases to be cupidity when duly ordered; for it is but love distorted. A *cupiditas* cannot be *ordinata qua cupiditas*. Cf. Chapter V, p. 141, note 211.

⁴⁰ ST. BERNARD, *In Quadrag. in Ps. Qui habitat*, Sermo XI, 3; P.L., CLXXXIII, 226 D.

⁴¹ ST. BERNARD, *De diligendo Deo*, VII, 19–20; P.L., CLXXXII, 985–986. Nothing can replace the meditation, line by line, of this admirable text. Its condensation defies analysis, and all I pretend to do here is to indicate its general movement. Another text may be added in the same vein, *De diversis*, Sermo XLII, 3; P.L., CLXXXIII, 662.

⁴² "Et horum omnium idcirco non est finis, quia nil in eis summum singulariter reperitur vel optimum. Et quid mirum si inferioribus et deterioribus contentus non sit, qui citra summum vel optimum quiescere non potest?" (ST. BERNARD, *De diligendo Deo*, VII, 18; P.L., CLXXXII, 985).

⁴³ "Prima regio est regio dissimilitudinis. Nobilis illa creatura in regione similitudinis fabricata, quia ad imaginem Dei facta, cum in honore esset, non intellexit et de similitudine ad dissimilitudinem descendit. Magna prorsus dissimilitudo, de paradiso ad infernum, de angelo ad jumentum, de Deo ad diabolum! Exsecranda conversio . . . Maledicta descensio . . . Vulnerati sumus ingredientes mundum, conversando in mundo, exeundo de mundo: a planta pedis usque ad verticem non est sanitas in nobis" (ST. BERNARD, *De diversis*, Sermo XLII, 2; P.L., CLXXXIII, 662). The expression "regio dissimilitudinis" is taken from St. Augustine. I looked for it for a long time without success, and at last Père F. Cayré found it for me. It occurs in the *Confessions*, Bk. VII, cap. X, n. 16: "Et reverberasti infirmitatem aspectus mei radians in me vehementer, et contremui amore et horrore: et inveni longe me esse a te in regione dissimilitudinis. . . ." Several editions (P. Knöll, P. de Labriolle) refer to *Jeremiah*, XXXI, 15. I find nothing in this verse to suggest such an expression; possibly XXXI, 40 is meant: "et omnem vallem cadaverum, et cineris, et universam regionem mortis. . . ." In any event "dissimilitudo" is not to be found there, nor is the word indicated in any of the Biblical concordances I have been able to consult. If we refer to the context we shall see that St. Bernard makes a very personal use of the expression he borrows; while all the time maintaining contact with one of St. Augustine's most profound ideas ("Mihi autem inhaerere Deo bonum est, quia, si non manebo in illo, nec in me potero", *Conf.*, VII, 11, 17), he powerfully reconstructs from within the whole doctrine of image, so as to make it the centre round which all his ascesis revolves.

St. Augustine would recognize himself without hesitation in St. Bernard; however, the "regio dissimilitudinis" of the *Confessions* is essentially the Platonic region of becoming, hovering between the non-being of mere nought and the immutable being of God. That of St. Bernard is essentially the region of sin and the deformity of the lost likeness. Of course there are plenty of ways to pass from one to the other. St. Augustine himself said that the contingence of created being explains the possibility of sin, and St. Bernard everywhere suggests that the loss of the likeness is a loss of being. It is none the less true that each moves on a plane, which, while not his exclusive property, is that of his preference. When we look at it from St. Bernard's standpoint the metaphysical and Hellenic aspect of Augustine's thought stands out with remarkable force.

Cf. WILLIAM OF SAINT-THIERRY, *De natura et dignitate amoris*, XI, 34; P.L., CLXXXIV, 401 A.

[44] "Frustra glorietur de libertati arbitrii, quae in mente est" (*In festo S. Martini episc.*, n. 3; P.L., CLXXXIII, 491 C). Free-will being the very image of God in us, this text amounts to placing the Divine image *in mente*.

[45] ST. BERNARD, *De gratia et libero arbitrio*, IV, 9; P.L., CLXXXII, 1006–1007. Cf. E. GILSON, *La philosophie de Saint Bonaventure*, Paris, J. Vrin, 1924, p. 395, note 1. As I have noted elsewhere, it is of interest to compare this text with those of Descartes on liberty (E. GILSON, *La liberté chez Descartes et la théologie*, Paris, Alcan, 1913, pp. 230–243). The source common to Bernard, Bonaventure and Descartes would be Gregory of Nyssa, according to Th. Raynaud, *op. cit.*, p. 239, note 2. Cf. GREGORY OF NYSSA, *De hom. opif.*, P. Gr.-Lat., XLIV, 184 BC.

The precise meaning of the doctrine is as follows. Man is made to the image of God in his free-will, and he will never lose it; he was made to the likeness of God in respect of certain virtues, enabling him to choose well (Divine Wisdom), and to do the good thing chosen (Divine Power); now these he has lost (see note 49). It is therefore by virtue of his free-will that he is chiefly made to the image of God, since this is the sole divine analogy that he can never lose without thereby ceasing to exist.

[46] ST. BERNARD, *De gratia et libero arbitrio*, IX, 28; P.L., CLXXXII, 1016. Cf. "An forte quaeris et tunicam inconsutilem, quae non dividitur, sed sorte provenit? Ego divinam arbitror imaginem, quae nimirum non assuta, sed insita atque ipsi impressa naturae, dividi scindique non potest. Ad imaginem nempe et similitudinem Dei factus est homo, in imagine arbitrii libertatem, virtutes habens in similitudine. Et similitudo quidem periit, verumtamen in imagine pertransit homo. Imago siquidem in gehenna ipsa uri poterit, non exuri; ardere, sed non deleri. Haec ergo non scinditur, sed sorte provenit. Et quocumque perveniat anima, simul et ipsa ibi erit. Nam similitudo non sic, sed aut manet in bono, aut si peccaverit anima, mutatur miserabiliter, jumentis insipientibus similata" (*In Annunt. B. Mariae Virg.*, Sermo I, 7; P.L., CLXXXIII, 386).

[47] ST. BERNARD, *De gratia et libero arbitrio*, VIII, 24; P.L., CLXXXII, 1014–1015.

[48] ST. BERNARD, *De gratia et libero arbitrio*, IV, 11; P.L., CLXXXII, 1007–1008.

[49] "De tribus ergo libertatibus quas acceperat, abutendo illa quae dicitur arbitrii, reliquis sese privavit" (ST. BERNARD, *De grat. et lib. arbitrio*, VII, 22; P.L., CLXXXII, 1013 D). Now these last two constitute the likeness: "Puto autem in his tribus libertatibus ipsam, ad quam conditi sumus, conditoris imaginem atque similitudinem contineri; et imaginem quidem in libertate arbitrii, in reliquis autem duabus bipertitam quandam consignari similitudinem" (ST. BERNARD, *De grat. et lib. arbitrio*, IX, 28; P.L., CLXXXII, 1016).—"Porro in aliis duabus libertatibus, quoniam non solum ex parte minui, sed et ex toto amitti possunt, accidentalis quaedam magis similitudo sapientiae atque potentiae divinae, imagini superducta cognoscitur" (*Ibid.*). St. Bernard, then, even with an imperfect conception of the "nature", knew how to distinguish between the essential and inseparable attributes of

man as man, impregnable therefore even to sin, and the gratuitous gifts which were open to corruption by original sin.

⁵⁰ ST. BERNARD, *De gratia et libero arbitrio*, VII, 21–22; P.L., CLXXXII, 1013–1014.

⁵¹ St. Bernard outlines on this point some metaphysical considerations which betray the influence of the theological controversies of his time. Not only does he assert the distinction between the form and that of which it is the form, but he goes so far as to say that the form is as distinct from its subject as are the *propria* in their various degrees: "Non igitur sua magnitudo anima, non magis quam sua nigredo corvus, quam suus candor nix, quam sua risibilitas seu rationalitas homo, cum tamen nec corvum sine nigredine, nec sine candore nivem, nec hominem qui non et risibilis sit et rationalis, unquam reperias. Ita et anima, et animae magnitudo, etsi inseparabiles, diversae tamen ad invicem sunt. Quomodo non diversae, cum haec in subjecto, illa subjectum et substantia sit" (ST. BERNARD, *In Cant. Cant.*, Sermo LXXX, 5; P.L., CLXXXIII, 1169). He adds at once that God alone is absolutely simple, and that, no doubt, is the key to the whole passage. The distinction introduced by St. Bernard between the soul and its greatness seems to be designed chiefly to reserve to the creature the metaphysical composition of subject and form which Gilbert de la Porrée had been accused of introducing into God; see *loc. cit.*, 8; P.L., CLXXXIII, 1170, where Gilbert is expressly mentioned.

⁵² Important elements in Bernard's synthesis were certainly furnished by St. Anselm. First. He distinguishes two principal affections of the will: the will to the useful (*commodum*) and the will to justice. The former is inseparable from the will, the latter is not (ST. ANSELM, *De voluntate;* P.L., CLVIII, 487 A). Second. The will to justice constitutes the soul's uprightness (*rectitudo*); justice in fact is the very will to maintain its uprightness (*De veritate*, XII; 482 CD), and freedom consists in our power to preserve it (*De libero arbitrio*, III; 493 A, and XIII, 505–506). Third. Liberty is therefore distinct from the will's justice: "aliud autem est voluntas, et aliud rectitudo, qua recta est" (*De conc. praesc. Dei*, cap. VI, 516 C); the loss of the soul's uprightness does not involve that of its free-will, which subsists, and can recover uprightness if God restores it (*Dial. de lib. arb.*, III; 493 C). All this passed into St. Bernard's doctrine, where, for the rest, it takes on another aspect by adaptation to the solution of new problems, less speculative than those which occupied St. Anselm and immediately connected with those raised by the practice of the Cistercian life.

⁵³ It plays an important part in St. Bonaventure's doctrine (E. GILSON, *La philosophie de saint Bonaventure*, Paris, J. Vrin, 1924, p. 416).

⁵⁴ ST. BERNARD, *In Cant. Cant.*, Sermo LXXXI, 1; P.L., CLXXXIII, 1171 C.

⁵⁵ "Quia ergo naturae ingenuitatem morum probitate defensare neglexit, justo auctoris judicio factum est, non quidem ut libertate propria nudaretur, sed tamen superindueretur, *sicut diploide confusione sua* (Ps. 108, 29). Et bene *sicut diploide*, ubi veste veluti duplicata, manente libertate propter vuluntatem, servilis nihilominus conversatio necessitatem probat" (ST. BERNARD, *In Cant. Cant.*, Sermo LXXXII, 5; P.L., CLXXXIII, 1179). "Ita bonis naturae mala adventitia, dum non succedunt, sed accedunt, turpant utique ea, non exterminant, conturbant, non deturbant" (*Ibid.*, 1179 D).

⁵⁶ "Porro communis voluntas caritas est. . . . Verum facile est nosse quam sint aliena a propria voluntate, quae propria sunt caritatis, cui illa recta fronte contrariam se constituit" (ST. BERNARD, *In tempore Resurrect.*, Sermo II, 8; P.L., CLXXXIII, 286 BC).

⁵⁷ "Voluntatem dico propriam, quae non est communis cum Deo et hominibus, sed nostra tantum: quando quod volumus, non ad honorem Dei, non ad utilitem fratrum, sed propter nosmetipsos facimus, non intendentes placere Deo et prodesse fratribus, sed satisfacere propriis motibus animorum. Huic contraria est recta fronte caritas, quae Deus est" (ST. BERNARD, *In tempore Resurrect.*, Sermo III, 3; P.L., CLXXXIII, 289).

⁵⁸ *Loc. cit.*, n. 3; 290.

⁵⁹ ST. BERNARD, *In temp. Resurrect.*, Sermo III, 4; P.L., CLXXXIII, 290.—We can hardly avoid asking whether St. Bernard is not glancing here at Abelard or at Gilbert de la Porrée.

⁶⁰ ST. BERNARD, *In Cant. Cant.*, Sermo LXXXII, 5; P.L., CLXXXIII, 1179 D.

⁶¹ *Op. cit.*, 6–7; 1180; 1181.

⁶² ST. BERNARD, *De praecepto et dispensatione*, cap. XIV, 356; P.L., CLXXXII, 880–881.

⁶³ ST. BERNARD, *De praecepto et dispensatione*, cap. XIV, 36; P.L., CLXXXII, 881.—Here we see clearly that the doctrine of freedom is an integral constituent of St. Bernard's mystical theology, and that both are a function of his monastic ideal, since this last is their indispensable condition. The contrary of our present misery is heavenly beatitude; the blessed are in full possession of the *libertas a miseria;* contemplatives alone are able to free themselves of it partially and for short intervals in this life. Ecstasy, then, might be defined as an imperfect and brief liberation from "*miseria*". Then it appears as a restoration of the *libertas complaciti* lost by sin. See on this subject the capital text of the *De gratia et libero arbitrio*, V, 15; P.L., CLXXXII, 1009–1010, notably: "Itaque in hac vita soli contemplativi possunt utcumque frui libertate complaciti: et hoc ex parte, et parte satis modica, viceque rarissima." And above: "Hi plane (quod negandum non est) etiam in hac carne, raro licet raptimque, complaciti libertate fruuntur qui cum Maria optimam partem elegerunt. . . ." &c. The fact that these evident references to the mystic states are found in the *De gratia et libero arbitrio* is enough to connect this treatise with the mystical writings of St. Bernard.

⁶⁴ The opposition of the "Porch of Solomon" to the Grecian Porch was classical; it goes back to the earliest days of Christian Latin literature, for we find it in Tertullian, *De praescript. haeret.*, c. VII, where divine Wisdom already confronts the teaching of the philosophers: "Nostra institutio de porticu Salomonis est, qui et ipse tradiderat Dominum in simplicitate cordis esse quaerendum. Viderint qui stoicum et platonicum et dialecticum christianismum protulerunt. Nobis curiositate opus non est post Christum Jesum, nec inquisitione post evangelium. Cum credimus, nihil desideramus ultra credere. Hoc enim prius credimus, non esse quod ultra credere debeamus" (Ed. P. de Labriolle, Paris, Picard, 1907, p. 18). Tertullian was to have a numerous following in the course of Christian history, or rather let us say that we encounter many similar temperaments: exclusive cult of Scripture, deep distrust of dialectics, amounting almost to hatred at times, exquisite literary taste, not excluding some of them from dealings with philosophy, but always forbidding dialectics, so fatal to a fine style.

⁶⁵ ST. BENEDICT, *Regula monasteriorum*, Prolog., ed. B. Linderbauer, Bonn, 1928, p. 15, l. 78.—The expression "schola primitivae ecclesiae" is found in the *Exordium magnum Ordinis Cisterciensis*, Dist. I, cap. 2; P.L., CLXXXV, 998 A.

⁶⁶ *Exordium magnum*, D. I, cap. 1–3; for what concerns St. Benedict, *op. cit.*, cap. 4.—Cf. WILLIAM OF SAINT-THIERRY, *Epistola aurea ad Fratres de Monte Dei*, I, C. l, n. 5–4; P.L., CLXXXIV, 310–311.

⁶⁷ *Exordium magnum*, D. I, cap. 4; col. 1000 A; "dilectionem Dei et proximi quae est perfectionis summa".

⁶⁸ ". . . conservationem caritatis. . . ." (ST. BENEDICT, *Regula, ed. cit.*, p. 16, l. 81).

⁶⁹ *Exordium magnum*, Dist. I, cap. 9; P.L., CLXXXV, 1005 A; Ovid.—Dist. III, cap. 5, 1056 C, and Dist. VI, cap I, 1180 A: Horace.

⁷⁰ WILLIAM OF SAINT-THIERRY, *Vita S. Bernardi*, lib. I, 3, 9: "Ubi vero de conversione tractantem, fratres ejus et qui carnaliter eum diligebant, persenserunt, omnimodis agere coeperunt, ut animam ejus ad studium possent divertere litterarum et amore scientiae secularis seculo arctius implicare. Qua nimirum suggestione, sicut fateri solet [notice the use of the present tense] propemodum retardati fuerant gressus ejus" (P.L., CLXXXV, 231).

Bérenger, the disciple of Abelard, reproached St. Bernard for having written in his youth certain "cantiunculas mimicas et urbanos modulos", and with always wanting to excel his companions in the art of writing (BERENGARIUS, *Apologeticus*, P.L., CLXXVIII, 1257 AB). It has been remarked that Bérenger, is a very dubious witness (VACANDARD, *Vie de saint Bernard*, Paris, 1927, t. I, p. 13). It is true, but does not apply here. Nothing is more likely than that Bernard, as a scholar at Châtillon, should have written profane verses in imitation of Ovid. As Manrique sagely observes: "Quae tamen, ut nullius fidei digna quippe ab auctore damnato et tunc furenti, per convicium objecta, ita vera fortasse esse potuerunt" (*Acta Bollandiana*, P.L., CLXXXV, 654 A).

[71] St. Bernard's austerity is too well known to need particularization. It is nevertheless important to bear in mind the intimate dependence of practice upon doctrine in this matter. The object in view was first of all to bring about a complete subordination of body to soul, by means of strict observance of the Cistercian Rule (see the horarium in D. Ursmer BERLIÈRE, *L'ascèse bénédictine*, p. 52), tempered nevertheless by the Abbot's discretion (ST. BERNARD, *In obitu Dom. Humberti monachi*, 4; P.L., CLXXXIII, 515-516) and moreover adapted to individual capacities (ST. BERNARD, *De diversis*, Sermo XXXVI, 2; P.L., CLXXXIII, 638 B). Through the body this mortification touched the sensibility. To leave the body outside the door when entering the monastery ("Hic foris dimitte corpora quae de seculo attulistis. Soli spiritus ingrediantur, caro non prodest quicquam") was to bridle not only concupiscence, but the senses themselves by which it entered the soul, so as to leave a clear place for the Divine love (WILLIAM OF SAINT-THIERRY, *Vita Bernardi*, I, 4, 20; P.L., CLXXXV, 238-239). (The last point in this text might have been suggested by GREGORY THE GREAT, *Moral.*, IV, 30, 57-60; P.L., LXXV, 667-670.) The famous examples of distraction that William here gives us are to be explained by the fact that to deaden his sensibility was, in St. Bernard's case, an indispensable condition of spiritual liberty. Cf. GEOFFROY DE CLAIRVAUX, *Vita Bernardi*, lib. III, cap. 8, n. 2; P.L., CLXXXV, 304 D-305 A. On poverty of spirit, see further on, p. 233, note 97.

[72] AELRED, *De spirituali amicitia liber*, P.L., CXCIV, 659-702. All the opening part is extremely interesting for the manner in which it combines the easily discernible influences of Cicero, St. Augustine, and St. Bernard. A brief summary of his youthful errors recalls in the first place St. Augustine: ". . . tota se mens mea dedit affetui et devovit amori; ita ut nihil mihi dulcius, nihil jucundius, nihil utilius quam amari et amare videretur" (c. 659 A. Cf. SAINT AUGUSTINE, *Conf.* III, I, 1). Next, just as Augustine had been carried away by the *Hortensius*, so was Aelred by the *De Amicitia*, and the reading of Cicero became for both the starting-point of a movement of conversion: "Et licet nec ad illud amicitiae genus me viderem indoneum, gratularbar tamen quamdam me amicitiae formulam reperisse, ad quam amorum meorum et affectionum valerem revocare discursus" (659 A). Finally comes the "conversion" itself; he enters the monastery and becomes a Cistercian. Having followed the Rule for a time he finds little savour left in the *De Amicitia;* nothing that is not Scripture can satisfy him; however the Fathers, although they spoke of it often enough, devoted no special treatise to friendship; and so he will write a treatise on spiritual friendship, that is to say he will rewrite Cicero's for the use of Christians (660 A; cf. 661 D-662 B).—In fact, it is clear that Aelred had Cicero under his eye while writing his dialogue; his borrowings, often of a literary character, have been noticed, and the modifications he made in the doctrine in order to Christianize it (see on this point R. EGENTER, *Gottesfreundschaft. Die Lehre von der Gottesfreundschaft in der Scholastik und Mystik des 12 und 13 Jahrhunderts*, Benno Filser, Augsburg, 1928, pp. 233-237). Egenter has shown that Aelred also makes use of the *De Officiis* of St. Ambrose (who was himself under the influence of Cicero), Augustine, Gregory the Great, Jerome, and an anthology of thoughts taken from Seneca.—On the unity of tone among the friends and followers of St. Bernard see the fine remarks of Dom A. WILMART, *Auteurs spirituels et*

textes dévots . . ., p. 322, n. 5. The Cistercian literary movement would make an interesting study for its own sake; we should encounter other great names besides those of the founders of the school whose doctrine is treated in this work. Alain de Lille died at Cîteaux (see the remarkable study of J. HUIZINGA, *Ueber die Verknüpfung des poetischen mit dem theologischen bei Alanus de Insulis*, Amsterdam, 1932, p. 3). Hélinand de Froidmont (died 1229), author of the celebrated *Vers de la mort*, was a Cistercian. William of Diguilleville, author of the *Pèlerinage de vie humaine* (1320), was a Cistercian. The mere titles of these works suggest the continuity of the school and the unity of spirit which runs through its literary, architectural and theological expressions.

On Aelred, see F. M..POWICKE, *Ailred of Rievaulx and his biographer Walter Daniel*, Manchester, 1922.—Dom A. WILMART, *Auteurs spirituels et textes dèvots.* . . ., pp. 287-297, XVI, L'oraison pastorale de l'abbé Aelred.

⁷³ ST. BERNARD, *De praecepto et dispensatione*, I, 1-2, and II, 3; P.L., CLXXXII, 861-863.—This explains St. Bernard's attitude towards those who wish to make exchange into another religious order. He does not favour abandonment of another order even to enter at Cîteaux; naturally he has the greater detestation for abandonment of Cîteaux for another order, for then it is a case of exchanging a severer rule for an easier one; it is apostasy. See the famous letter *Epist.* I; P.L., CLXXXII, 67-79. For a survey of the whole question see E. VANCANDARD, *Vie de saint Bernard*, t. I, ch. IV-V, pp. 99-173.

⁷⁴ The Rule therefore is not to be easily altered. Those of its precepts which merely re-affirm the commandments of God are strictly unalterable, since they come from God. As regards the provisions added by St. Benedict, they have no other end than to lead us more easily to the end of all Christian life: the acquisition and preservation of charity: "Porro inventa atque instituta fuerunt, non quia aliter vivere non liceret, sed quod ita magis expediret, nec plane ad aliud quam ad lucrum vel custodiam caritatis." Such is the criterion by which we may distinguish the provisions of monastic rules. In so far as they serve to promote charity, they are inviolable and binding; should they happen to be opposed to it they must be changed or suppressed, since in that case they defeat their end (ST. BERNARD, *De praecepto et dispensatione*, II, 5; P.L., CLXXXII, 863-864).

⁷⁵ "Petrus Abaelardus christianae fidei meritum evacuare nititur, dum totum quod Deus est, humana ratione arbitratur se posse comprehendere" (ST. BERNARD, *Epist*, CXCI, I; P.L., CLXXXII, 357 B).—"Nihil videt per speculum et in aenigmate, sed facie ad faciem omnia intuetur, ambulans in magnis et mirabilibus super se" (ST. BERNARD, *Epist.* CXCII; P.L., CLXXXII, 358 C).—St. Bernard's antagonism to the philosophic spirit is clearly expressed in his treatise: *De erroribus Abaelardi*, IV, 10 and V, 12-13; P.L., CLXXXII, 1062 and 1063-1064.—On the relations between Bernard and Abelard see VACANDARD, *Abélard, sa lutte avec saint Bernard, sa doctrine, sa méthode*, Paris, Roger et Chernovitz, 1881. We may also read with interest but prudent reserve: P. LASSERRE, *Un confiit rèligieux au XII siècle*, Paris, Artisan du livre, 1930.

St. Bernard had no hostility to studies as such. In itself, on the contrary, the study of letters is good, for it adorns the soul, instructs the man, and makes him capable of instructing others. But it is good only on condition that two things precede it: the fear of God and charity (*In Cant. Cant.*, Sermo XXXVII, 1-2; P.L., CLXXXIII, 971-972). It is difficult to be sure what Bernard means exactly by this study of "letters"; it evidently includes the Humanities but doubtless not the study of Plato and Aristotle, the thing that led Abelard and Gilbert de la Porrée into error.—For a bibliography of the question see M. GRABMANN, *Die Geschichte der scholastischen Methode*, Herder, t. II (1911), pp. 104-108.

St. Bernard's anti-philosophism, although not universal, is very widespread in the ancient Cistercian school. Among his followers the one who most fully developed it was Gilbert of Holland (died towards 1172). He continued Bernard's Commentary on the Canticle of Canticles, from III, *In lectulo*, to V, *Dilectus meus candidus* (and his work also was interrupted by death). His conception of the inter-relation of faith and reason is developed at length in connection with *Cant.*, III, 2; *Circuibo civitatem.* The "circuit" consists in seeking God from the starting-point of faith, by means of reason, so to attain to understanding. Here therefore we have a commentary, for the rest very personal, on the *Fides quaerens intellectum* of St. Anselm. Reason ought to remain within the limits of faith (*Cant. Cant.*, IV, 2; P.L., CLXXXIV, 26 D) which it retains in its memory and explores, but the eventual understanding is to contain nothing beyond what is already contained in faith: "Fides, ut sic dicam, veritatem rectam tenet et possidet; intelligentia revelatam (unveiled) et nudam contuetur; ratio conatur revelare. Ratio inter fidem intelligentiamque discurrens, ad illam se erigit, sed ista se regit . . ." &c. (*ibid.*, c. 27 A). The city in which the soul never ceases to circulate is the universe, and very especially the society of saints: the Church. We may confine ourselves to the rational exploration of the universe, but we are warned of its dangers by the example of the Pagan philosophers (GILBERT OF HOLLAND, *In Cant. Cant.*, IV, 5; P.L., CLXXXIV, 29. Cf. *op. cit.*, V, 2; 32–33). Pure philosophy is therefore to be distrusted. Any doctrine which makes no mention of Christ is *suspecta*, and even *despecta* (*op. cit.*, V, 3, 33 C. Cf. St. Augustine, *Conf.* III, 4, 8). On the other hand, the Jewish Law itself is insufficient, at least as the Jews understand it, for it contains the truth, but they do not recognize it there: "velamen est magis in eorum mente quam lege" (*ibid.*, 33 D). The Bride therefore has in the end but one way at her disposal, that which leads to the Bridegroom by revealing the meaning of the Law, that is to say Charity. This interesting synthesis of Augustine, Anselm, and St. Bernard deserves to be studied for its own sake. Gilbert was not a great mystic, perhaps no mystic at all (*In Cant. Cant.*, II, 8; P.L., CLXXXIV, 22), and in his commentary he prudently remains on the level of the "moral interpretation". But he has a strong and well-poised mind, and his writings are well worth reading.

[76] ST. BERNARD, *In Cant. Cant.*, Sermo XXXVI, 3; P.L., CLXXXIII, 968. He cites in this connection a verse of Persius: "Scire tuum nihil est, nisi te scire hoc sciat alter" (*Sat.* I. v. 27).

[77] ST. BERNARD, *In Cant. Cant.*, Sermo XXXVI, 1; P.L., CLXXXIII, 967.

[78] ST. BERNARD, *In fest. Pentecost.*, Sermo III, 5; P.L., CLXXXIII, 331.—Cf. "Hi sunt magistri nostri (sc. Petrus et Paulus), qui a magistro omnium vias vitae plenius didicerunt et docent nos usque in hodiernum diem. Quid ergo docuerunt vel docent nos apostoli sancti? Non piscatoriam artem . . . non Platonem legere, non Aristotelis versutias inversare, non semper discere et nunquam ad veritatis scientiam pervenire. Docuerunt me vivere. Putas, parva res est scire vivere? Magnum aliquid, imo maximum est" (*In Festo SS apost. Petri et Pauli*, Sermo I, 3; P.L., CLXXXIII, 407).

[79] ST. BERNARD, *De diversis*, Sermo XL, 1; P.L., CLXXXIII, 647.

[80] *Dilectionem*, in the sense of love of God. *Dilectio* is opposed in St. Bernard to carnal love—a terminology become classical since St. Augustine and codified by Isidore of Seville, *Etymol.*, VIII, 2, 7: "Omnis autem dilectio carnalis non dilectio sed magis amor dici solet" (Ed. W. M. Lindsay, Oxford, 1911, *ad loc*).

[81] ST. BERNARD, *De diversis*, Sermo CXXI; P.L., CLXXXIII, 743. The Benedictine conception of the monastic life as *schola Christi* is not the exclusive property of St. Bernard or even of the Cistercian school; it may be found in other Benedictines (for example in John the Man of God, in Dom A. WILMART, *Auteurs spirituels ex textes dévots du moyen âge latin*, Paris, Bloud et Gay, 1932, p. 95, l. 38); it is familiar, outside the Order, to St. Peter Damian and many others; it is none the less true that it is an intregal part of the Cistercian doctrine and there underwent a remarkably thorough elaboration.

[82] WILLIAM OF SAINT-THIERRY, *Epistola aurea*, I, 2; P.L., CLXXXIV, 309–310. William moreover knows exactly against whom the Cistercian

schools should set up their school of charity: that is to say against those literary
schools that teach the art of love according to Ovid. This latter proclaimed
himself the master of the art of loving:

> Sed quicumque meo superarit Amazona ferro
> Inscribat spoliis "Naso magister erat".
>
> (Ars Amatoria, II, 743–744.)

One of William's fundamental theses is that the only true master of the
art of loving is, not this pagan Ovid so eagerly devoured in the schools, but
Nature, and God, Who is the Author of nature. The whole opening of his
De natura et dignitate amoris is a vindication of the rights of Christian love
against pagan love, and of the schools of charity against the schools of letters.
Cf. the opening assertion: "Ars est artium ars amoris, cujus magisterium ipsa
sibi retinuit natura, et Deus auctor naturae" (op. cit., I, 1; P.L., CLXXXIV,
379 C), and the allusion which follows: "doctor artis amatoriae . . ." (I, 2;
381 A), which evidently points to Ovid. This whole critique of the Ars
Amatoria is so clearly and fully developed that William's intention is quite
unmistakable. According to the picturesque and definitive expression of its
ancient editor: "Est alius ejusdem liber De natura et dignitate amoris quem
secundum ipsius materiam: Anti-Nasonem possumus appellare" (P.L.,
CLXXXIV, 363–364). The thing is evident to readers of the text, and
Mabillon took the trouble to point it out. History, however, seems hardly
to have considered a fact so important for any due appreciation of the
humanist background of Cistercian mysticism.

⁸³ WILLIAM OF SAINT-THIERRY, Epist. aurea, I, 2, 5; P.L., CLXXXIV,
311.—For the "vacare Deo", op. cit., I, 4, 10; 314 A.

⁸⁴ Op. cit., I, 7, 18; P.L., CLXXXIV, 320. Cf. I, 13–14, 41–42; P.L.,
CLXXXIV, 334–335.

⁸⁵ "Haec est specialis caritatis schola, hic ejus studia excoluntur, disputa-
tiones agitantur, solutiones non ratiocinationibus tantum, quantum ratione
et ipsa rerum veritate et experientia terminantur" (WILLIAM OF SAINT-
THIERRY, De nat. et Dig. amoris, IX, 26; P.L., CLXXXIV, 396).

⁸⁶ "Fons siquidem vitae caritas est; nec vivere animam dixerim, quae de
illo non hauserit. Haurire porro quomodo potest, nisi fuerit praesens ipsi
fonti qui caritas est, quae Deus est? Praesens igitur Deo est qui Deum amat,
inquantum amat" (ST. BERNARD, De praecepto et dispensatione, XX, 60;
P.L., CLXXXII, 893).—Cf. "quia habet te quis, inquantum amat te"
(WILLIAM OF SAINT-THIERRY, De contemplando Deo, VIII, 16; P.L.,
CLXXXIV, 376 A).—Both here move in the circle of ideas familiar to ST.
AUGUSTINE, Sermo XXIII, VII, 7–VIII, 8; P.L., XXXVIII, 158–159.

⁸⁷ The word asceticism is always used, in this exposition, in the sense of
bodily mortification. The word ascesis is used in the sense of voluntary and
systematic discipline of mind and will.

⁸⁸ "Praesens igitur Deo est qui Deum amat, in quantum amat. In quo
enim minus amat, absens profecto est. In eo autem minus Deum amare con-
vincitur, quod carnis adhuc necessitatibus occupatur. Illa vero circa corpus
occupatio quid est, nisi a Deo quaedam absentatio? Et absentatio quid, nisi
peregrinatio? Et peregrinamur ergo a Domino, et in corpore peregrinamur;
cujus nostra nimirum, et intentio praepeditur aerumnis, et curis caritas
fatigatur" (ST. BERNARD, De praecepto et dispensatione, XX, 60; P.L.,
CLXXXII, 893 A).—It might be objected that the soul is bound in duty
to love its body, not to despise its own flesh. True: but to love its own flesh
is to keep it in its proper place, in due order; under the dominion of the
mind. Who spares his flesh the better,—the Cistercian who mortifies to save
it, or the man we call carnal who condemns his own to eternal punishment?
(ST. BERNARD, In Psal. Qui habitat, Sermo X, 3; P.L., CLXXXIII, 222–
223). The natural necessity of loving the body is therefore always respected
by St. Bernard, all that he asks is that this love be duly ordered: "Diligat
anima carnem suam; sed multo magis suam ipsius animam servet" (loc. cit.,
222 D). Cf. De diversis, Sermo XXIII, 1; P.L., CLXXXIII, 600. Pro
dominica 1 Novembris, Sermo II, 2; P.L., CLXXXIII, 347.

⁸⁹ M.-J. FESTUGIÈRE, *L'idéal religieux des Grecs et l'Evangile*, Paris, J. Gabalda, 1932, pp. 23-24.—E. GILSON, *L'esprit de la philosophie médiévale* (deuxième série), Ch. I. (English translation, Chap. XI)—The history of Christian Socratism ought to be written; see, for example, ORIGEN, *Comm. in Cant. Cant.*, lib. 88; edit. Baehrens, p. 146, 12-150, 22. (Cf. ROUËT DE JOURNEL, *Enchir. Ascet.*, pp. 62-63.) St. Bernard goes so far as to connect this theme with the teaching of St. Paul, who certainly had no thought of it. His reasoning runs thus: St. Paul teaches that God is to be known from His creatures; He can be known then so much the better from the creature that resembles Him the most, that is to say man made to His image; and that is why man must know himself if he wishes to know his Author (ST. BERNARD, *De diversis*, Sermo IX, 2; P.L., CLXXXIII, 566).

⁹⁰ Cf. WILLIAM OF SAINT-THIERRY, *De natura corporis et animae*, Prolog., P.L., CLXXX, 695-696: "Fertur celebre apud Graecos Delphici Apollinis responsum: 'Homo, scito teipsum. Hoc, et Salomon, imo Christus in Canticis: 'Si non, inquit, cognoveris te, egredere'" (Cant. I). William here presents us with a curious instance of the convergence of the Greek and the Biblical traditions. We know, moreover, from what source he draws, since he is the author of the compilation extracted from St. Ambrose: *Commentarius in Cantica Canticorum e scriptis sancti Ambrosii a Guillelmo, quondam abbate sancti Theodorici, postea monacho Signiacensi, collectus* (P.L., XV, 1947-2060). The whole doctrine of self-knowledge, which I have elsewhere called *Christian Socratism*, and which is of considerable importance in St. Bernard, William, Hugh and Richard of Saint-Victor, is developed at length by St. Ambrose in his commentary *In Ps. CXVIII*, Sermo II, 13-14, P.L., XV, 1278-1279: the oracular utterance of Delphi was stolen from Moses, who had said as much in *Deut.*, XV, 9; whence the commentary of the C.C., I, 7: "Nisi noscas te. . . ." (cf. *op. cit.*, Sermo X, 10-16; col. 1402-1406); man must learn to know himself in his greatness, as one who is made to the image of God. The same theme is developed in the *Liber de Isaac et Anima*, cap. IV, 11-16; P.L., XIV, 533-535, always in connection with the Canticle of Canticles. William collected these texts in his Ambrosian compilation: *In C.C.*, cap. I, 33-38; P.L., XV, 1959-1962. We may add other texts of ST. AMBROSE, *Hexaemeron*, VI, 39; XIV, 271-272. VIII, 50: "Cognosce ergo te, decora anima, quia imago Dei es . . ." (*ibid.*, col. 277-278). Such a text has only to be compared with those cited by P. Festugiere (preceding note) to reveal one of the essential differences between Christian Socratism and Greek Socratism. The Greeks say: Know thyself that thou may'st know that thou art not a god, but only a mortal. The Christians say: Know thyself that thou may'st know thyself a mortal, but the image of a God.

⁹¹ ST. BERNARD, *De diversis*, Sermo XII, 2; P.L., CLXXXIII, 571 CD. We recognize in this text (n. I; C. 571 B) the invitation to cultivate the *Nosce teipsum* which Bernard heard in the Canticle of Canticles: "Si ignoras te, O pulchra inter mulieres, egredere, et abi post greges sodalium tuorum" (*Cant. I, 7*).

⁹² ST. BENEDICT, *Regula*, VII, ed. B. Linderbauer, pp. 27-28; commented by St. Bernard, *De gradibus humilitatis*, cap. I; P.L., CLXXXII, 941-942.

⁹³ ST. BENEDICT, *Regula*, cap. VII: *De humilitate*, ed. B. Linderbauer, pp. 27-31.—ST. BERNARD, *De gradibus humilitatis*, cap. I, 1; P.L., CLXXXII, 941 C: "Locuturus ergo de gradibus humilitatis quos beatus Benedictus non numerandos sed ascendendos proponit. . . ." This treatise, the first of the great works of St. Bernard, is an ascetic commentary on Chapter VII of the Rule. It will be noticed that the practice of humility includes the training of the whole man, body and soul. That is how it came about that, with a view to facilitate knowledge of self, of which humility is the first stage, a Cistercian was moved to write what amounts to a treatise of anatomy according to the science of the time (see WILLIAM OF SAINT-THIERRY, *De natura corporis et animae*, P.L., CLXXX, 695-726). (Cf. ST. AMBROSE, *Hexaemeron*, lib. VI, cap. 9; P.L., XIV, 280-288.) It is a compilation (as the author avows) of texts taken from old writers: philosophers, physicians,

Fathers of the Church, which should serve for commentary on the Delphic oracle: "Scito te ipsum" (Prolog., opening). Mabillon had already noted this (P.L., CLXXXIV, 363-364).

⁹⁴ Humility is necessary for the attainment of truth because it corresponds to the truth about ourselves; and the truth about our miserable state teaches us charity because it opens our eyes to the misery of our neighbour (ST. BERNARD, *De gradibus humilitatis*, I, 1; P.L., CLXXXII, 941-942). (Cf. *op. cit.*, II, 3; c. 943, a text which expressly refers to the Rule of St. Benedict.) On the other hand, and still more directly, humility is charity because it consists in submission to the will of God, and therefore in union with that will and in the "common will" as by definition (St. BERNARD, *De diversis*, Sermo XXVI, 2: P.L., CLXXXIII, 610).

⁹⁵ ST. BERNARD, *De gradibus humilitatis*, I, 2; P.L., CLXXXII, 942. —Cf.: "Et quemadmodum ex notitia tui venit in te timor Dei, atque ex Dei notitia Dei itidem amor: sic e contrario de ignorantia tui superbia, ac de Dei ignorantia venit desperatio. Sic autem superbiam parit tibi ignorantia tui, cum meliorem quam sis, decepta et deceptrix tua cogitatio te esse mentitur" (*In Cant. Cant.*, Sermo XXXVII, 6; P.L., CLXXXIII, 973 C.)—*De moribus et officio Episc.*, V, 17-20; P.L., CLXXXII, 820-822.

⁹⁶ ST. BERNARD, *De gradibus humilitatis*, V, 16; P.L., CLXXXII, 950.

⁹⁷ ST. BERNARD, *Apologia*, XII, 28; P.L., CLXXXII, 915. Historians have made much of this aspect of St. Bernard's thought, and it is in fact important. But it has to be noted in the first place that St. Bernard had inherited this love of poverty from St. Stephen Harding (*Exordium magnum*, Dist. I, cap. 15; P.L., CLXXXV, 1011 A). This inexorable opposition to the architectural and liturgical luxury of the Cluniacs is sometimes dubbed "puritanism" (G. G. COULTON, *Five Centuries of Religion*, Vol. I, p. 300). The formula is tempting, but only on condition that it is taken in a sense so wide that it becomes vague. The "puritanism" of St. Bernard was prompted by motives that the authentic puritans would not all have recognized, for it is essentially a function of monastic poverty and the mystical life: "Denique quid haec ad pauperes, ad monachos, ad spirituales viros?" (ST. BERNARD, *Apologia*, XII, 28; P.L., CLXXXII, 915 D). It is somewhat amusing to note that even in this Chapter St. Bernard recollects Persius, *Sat.* II, 69. If there exists a Cistercian architecture, grand in its bareness and of great moment in the history of art, we owe it therefore, in the first place, to the Cistercian ideal of poverty (*Exordium magnum*, Dist. I, cap. 23; P.L., CLXXXV, 1018-1019), but quite as much to the spirit of mortification of sense which a life of contemplation involves. How rise above sense in the midst of so many sculptured images? The nudity of the Cistercian walls removes the sensible obstacles to meditation: "Tam multa denique, tamque mira diversarum formarum ubique varietas apparet, ut magis legere libeat in marmoribus quam in codicibus, totumque diem occupare singula ista mirando, quam in lege Dei meditando" (*Apologia*, XII, 29; P.L., CLXXXII, 916 B). Thus Cistercian architecture is all of a piece with Cistercian spirituality and by no means to be divorced from it.

The violent expressions of St. Bernard against the luxury of churches to the detriment of the poor have often led to misunderstanding on the part of certain historians who fall in with them elsewhere without being aware of their origin. Thus, S. Parkes CADMAN, *Christianity and the State* (N.Y., Macmillan, 1924), p. 109, rediscovers them in the writings of Wycliffe and declares that these lines contain the half of his programme. The two halves must have differed widely.

⁹⁸ ST. BERNARD, *In Cant. Cant.*, Sermo XXIII, 6; P.L., CLXXXIII, 887 A. Cf. GREGORY THE GREAT, *Moral.*, XXI, cap. 15, n. 22; P.L., LXXVI, 203.—ST. THOMAS AQUINAS, *In II Sent.*, Dist. 44, qu. I, art. 3, obj. I.

⁹⁹ ST. BERNARD, *De diligendo Deo*, cap. VIII, 93; P.L., CLXXXII, 987-988, which concludes thus: "Sic amor carnalis efficitur et socialis cum in commune protrahitur" (c. 988 C).

[100] ST. BERNARD, *De gradibus humilitatis*, III, 6; P.L., CLXXXII, 945,
—Cf. "Non ergo debet absurdum videri si dicitur Christum non quidem
aliquid scire coepisse quod aliquando nescierit, scire tamen alio modo miseri-
cordiam ab aeterno per divinitatem et aliter id tempore didicisse per carnem"
(*op. cit.*, n. 10, c. 946 D). It is necessary to emphasize in *didicisse* the force that
expresses the value attributed by St. Bernard to experiential knowledge. The
whole of this development is a commentary on *Isaiah*, LIII, 3; "virum dolorum,
et *scientem* infirmitatem. . . ." Cf. WILLIAM OF SAINT-THIERRY,
De natura et dignitate amoris, XI, 34; P.L., CLXXXIV, 401 B. This beautiful
text of William's, even if it was inspired by Bernard's, has a character which
is all its own; for its accent is very personal, and in the development of his
own doctrine it plays another part.

[101] *Op. cit.*, III, 12; P.L., CLXXXII, 948 AB.

[102] ST. BERNARD, *De diversis*, Sermo XXIX, 2–3; P.L., CLXXXIII,
620–621.—Cf. *In Cant. Cant.*, XX, 6; "Ego hanc arbitror praecipuam . . ."
&c. (P.L., CLXXXIII, 870–BC).—A passage of similar contents, but
different tone, may be found in WILLIAM OF SAINT-THIERRY, *De
contemplando Deo*, VI, 13; P.L., CLXXXIV, 374. St. Bernard's sermon is
probably later than the treatise, but how shall we know whether it was
suggested by it?

[103] ST. BERNARD, *In Cant. Cant.*, Sermo XLIII, 3; P.L., CLXXXIII,
994.—*De diversis*, Sermo XXIX, 4; P.L., CLXXXIII, 621.

[104] ST. BERNARD, *In Cant. Cant.*, Sermo XX, 6 and 8; P.L., CLXXXIII,
870 and 871. Note that this carnal love for Christ is excellent in itself (*ibid.*
9), and a great gift of the Holy Spirit (8). It is inferior to the others only because
of its connection with the animal nature through the sensibility. Its weakness
is evident in the fact that it does not suffice to itself, for if it is not ruled by
faith, which brings "prudence", it may very easily swerve aside (*De div.*,
Sermo XXIX, 4; P.L., CLXXXIII, 621).

[105] ST. BERNARD, *De diligendo Deo*, III, 7; P.L., CLXXXII, 978. Note
these manifestly mystical expressions: "in hortum introducta dilecti sponsa . . ."
". . . cordis thalamum frequenter libenterque (sponsus) ingreditur . . ."

[106] ST. BERNARD, *De diligendo Deo*, IV, 11; P.L., CLXXXII, 981;A.

[107] ST. BERNARD, *De diligendo Deo*, IV, 11–12; P.L., CLXXXII, 980–
981. On the relation of the *Jesu dulcis memoria* to the doctrine of St. Bernard,
see E. GILSON, *Les Idées et les lettres*, Paris, J. Vrin, 1932, pp. 39–57. The
editor of St. Bernard sees in the text of the *De diligendo Deo*, IV, p. 22, l. 15
—p.23, l. 2, "perhaps a tacit reference to the hymn *Jesu dulcis memoria*, which
we know now to be earlier than the time of St. Bernard" (p. 22, n. 16). The
fact is the other way round. This error as regards the date of the *Jesu dulcis
memoria* is the result of a series of quid pro quo's, the whole story of which
has been disentangled by M. Reginald VAUX, *Jesu dulcis memoria*, in *The
Church Quarterly Review*, April, 1929, pp. 120–125.

[108] ST. BERNARD, *De diligendo Deo*, IV, 13; P.L., CLXXXII, 981–982.

[109] ST. BERNARD, *In temp. Resurect.*, Sermo III, 3; P.L., CLXXXIII,
289–290. Hell, in fact is the "land of unlikeness" complete and fixed for
ever. Retaining the image of God, that is to say free-will, which is inalienable,
the damned have lost, beyond hope of recovery, the *libertas consilii* and the
libertas complaciti, that is, the Divine likeness. In other words they are eternally
fixed in their "proper willing", eternally excluded from the "common will"
with God, and, since this common will is charity, they are eternally excluded
from the substantial Charity which is God. Now God is beatitude; therefore
eternal "proper willing" is equivalent to eternal exclusion from beatitude,
and that is eternal misery: hell. For the bases of this doctrine see ST.
BERNARD, *De gratia et libero arbitrio*, IX, 30–31; P.L., CLXXXII, 1017–1018.

[110] P. ROUSSELOT, *Pour l'histoire du problème de l'amour au moyen âge*
(Baeumker-Beitrage, VI, 6), Münster i. W., 1908, p. 51.

[111] *Op. cit.*, pp. 51–52.

[112] ST. BERNARD, *De diligendo Deo*, XIV, 38; P.L., CLXXXII, 998 A.
Cf. P. ROUSSELOT, *op. cit.*, p. 52.

[113] ST. BERNARD, *De diligendo Deo,* IX, 26–X, 27; P.L., CLXXXII, 989–990.—Cf. *op. cit.,* XV, 39; 998 D: "et nescio si a quoquam hominum quartus (gradus) in hac vita perfecte apprehenditur, ut se scilicet diligat homo tantum propter Deum."

[114] I do not believe that St. Bernard had any real hesitation on this point. In any event his position is clear in the Sermons on the Canticle of Canticles: "At talis visio non est vitae praesentis, sed in novissimis reservatur, his dumtaxat qui dicere possunt: *Scimus quia cum apparuerit similes ei erimus, quia videbimus eum sicuti est* (I *John,* III, 2). Et nunc quidem apparet quibus vult; sed sicuti vult, non sicuti est. Non sapiens, non sanctus, non propheta videre illum, sicuti est, potest, aut potuit in corpore hoc mortali; poterit autem in immortali, qui dignus habebitur. Itaque videtur et hic, sed sicut videtur ipsi, et non sicuti est" (ST. BERNARD, *In Cant. Cant.,* Sermo XXXI, 2; P.L., CLXXXIII, 941). This very firm text should be adopted, it would seem, as a canon of interpretation for the rest. The rule is that sight of God in this life is not impossible, but that *no man* has ever seen Him "as He is". When these formulas are compared with the apparently contrary views expressed by St. Bernard as regards St. Benedict, it will be seen in effect that he attributes to the latter a knowledge of things in God, a mystical vision akin to that of the angels, and more than human, since it belongs to man to know God in things, not things in God. The "raptus" of St. Benedict consisted therefore in a brief "vision in God", which certainly supposes a certain sight of God, but not of God "*sicuti est*" (see *De diversis,* Sermo IX, 1; P.L., CLXXXIII, 565 CD). Similarly, when closely scrutinized, the text in which St. Bernard cites Moses, Philip, Thomas and David as having seen God, does not, in his terminology, imply that they saw Him as He is: *In Cant. Cant.,* Sermo XXXIII, 8–9; P.L., CLXXXIII, 949–950; and Sermo XXXIV, 1; where we see that even Moses obtained a far lower kind of vision of God than he looked for (*op cit.,* P.L., CLXXXIII, 959–960). We may therefore hold fast to this: that St. Bernard firmly refused to identify mystic union, even *raptus,* with the beatific vision.

[115] It was not given even to the saints of the Old Testament to enjoy the Divine presence "sicuti est, sed sicuti dignata est"; moreover: "haec demonstratio, non quidem communis, sed tamen foris facta est, nimirum exhibita per imagines extrinsicus apparentes, seu voces sonantes. Sed est divina inspectio, eo differentior ab his quo interior, cum per se ipsum dignatur invisere Deus animam quaerentem se, quae tamen ad quaerendum toto se desiderio et amore devovit" (ST. BERNARD, *In Cant. Cant.,* Sermo XXXI, 4; P.L., CLXXXIII, 942).—Cf. the precise formula which follows: "Non tamen adhuc illum dixerim apparere sicuti est, quamvis non omnino aliud hoc modo exhibeat quam quod est" (*ibid.* 7; 943 D). On the visions accorded to the Fathers of the Old Testament, cf. PSEUDO-DIONYSIUS, *Coel. hier.,* trad. J. Scot. Erigena, P.L., CXXII, 1047 BC.

[116] ST. BERNARD, *In Cant. Cant.,* Sermo XXXI, 2; P.L., CLXXXIII, 941.

[117] ST. BERNARD, *In Cant. Cant.,* Sermo XXXI, 3; P.L., CLXXXIII. 941 CD.

[118] *Op. cit.,* 3–4; 941 D–942 C.

[119] ST. BERNARD, *In Cant. Cant.,* Sermo XXIII, 9; P.L., CLXXXIII, 888–889. Cf. Sermo XXXI, 2; 941.

[120] ST. BERNARD, *De consideratione,* II, 3; P.L., CLXXXII, 745 D. Cf.: "Hodie legimus in libro experientiae. . . . hunc proprium experimentum . . . Audi expertum . . ." (*In Cant. Cant.,* Sermo III, 1; P.L., CLXXXIII, 794.—Sermo XXII, 2; 878–879). See J. SCHUCK, *Das religiöse Erlebnis beim hl. B. von Clairvaux,* pp. 23–24.

[121] The Holy Spirit, the bond of the Father and the Son, will therefore, in the doctrine of St. Bernard, be also the bond uniting the soul to God. He fulfils precisely the same function in William of Saint-Thierry, but does so in another manner. In the *De diligendo Deo* (XII, 35; P.L., CLXXXII, 996; really the *Epistola de caritate* addressed in the Carthusians in response to the *Meditationes* of Guigo I) St. Bernard bases his doctrine on the conception of the Holy Spirit as the law of the Divine life. William of Saint-Thierry, at the

I

time when he wrote his *De contemplando Deo*, was either as yet unacquainted with this doctrine, or preferred to follow a more direct route. He puts the problem thus: Jesus Christ willed that His disciples should be one in Him and in the Father, even as He and the Father are one (*John*, XVII, 21). Now the Father and the Son are one by the Holy Spirit. It is therefore by the Holy Spirit that we are enabled to enter into union with God. The solution then is evidently this: that in receiving the Holy Spirit under the form of a gift, namely the gift of grace, we thereby participate in the Divine Life; for, since the Holy Spirit dwells in us, the love of the Father for the Son, and of the Son for the Father dwells in us also. God therefore loves Himself then in us, our love for Him being nothing but the gratuitous gift of the love wherewith He loves Himself: "Tu te ipsum amas in nobis, et nos in te, cum te per te amamus, et in tantum tibi unimur, in quantum te amare meremur" (WILLIAM OF SAINT-THIERRY, *De contemplando Deo*, VII, 15; P.L., CLXXXIV, 375 B). Now this love of God for God is the Holy Spirit, and therefore God Himself; whence it follows that the gift of charity makes us of divine race (*Acts* XVII, 29), makes gods of us (*Ps.* LXXXI, 6), authorizes us to call God Father in virtue of this adoption, even as the Son calls God Father by right of His nature, and unites us to Him, not only by love but by beatitude (*op. cit.*, VIII, 16; 375 D), which is inseparable from love. William of Saint-Thierry therefore finds in the life of grace, gift of the Holy Spirit, the short way, the "compendium", which leads to the affective mystical experiences described in his treatise (IX, 20; 378 CD). In the absence of all certain chronological data which would enable us to correlate the works of William with those of Bernard, no hypothesis on their probable filiations can be put forward. In spite of the remarkable coincidence of the standpoints adopted I have been unable to detect the least trace of any influence of either on the other, whether in respect of reasoning or wording. Till proof to the contrary is forthcoming I remain convinced of their complete independence. Internal criticism would thus confirm the hypothesis of Dom. A. Wilmart which refers the composition of this treatise to the pre-Cistercian period of William's life (*art. cit.*, "Revue Mabillon", 1924, p. 166).

[122] ST. BERNARD, *De diligendo Deo*, XII, 35; P.L., CLXXXII, 996.— On the rôle of the Holy Spirit as bond: *In Cant. Cant.*, Sermo VIII, 4; P.L., CLXXXIII, 811–812. The translation in the text is that of E. G. GARDNER, *The Book of St. Bernard on the Love of God*, London, Dent, p. 121.

[123] ST. BERNARD, *De diligendo Deo*, XIII, 36; P.L., CLXXXII, 995–996. English translation substantially E. G. Gardner's.

[124] ST. BERNARD, *De diligendo Deo*, XIV, 37; P.L., CLXXXII, 997. Let us never lose sight of the ultimate foundations of the doctrine: (*a*) the image of God in us—free-will—still subsists; (*b*) the two-fold likeness to God in us—the *libertas consilii* and the *libertas complaciti*—have been lost (*De gratia et libero arbitrio*, IX, 31; P.L., CLXXXII, 1018 B); (*c*) the image, although still subsistent, has been defiled and defaced by sin, and would remain so for ever were it not for the grace of Jesus Christ (*op. cit.*, X, 32; 1018 C); grace helps man to recover the two lost liberties and consequently also the Divine likeness (*op. cit.*, X, 34; 1019). If we compare this conclusion with the doctrine of the *De diligendo Deo*, they mutually light up each other. If the whole problem of the mystical life consists in making our own the law of God, Who is Charity, it is clear that it equally consists in endeavouring to wipe away the stains on the divine image, since this is not to be done without exchanging our own will for the common will, or charity. The doctrine of the renewal of the image in perfect likeness is altogether one with the doctrine of liberty; both aim at the goal of mystical union, while expecting the beatific vision.

[125] Here once more William of Saint-Thierry rejoins St. Bernard, but by such independent ways that it can hardly be supposed that he was under his influence on this point. In any event he knew how to preserve his originality intact. His position may be briefly summarized thus: (*a*) Like naturally desires its like; man therefore, created to the image of God, naturally loves God, and inasmuch as His image shines forth in man, God loves man (*De*

nat. et dign. amoris, II, 3; P.L., CLXXXIV, 382 BC). (*b*) To this Christian application of a Greek principle there is added an Augustinian thesis, playing a capital rôle in William that it does not play in Bernard: in the created image there is found the memory; corresponding to the Father, it is, as it were, the centre of the soul in which it generates reason (the Son), and the will (the Holy Spirit) proceeds from the one and the other(*loc. cit.*, 382 CD). (*c*) The starting point of mystical contemplation must therefore be an effort of recollection, seeking God where He resides, that is, in the memory, and where He is to be found as Charity (*De contemplando Deo*, the whole admirable mystical *De profundis* cf the Prooemium, 1–3; P.L., CLXXXIV, 365–367). (*d*) That is why the birthplace of love is God: in Him love is at home, a citizen, indigenous; but created in man by God and strengthened by grace, it is in us naturally, albeit received (*De nat. et dign. amoris*, II, 3; P.L., CLXXXIV, 382 B), so that it may be said, against Ovid, that there is but one master of the art of loving "natura, et Deus auctor naturae" (*op. cit.*, I, 1; 379 C). (*e*) This natural art, lost by the fall, has to be re-learnt; its re-education can be effected only by grace under one sole master, Jesus Christ; but not without the ministry of a man who reminds us of His lessons: "Amor ergo, ut dictum est, ab auctore naturae naturaliter est animae inditus; sed postquam legem Dei amisit, ab homine est docendus. Non est autem docendus, ut sit tanquam qui non sit; sed ut purgetur, et quomodo purgetur; et ut proficiat, et quomodo proficiat; ut solidetur, et quomodo solidetur, docendus est" (*op. cit.*, I, 2; 381 A; cf. VIII, 21; 398 A). (*f*) What therefore man has to do is step by step to recover awareness of this natural law, innate in his own being, and this he does by exploring the depths of his "memory", where this law remains written. We may therefore say that while the mysticism of St. Bernard is mainly based on a doctrine of freedom, that of William of Saint-Thierry rests especially on a doctrine of "memory", and is thus more closely affiliated with the Augustinian tradition than is that of St. Bernard.

[153] ST. BERNARD, *De gradibus humilitatis*, VII, 20; P.L., CLXXXII, 952 C.
[154] ST. BERNARD, *De grad. humilitatis*, VIII, 23; P.L., CLXXXII 954–955.—The Scriptural texts alleged are, in order, *Matt.*, VI, 9; *Ps.* CXVIII, 75; *Ps.*, CXXXII, 1; *Isa.*, XXIV, 16.
[155] ST. BERNARD, *De grad. humilitatis*, VIII, 24; P.L., CLXXXII, 955. Cf. *Job.*, XIV, 15.
[156] EXCESSUS.—A generic term signifying, in a general way, any exceeding of the limits of a state in order to attain another. To free oneself of one's passions is already an *excessus*. However, the word takes on a mystical sense only when it indicates the passage from a normal human state, even were this attained by the aid of grace, to a state that is more than human. The two most important *excessus* are, that which liberates man from his external senses (ecstasy properly so called), and that which takes him beyond thought itself (*abductio interioris sensus*).
We see therefore that strictly speaking, we should distinguish ecstasy from *excessus*, taken absolutely; but the terms are too closely connected to allow us always to observe the precaution.
EXTASIS.—A word rare in St. Bernard. He uses it, however, to designate the state in which the corporeal senses cease to exercise their functions. In this sense it belongs to the genus *excessus*. It is *excessus* which takes us out of external sensibility: "Proinde et ego non absurde sponsae extasim vocaverim mortem, quae tamen non vita, sed vitae eripiat laqueis" (*C.C.*, LII, 4; P.L , CLXXXIII, 1031).—If the *extasis* is complete it takes us out, not only of the external senses, but also of the internal sense. It is then identical with the *excessus mentis*.
[157] ST. BERNARD, *In Cant. Cant.*, Sermo V, 1–9; P.L., CLXXXIII, 798–802.
[158] ST. BERNARD, *In Cant. Cant.*, Sermo VI, 1; P.L., CLXXXIII, 803.
[159] ST. BONAVENTURE, *Itinerarium mentis in Deum*, Prolog. 3–4; ed. minor, Quaracchi, 1911, pp. 201–202.

¹⁶⁰ ST. BERNARD, *In Cant. Cant.*, Sermo VIII, 8; P.L., CLXXXIII, 814.
¹⁶¹ *"Osculetur*, inquit, *me osculo oris sui (Cant.*, I, 1). Quis dicit? Sponsa. Quaenam ipsa? Anima sitiens Deum" (ST. BERNARD, *In Cant. Cant.*, Sermo VII, 2; P.L., CLXXXIII, 807 A).—By this thirst for God we must further understand an absolute contempt for all that is not God, and the desire, excluding all other feelings, to be united to Him. Cf. *In Cant. Cant.*, Sermo LXXIV, 3; P.L., CLXXXIII, 1140 A. Sermo LXXXV, 12; 1194 A.
¹⁶² ST. BERNARD, *In Cant. Cant.*, Sermo VII, 2; P.L., CLXXXIII, 807 C.
¹⁶³ ST. BERNARD, *In Cant. Cant.*, Sermo VIII, 2–3; P.L., CLXXXIII, 811–812.
¹⁶⁴ EBRIETAS, EBRIA.—The state of a soul inflamed with such love that, forgetting her fear and reverence for God, she dares to long for the kiss of the mystic union.
"Quid enim? Respicit (Deus) terram et facit eam tremere *(Ps.* CIII, 32) et ista (anima) se ab eo postulat osculari! Ebriane est? Ebria prorsus. Et forte tunc, cum ad ista prorupit, exierat de cella vinaria. . . ." *(In Cant. Cant.*, Sermo VII, 3; P.L., CLXXXIII, 807).
¹⁶⁵ ST. BERNARD, *In Cant. Cant.*, Sermo VII; P.L., CLXXXIII, 808; see especially *op. cit.*, IX, 2; 815–816.
¹⁶⁶ ST. BERNARD, *In Cant. Cant.*, Sermo VIII, 4; P.L., CLXXXIII, 811–812.
¹⁶⁷ ST. BERNARD, *In Cant. Cant.*, Sermo VIII, 6; P.L., CLXXXIII, 812–813.
¹⁶⁸ See above, p. 232, note 89.
¹⁶⁹ Since the Cistercian mysticism is sometimes accused of pantheistic tendencies, it will not perhaps be superfluous to note that it consists in a full development in us of the life of grace. Now grace is not God save in the sense that it is a "gift" of God. The distinction is strongly marked in St. Bernard between God, Who is substantial Charity, and grace, a quality of charity. The metaphysical gulf between God, Who is Charity, and man, who receives a created charity, is therefore clearly delineated: "Dicitur ergo rectae et charitas, et Deus, et Dei donum. Itaque caritas dat caritatem, substantiva accidentalem. Ubi dantem significat, nomen substantiae est; ubi donum qualitatis" (ST. BERNARD, *De diligendo Deo*, XII, 35; P.L., CLXXXII, 996).—William of Saint-Thierry has the same distinction expressed in very similar terms: "Quidquid de Deo potest dici, potest dici et de caritate; sic tamen ut, considerata secundum naturas doni et dantis, in dante nomen sit substantiae, in dono qualitatis" (WILLIAM OF SAINT-THIERRY, *De nat. et dignit. amoris*, V, 12; P.L., CLXXXIV, 587–588). Since the two works are almost contemporary we cannot tell here, any more than we can elsewhere, whether the coincidence indicates an influence, or in which direction such influence went.
¹⁷⁰ Cf. Marg. SMITH, *An Introduction to the History of Mysticism*, S.P.C.K., 1930.—There is no question here of denying the existence of poetic sentiments corresponding, on quite another plane, of course, to the mystic states. But there we have something very different, and not to be termed mystical without radical impropriety.
¹⁷¹ ST. BERNARD, *De diligendo Deo*, X, 28; P.L., CLXXXII, 991 B.
¹⁷² ST. BERNARD, *loc. cit.*
¹⁷³ ST. BERNARD, *De gratia et libero arbitrio*, XIV, 49; P.L., CLXXXII, 1027 D.
¹⁷⁴ Numerous references to the use of this phrase may be found in W. W. WILLIAMS, *ed. cit.*, p. 50, note 1.
¹⁷⁵ ST. BERNARD, *In Cant. Cant.*, Sermo LXXI, 9–10; P.L., CLXXXIII, 1125–1126. The lines inscribed for the epigraph of this book are taken from this text.
¹⁷⁶ See on this point A. HARNACK, *Lehrbuch der Dogmengeschichte*, Vol. III, p. 342.
¹⁷⁷ "Ille autem qui idem ipse est, qui dixit: *Ego sum qui sum (Exod.*, III 14), veraciter est, cui est esse quod est. Quae ergo participatio, quae convento,

illius qui non est ad illum qui est? Quomodo possunt tam diversa conjungi? *Mihi*, ait sanctus, *adhaerere Deo bonum est* (*Ps.*, LXXII, 28). Immediate ei conjungi non possumus, sed per medium aliquod poterit fieri fortassis ista conjunctio" (ST. BERNARD, *De diversis*, Sermo IV, 2–3; P.L., CLXXXIII, 552 CD).—For the formula which follows see *ibid.*, 553 A. The source of the formula is evidently St. Paul, 1 *Cor.*, VI, 17: "Qui autem adhaeret Domino, unus spiritus est." This text alone would have sufficed to determine one of the fundamental positions of the Cistercian mysticism; love alone is capable of establishing between God and man the unity of spirit which is the term of the spiritual life. Let us add that the Pauline text was an irresistible invitation to Bernard to comment on the Canticle of Canticles in this sense. St. Paul (1 *Cor.*, VI, 16) compares carnal union of man and wife with spiritual union: the Canticle then could be interpreted in the same way. It happened, on the other hand, as we have already seen, that Cicero had described friendship as the sentiment which makes of two minds one (see Chapter I, p. 12). Bernard therefore had a double reason for seeing in love the principle of the spiritual unification of the creature with the Creator.

[178] I say the manner in which they are linked up, not the mere fact that they are so. William of Saint-Thierry equally links up the mystical union with image of God in man, but his doctrine is rather a description of the manner in which the "memory" of God, obliterated by sin, is gradually recovered by the soul. The likeness is restored in two different ways in the two doctrines, because it is not situated exactly at the same point. In St. Bernard it lies in a good use of free-will, and the restoration effected is therefore essentially the restoration of liberty. In William it is especially in the Augustinian "memory" of God, which gives birth to reason; therefore the restoration of the obliterated image consists in recalling the presence of God. Each doctrine reaches the same conclusions and leaves room for all the essentials of the other, but each travels by its own particular route.

[179] Père ROUSSELOT, *Pour l'histoire du problème de l'amour au moyen âge*, pp. 53–54. It is of great interest to read these two pages closely, for their author never ceases to correct himself line by line, and lastly corrects the whole text by a note (p. 53, note 1), which contains the essential elements of the solution. Père Rousselot clearly sees that St. Bernard speaks of an annihilation and that nevertheless the individual personality, which *seems* an obstacle to the mystic union, is carefully safeguarded. Further, if "the undoing of souls is their state of perfection" (p. 54, note) it is because what is undone in them is unlikeness. Père Rousselot puts his finger on the true reply when he writes, "that amounts to saying that one cannot fully possess God without fully possessing oneself, and that this *proprium* that has to be got rid of in order to arrive at the perfection of love, is not the natural appetite, but a solicitude that impedes, contracts and restrains the natural appetite" (p. 53, note 1). True, and if Père Rousselot had reconstructed the whole book on this basis, many of the contradictions he believed himself to have discovered would at once have vanished. They were, in large measure, of his own making.

[180] The destruction of the false ego by love is certainly what St. Bernard would express in the text we are analyzing and are about to cite. Père Rousselot moreover (*op. cit.*, p. 66) has the credit of pointing out a text of St. Augustine's which shows that St. Bernard has simply followed up his indications on this important point. The text is so much the more significant inasmuch as Augustine is commenting on the Canticle of Canticles, VIII, 6; "Valida est sicut mors dilectio." Here is the passage: "Propterea viribus ejus (*sc.* mortis) caritas comparata est, et dictum est, *valida est sicut mors dilectio*. Et quia ipsa caritas occidit quod fuimus, ut simus quod non eramus, fecit in nobis quamdam mortem dilectio" (ST. AUGUSTINE, *Enarr. in Ps. CXXXI*, 12; P.L., XXXVII, 1628). We must carefully distinguish the idea of *death*, in the sense of destruction of the *proprium*, or unlikeness, from the idea of *languor*, the state of the lover in the absence of the beloved, and from the idea of the *invincibility* of love, which involves for man, or even for God, an overthrow which should rather be considered as a triumph. P. Rousselot

seems to have considered these ideas as flowing from each other (pp. 66–67), but in fact they correspond to states of spiritual life which are essentially distinct or even opposed.

[181] Père Rousselot very clearly sees that thus it must be in St. Bernard: "There is no longer any *suum*, the being is emptied of itself; the man who loves God is carried away into the very centre of all; he has no longer any other inclinations save those of the absolute spirit; he must needs in any event love what is better; he has become identified with the pure Reason" (*op. cit.*, p. 70). Let us leave on one side a terminology that makes of the *Deus charitas* a Pure Reason; that is a detail. What is important is to see what is meant by *suum*. If you are imprudent enough to understand it as involving the very personality of the ecstatic, you are led, like. P. Rousselot, to set up the "Graeco-Thomist" conception of love in strong opposition to the "ecstatic", and moreover to destroy the unity of Cistercian thought. If what is eliminated is only the false *suum*, that of unlikeness, then it follows at once that the most ecstatic of loves excludes neither the subsistence of the part as part, nor the inclusion of the love that the part bears itself in that which it bears to the whole. The soul then loves itself only for God's sake. What needs to be added is that in this case the words *part* and *whole* are equivalent to *image* and *original*, a remark that avails equally for St. Thomas and for St. Bernard. The opposition proposed to be set up between the two schools on this point entails, as a first consequence, the ruin of the coherence of both; their differences are real, but they lie elsewhere, and moreover are incomparably less deep-seated than that would amount to.

[211] This is the famous doctrine of *cupiditas ordinata*, so dear to the heart of Fénelon; but what does it mean? We must scrutinize the inner significance of the chief words involved:

ORDINATUS, ODINARE.—The affections are ordered when they follow each other in the order that favours the attainment of our last end. Their order then should be: fear, joy, sadness, love.—"Ordinantur autem sic. In initio timor, deinde laetitia, post tristitia, in consummatione amor. Compositio quarum talis est. De timore et laetitia nascitur prudentia, et est timor causa prudentiae, laetitia, fructus. De tristitia et amore nascitur fortitudo, et est, tristitia causa fortitudinis, amor fructus. Clauditur circulus coronae. De amore et timore nascitur justitia, et est timor causa justitiae, amor fructus" (ST. BERNARD, *De diversis*, Sermo L, 2; P.L., CLXXXIII, 673). The doctrine means therefore that cupidity is evil if not preceded by fear of God. It is evil because it does not tend to lead us to our end. If, on the contrary, fear precedes it, then it becomes good because it becomes love.

The ordering of the affections is moreover closely akin to their "purgation". See the following expressions:

PURGATUS, PURGARE.—The purgation of the affections consists in referring them to their appointed end. Love what ought to be loved, and love more what ought to be loved more; fear what ought to be feared, and fear more what ought to be feared more, &c.

"Sunt autem affectiones istae quatuor notissimae, amor et laetitia, timor et tristitia. . . . Purgantur autem sic. Si amantur quae amanda sunt, si magis amantur quae magis amanda sunt, si non amantur quae amanda non sunt, amor purgatus erit. Sic et de caeteris" (*De diversis*, Sermo L, 2; P.L., CLXXXIII, 673).

[212] St. Bernard here moreover places himself in direct opposition with one of Abelard's theses condemned in 1140 at the Council of Sens. In accordance with the spirit of his doctrine (see Appendix, p. 158) Abelard taught: "Quod etiam castus timor excludatur a futura vita" (see in P. RUF and M. GRABMANN, *Ein neuaufgefundenes Bruchstück der Apologia Abaelards*, Munich, 1930, p. 10, 1. 24-25). Cf. J. RIVIERE, *Les "capitula" d'Abélard*, Recherches de théologie ancienne et médiévale, V (1933), p. 17.

[213] The most important text on this point is the fully developed meditation to be found in *In Cant. Cant.*, Sermo XXIII, 11-16; P.L., CLXXXIII,

890–893. It proceeds entirely on the mystical plane, not, that is to say, by way of simple "consideration", but of "contemplation" properly so-called (see, as to meaning of these terms, *De consideratione*, Lib. II, cap. 5; P.L., CLXXXII, 745. *In Cant. Cant.*, Sermo LII, 5; P.L., CLXXXIII, 1031). It consists therefore of a series of glimpses, of intuitive certitudes, putting the soul in the presence of facts which it intuitively grasps. These are in order: 1. Providence: God as the ordering power of the universe: "et locus iste altus et secretus, sed minime quietus" (*loc. cit.*, 11); 2. God as justiciary: the place of fear and trembling (*loc. cit.*, 13). This place is higher than the first because there God teaches, here He touches; the first is an *acessus* to wisdom, the second is an *ingressus* thereto, for wisdom begins with the "feeling" (*affectio*) of God (*loc. cit.*, 14); 3. From fear of judgment the soul throws itself upon certitude of mercy, of non-imputation of sin: "Omne quod nihi ipse non imputare decrevit, sic est quasi non fuerit" (*op. cit.*, 15; see on this point p. 242, note 217). The soul is then wholly filled with (*a*) full confidence in its own salvation (*fiducia*); (*b*) an infused joy, outweighing in sweetness the foregoing fears; (*c*) a devotion "quod non est aliud nisi concepta de spe indulgentiae exultatio" (*op. cit.*, 15); (*d*) peace, finally, supervening on the flight of all doubts: "visio ista . . . inquietam curiositatem non excitat, sed sedat; nec fatigat sensus, sed tranquillat. Hic vere quiescitur. Tranquillus Deus tranquillat omnia" (*op. cit.*, 16). Cf. *In Cant. Cant.*, Sermo XVI, 7; P.L., CLXXXIII, 851–852; Sermo VI, 8–9; 806—*De diversis*, Sermo XVI, 7; P.L., CLXXXIII, 582–583.

214 ST. BERNARD, *De diligendo Deo*, VII, 17; P.I.., CLXXXII, 984–985.

215 This inevitable alternation of ecstasy and languor is therefore at the opposite pole to pure love. St. Bernard calls it:

VICISSITUDO.—Alternate presences and absences of the Bridegroom, due to the fact that the soul is united to a non-glorified body.

"Ergo si cui nostrum cum sancto propheta adhaerere Deo bonum est (*Ps.*, LXXII, 28), et, ut loquar manifestius, si quis in nobis est ita desiderii vir, ut cupiat dissolvi et cum Christo esse, cupiat autem vehementer, ardenter sitiat, assidue meditetur; is profecto non secus quam in forma Sponsi suscipiet Verbum in tempore visitationis, hora videlicet qua se astringi intus quibusdam brachiis sapientiae, atque inde sibi infundi senserit sancti suavitatem amoris. Siquidem desiderium cordis ejus tribuetur ei, etsi adhuc peregrinanti in corpore, ex parte tamen, idque ad tempus, et tempus modicum. Nam cum vigiliis, et obsecrationibus, et multo labore et imbre lacrymarum quaesitus adfuerit, subito dum teneri putatur elabitur; et rursum lacrymanti et insectanti occurrens, comprehendi patitur, sed minime retineri, dum subito iterum quasi e manibus evolat. Et si institerit precibus et fletibus devota anima, denuo revertetur, et voluntate labiorum ejus non fraudabit eam; sed rursum mox disparebit, et non videbitur, nisi iterum toto desiderio requiratur. Ita ergo et in hoc corpore potest esse de praesentia sponsi frequens laetitia, sed non copia; quia etsi visitatio laetificat, sed molestat vicissitudo. Et hoc tandiu necesse est pati dilectam, donec semel posita corporeae sarcina molis, avolet et ipsa levata pennis desideriorum suorum, libere iter carpens per campos contemplationis, et mente sequens expedita dilectum quocumque ierit" (ST. BERNARD, *In Cant. Cant.*, Sermo XXXII, 2; P.L., CLXXXIII, 946).—

"Nunc vero constat in anima fieri hujusmodi vicissitudines euntis et redeuntis Verbi, sicut ait: *Vado et venio ad vos* (*John*, XIV, 28); item: *Modicum et non videbitis me; et iterum modicum et videbitis me* (*John*, XVI, 17). O modicum et modicum! O modicum longum!" (*op. cit.*, Sermo LXXIV, 4; P.L., CLXXXIII, 1140).

216 ST. BERNARD, *De diligendo Deo*, VII, 17; P.L., CLXXXII, 984 D. Père Rousselot saw hesitations of thought in this formula which in fact only indicate his own (*op. cit.*, p. 52). We cannot "with equal probability maintain either that Bernard condemned the desire to possess God as something opposed to the purity of love, or that he excepted this particular desire from his condemnations". Love is the *desire* to possess God, but pure love is the *possession* of God. There can be no question therefore of "condemning" this desire, but only of testifying that while it subsists love has not yet attained its term, and that when it attains it the desire of the term, *ipso facto*, disappears. St. Bernard consequently considers that the promise of reward is required in proportion as the love is not yet pure, that is to say where it has not yet been obtained. The spiritual life therefore is a perpetual alternation of hope of rewards (languor), of rewards (amor purus), of new desires and new rewards: "Praemium sane necdum amanti proponitur, amanti debetur, perseveranti redditur" (*loc. cit.*, 948 B). Obviously we are far from what Fénelon was to consider as an "habitual state of the righteous in this life", characterized by "a fully disinterested love sometimes called pure to express the fact that it is ordinarily excited by no other motive than a single-minded love of the Sovereign Goodness of God, in itself and for itself" (FÉNELON, *Explication des Maximes des saints sur la vie intérieure*, critical edition by Albert Chérel, Paris, Bloud, 1911, pp. 133 and 135). Fénelon talks of it at ease. Had he spoken otherwise than by hearsay he would never have dreamt of describing St. Bernard's ecstasy as a state.

²¹⁷ On the radical distinction between the non-imputation of sin according to St. Bernard on the one hand and Luther on the other, see the excellent remarks of W. W. Williams, to which I have nothing essential to add: *De diligendo Deo*, *ed. cit.*, p. 6. St. Bernard, says his editor, "has no notion of a mere forensic righteousness". It is the least that can be said, but it suffices.

²¹⁸ "To conclude, God's will is the sovereign object of the indifferent soul; wheresoever she sees it she runs after the odour of its perfumes, directing her course ever thither where it most appears, without considering anything else. She is conducted by the Divine will, as by a beloved chain; which way soever it goes, she follows it; she would prize hell more with God's will than heaven without it; nay she would even prefer hell before heaven if she perceived only a little more of God's good-pleasure in that than in this, so that if by supposition of an impossible thing she should know that her damnation would be more agreeable to God than her salvation, she would quit her salvation and run to her damnation" (ST. FRANCIS DE SALES, *Traité de l'amour de Dieu*. Bk. IX, Chap. IV. Translated by the Rev. H. B. Mackey, O.S.B. 3rd edn,, p. 375, London, Burns & Oates).—Cf. FÉNELON, *Explication des Maximes des saints*, edit. A. Chérel, pp. 136–138.

²¹⁹ "In truth there are many who take no delight in divine love unless it be candied in the sugar of some sensible sweetness, and they would willingly act like children, who, if they have a little honey spread upon their bread, lick and suck off the honey, casting the bread away; *for if the delight could be separated from the love*, they would reject love and take the sweetness only. Wherefore as they follow love for the sake of its sweetness, when they find not this they make no account of love" (ST. FRANCIS DE SALES, *Treatise on the Love of God*, Translated by the Rev. H. B. Mackey, O.S.B., London, Burns & Oates, 3rd edn., Bk. IX, Chap X, p. 392).—"Now, Theotimus, after the same manner it fares with a soul which is overcharged with interior anguishes, for although she has the power to believe, to trust, and to love her God, and in reality does so, yet she has not the strength to see properly whether she believes, hopes and loves, because her distress so engages her, and makes head against her so desperately, that she can get no time to return into her interior and see what is going on there. And hence she thinks that she has no faith, nor hope, nor charity, but only the shadows and fruitless impressions of those virtues, which she feels in a manner without feeling them, as if foreign instead of natural to her soul" (*op. cit.*, Bk. IX, Chap. XII, p. 395). —"Such then are the feelings of the soul which is in the midst of spiritual anguishes. These do exceedingly purify and refine love, for being deprived of all pleasure by which its love might be attached to God, it joins and unites us to God immediately, will to will, heart to heart, without any intervention of satisfaction or desire. Alas! Theotimus, how the poor heart is afflicted when being as it were abandoned by love, she seeks everywhere, and yet seems not to find it. She finds it not in the exterior senses, they not being capable of it; nor in the imagination, which is cruelly tortured by conflicting impres-

sions; nor in the understanding, distracted with a thousand obscurities of strange reasonings and fears; and though at length she finds it in the top and supreme region of the spirit where it resides, yet the soul does not recognize it, and thinks it is not love, because the greatness of the distress and darkness hinders her from perceiving its sweetness. She sees it without seeing it, meets it but does not know it, as though all passed in a dream only, or in a type. In this way Magdalen, having met with her dear Master, received no comfort from him, because she thought that it was not he indeed, but the gardener only" (*ibid.*, pp. 396–397).

220 This initial difference of standpoint explains why the citations from St. Bernard with which Fénelon so plentifully strews his writings are almost always given a sophistical twist. It is not done intentionally, but was simply bound to happen because pure love does not mean the same thing in the two doctrines. I would not intrude into the *hortus conclusus* where I have no right of access, but perhaps it is permissible to say that the spiritual life of Fénelon, and even the tenderness of a St. Francis de Sales, would have appeared to St. Bernard as nothing but permanent states of *languor*. That is the reason why, lacking the triumphant certainty that ecstasy alone can bring, the only means left to them to persuade themselves of the purity of their love lay in the acceptance of dryness. St. Francis de Sales himself relies only on *anguishes* to make love *pure* and *clear* (see p. 146); this pure love seems more like that of the courtly poets or of the *Astraea* than that of St. Bernard, for whom love is purified, not by dryness or languor, but by ardour.

221 "Exponit beatus Gregorius, quia amor ipse, notitia est" (ST. BERNARD, *De diversis*, Sermo XXIX, 1; P.L., CLXXXIII, 620 C). Cf. GREGORY THE GREAT, *Hom.* 27 *in Evang.*, P.L., LXXVI, 1207; "Dum enim audita supercaelestia amamus, amata jam novimus, quia amo ipse notitia est." Note moreover that Gregory, like Bernard, depends here on I *John*, IV, 7–8.

222 "Nam neque hoc luminare magnum (solem loquor istum, quem quotidie vides) vidisti tamen aliquando sicuti est, sed tantum sicut illuminat, verbi causa aerem, montem, parietem. Quod nec ipsum quidem aliquatenus posses, si non aliqua ex parte ipsum lumen corporis tui, pro sui ingenita serenitate et perspicuitate, coelesti lumini simile esset. Non denique alterum membrum corporis capax est luminis, ob multam utique dissimilitudinem. Sed nec ipse oculus cum turbatus fuerit, lumini propinquabit, nimirum ob amissam similitudinem. Qui ergo turbatus, nullatenus serenum solem videt propter dissimilitudinem, serenus aliquatenus videt propter nonnullam similitudinem. Profecto si pari prorsus puritate vigeret, videret omnino inoffensa acie eum sicuti est, propter omnimodam similitudinem. Ita et solum justitiae illum, qui illuminat omnem hominem venientem in hoc mundum, videre in hoc mundo, sicut illuminat, illuminatus potest, tanquam jam in aliquo similis; sicuti est, omnino non potest, tanquam nondum perfecte similis" (ST. BERNARD, *In Cant. Cant.*, Sermo XXXI, 2; P.L., CLXXXIII, 941).

223 This great good is that which St. Bernard sometimes designates in a single word, recalling that in virtue of this we are made to the image of God: DIGNITAS.—Emphatically, free-will. "Dignitatem in homine liberum arbitrium dico: in quo ei nimirum datum est non solum caeteris praeeminere, sed et praesidere animantibus" (*De diligendo Deo*, II, 2; P.L., CLXXXII, 976). Cf. *De gratia et libero arbitrio*, IX, 28; P.L., CLXXXII, 1016.

The expression is probably of Stoic origin. On the "pre-eminence" conferred on man by free-will, see CICERO, *De nat. deorum*, II, 11 (cited by W. W. WILLIAMS, *ed. cit.*, p. 11, note 15).

224 On the meaning of "recta" and "curva"—state of the soul which has lost the divine likeness and stoops to earth—see ST. BERNARD, *In Cant. Cant.*, P.L., CLXXXIII, 897–898.

225 Barton R. V. MILLS, *Saint Bernard. The Twelve Degrees of Humility and Pride*, London, Society for Promoting Christian Knowledge, 1929, Introduction, p. XIV.

226 The importance of these texts has been noticed by Ch. de REMUSAT, *Abélard*, Paris, 1845, t. II, pp. 424 et seq.; E. VACANDARD, *Abélard*, Paris,

I*

1881, pp. 297-303, and by Père ROUSSELOT, *Pour l'histoire du problème de l'amour au moyen âge*, pp. 72-74. One can but subscribe to the analysis of them given by this historian and to the conclusion drawn: "Abelard therefore curtails and suppresses as far as may be, all reasons for loving God which have their root in our *nature* and our *being*. His doctrine appears to me to be in strict contradiction with that we have seen to have been promulgated by St. Thomas: 'If God were in no wise man's good, man would have no reason to love God'" (*op. cit.*, p. 74).

[227] I allude here to the memory of Abelard which still tortured her long after their separation, and which a moralist would consider as a "cupidity" no longer able to achieve satisfaction. But Heloïse very cleverly parried the objection when she interpreted this ardour as a chastisement from God. It was not there for nothing.

[228] The interest of the passage has been strongly brought out by W. W. WILLIAMS, *De diligendo Deo, ed. cit.*, pp. 3-4. On p. 5 there are interesting remarks on the question whether, in the *De diligendo Deo*, St. Bernard is intentionally combating Abelard, notably on the problem of redemption. As I have already said (p. 166), I recognize an opposition between the two doctrines, but no sign of any refutation cf Abelard, even indirect, in the *De diligendo Deo*. Moreover Abelard's position on this matter was only fully defined in his Commentary on St. Paul (1136/40) which is almost certainly later than the *De diligendo Deo* (1127/41). It is more likely that the latter is combated by Abelard in the Commentary than vice versa.

[229] Good judges believe so. Ed. Wechssler points out that the activity of St. Bernard and Hugh of Saint-Victor began towards 1120-1130 and that towards the middle of the century there appeared the first great poets whose works contain mystical elements: Jaufré Rudel, Bernard de Ventadour, and Pierre Rogier: "Dieses Zusammentreffen war kein Zufall" (*Das Kulturproblem des Minnesanges . . .*, p. 243). No doubt; but the first thing we want to know is whether the meeting took place.

[230] We shall find an indispensable corrective for illusions of this kind in the admirably balanced pages of A. JEANROY, *La première génération des Troubadours*, in *Romania*, t. LVI, pp. 481-482.

[231] It is useless to insist on this obvious point. It has been developed well and at length by Ed. WECHSSLER, *Das Kulturproblem des Minnesangs. Studien zur Vorgeschichte der Renaissance*, Bd. I, Minnesang und Christentum. Halle a. S., Max Niemeyer, 1909. XI Kap. Minne und christlicher Spiritualismus, pp. 219-241.

[232] J. Anglade does not hide the fact: "Some are more precise in the expression of their desires; certain of their demands are remarkable for their naïveté, and sometimes for their crudity" (*Les Troubadours*, Paris, Colin, 1908, p. 82). He instances further on the partially sensual character of the conception of love in the Troubadour Cercamon (p. 101). Marcabrun is a "misogynist", and wrote ferocious satires against love (pp. 101-102). All this may be verified in the texts, many of them being now easily accessible. See in A. JEANROY, *Les Chansons de Guillaume IX, duc d'Aquitaine*, Paris, Champion, 1913: V, *Farai un vers . . .*, pp. 8-13; VI, *Ben vuelh . . .*, st. 5 and 6, pp. 14-15; his biographers describe him as a kind of Rabelais (p. IV). —W. P. SHEPARD, *Les poésies de Jausbert de Puycibot*, Paris, Champion, 1924; V, Jausbert, *razon ai adrecha*, st. 7 and 8, pp. 16-17.

[233] A. WALLENSKÖLD, *Les chansons de Thibaut de Champagne, roi de Navarre*, Paris, Champion, 1925. All the following citations in the text are taken from this edition.

[234] A. LÅNGFORS, A. JEANROY, and L. BRANDIN, *Recueil général des jeux-partis francais*, Paris, Champion, 1926, t. I, p. 39, v. 36.

[235] Even the poet of the *Princesse lointaine*, the ethereal Jaufré Rudel, makes himself understood by those who wish to understand him. Cf. A. JEANROY, *Les chansons de Jaufré Rudel*, Paris, Champion, 1915; Jaufré's dreams are as erotic as those of Thibaut de Champagne (I, 3, p. 2); if he ever attains his "*amour de terre lointaine*", he hopes that this will be "*dinz vergier o sotz cortina*"

(II, 2, p. 4; cf. V, 6, pp. 14–15), places one would think but little propitious to metaphysics (cf. p. VI, the just observations of M. Jeanroy against C. Appel, who believes this poem to be dedicated to the Virgin!); the famous "joy", occasionally compared with the mystical "gaudium", is of a very precise nature (III, 5, pp. 7–8). The least to be said of Chanson IV is that it is equivocal (st. 5–7, pp. 11–12), and throws a suspicious light on the poet's morals.—Cercamon is more brutal (A. JEANROY, *Les poésies de Cercamon*, Paris, Champion, 1922, IV, 7, pp. 13–14), showing no pity for husbands whom he treats as they do others; the song of dubious authorship, bound up with his works, whether by him or another, very clearly expresses what these poets expected of their love (VIII, 9, p. 29).—Peire Vidal is made of the same metal as Jaufré or Cercamon; when he fails in one country he goes off to another (J. ANGLADE, *Les poésies de Peire Vidal*, Paris, Champion, 2nd edn., 1923, VIII, pp. 19–23); his preference goes to the young Castilian ladies, whom he loves far better than the rich old women (VI, 6, pp. 15–16) or, as he says less amiably elsewhere, than a thousand camels laden with gold (XVI, 6, p. 49). This view of the matter may perhaps be defended, but if this is spirituality it is spirituality of a very modest type. Cf. XVII, 8, p. 55; XX, 2, pp. 62–63; XXXIX, 6, p. 124, XL, 5, p. 128. If half is true of what is reported of this fine talker, braggart, and scatterbrain (*op. cit.*, pp. 162–165) he could never have read much of the mystical writings of St. Bernard.

²³⁶ Thibaut de Champagne is here taken as our example, but the same thing can be verified from other texts. See A. LÅNGFORS, *Recueil général des jeux-partis français*, Paris, 1926, No. XX, t. I, pp. 20–22.—Like Thibaut, whom he cites, Jehan Bretel prefers beauty to intelligence (XXVII, 5, p. 100), and his interlocutors do not seem to be particular in the choice of their loves (XXXVI, t. I, pp. 133–135); but do not content themselves with words (XLVII, t. I, pp. 175–177). It would be superfluous to analyze from this standpoint a collection otherwise instructive enough but showing such a total absence of any kind of amoristic idealism. If there was a touch of Don Quixote in the Troubadours there was a good dose of Sancho Panza among the authors of these *jeux partis* of an Epicureanism so flatly bourgeois (CIV, t. II, pp. 18–20 (Lambert Ferri); CXIII, t. II, pp. 51–54 (Adam de la Halle). No one, not even among the monks, but loses his virtue (CXXVII, t. II, pp. 104–106) (Guillaume le Vinier).

²³⁷ The problem moreover has already been studied by Ed. WECHSSLER, *Das Kulturproblem des Minnesangs*, Ch. XIV, pp. 316–317. He cites in this connection the tripartite division of Guiraut de Calanson into (1) heavenly love, (2) natural love (of parents for children), (3) carnal love. M. Ed. Wechssler adds this other quadripartite division of Malfré Ermengaud: (1) love of God and the neighbour, (2) love of temporal goods, (3) love of man and woman, (4) love of children for parents. Assuredly these two divisions suppose an influence of Christianity on the thought of the poets, but that is a long way from establishing a connection between the thought of Guiraut and that of St. Bernard. For their tripartite divisions in no way correspond.

There exist, to our knowledge, four divisions of love in St. Bernard; two divisions into three, one into four, and one into five.

1. Divisions into three:
   (a) Amor dulcis, prudens, fortis (*De diversis*, Sermo XXIX, I; P.L., CLXXXIII, 620).
   (b) Carnalis rationalis, spiritualis (*C.C.*, XX, 9; P.L., CLXXXIII, 871–872).
2. Division into four (*by far* the most important):
   (1) Amor sui; (2) Amor Dei propter se; (3) Amor Dei propter ipsum; (4) Amor sui propter Deum tantum (*De dilig. Deo*, cap. VIII–IX; P.L., CLXXXII, 987–992).
3. Division into five:
   (1) Amor parentum; (2) Amor sociorum (socialis); (3) Amor generis humani (generalis); (4) Amor inimicorum (violentus); (5) Amor Dei (sanctus). These five kinds of love correspond to the five senses (*De diversis*, Sermo X, 2–4; P.L., CLXXXIII, 568–569).

The only tripartite division in Bernard which, to satisfy M. Anitchkof, could be compared with Guiraut's is the division 1 *a*. Now the two divisions are in no kind of relation with each other, for this simple reason, that Guiraut's is a division of love in general, while Bernard's is a division of divine love. We should read them therefore thus:

GUIRAUT		BERNARD	
	⎧ Heavenly		⎧ Carnal
Love	⎨ Natural	Heavenly love	⎨ Rational
	⎩ Carnal		⎩ Spiritual'

The two divisions therefore in no way correspond. In Guiraut Riquier, on the contrary, spiritual love is clearly affirmed, but we are then at the end of the thirteenth century, and J. Anglade has very justly remarked that the advent of religious love in the poetry of the Middle Ages marks the end of the age of the Troubadours (*Les Troubadours*, pp. 296–297); Guiraut Riquier comments on and refutes Guiraut de Calanson; he therefore tolls the knell of courtly love, and if it is desired to reckon among the proofs of the influence of mysticism on courtly love, it will have to be said that the influence consisted in making an end of it. This at least seems to be an almost incontrovertible assertion as far as concerns the Provençal and French literatures.

²³⁸ Jaufré RUDEL: "my fate is to love without being loved" (J. ANGLADE, *op. cit.*, p. 106). That alone is enough to exclude the hypothesis, once proposed, that the poem was addressed to the Virgin. The lamentations of the courtly poets over their unrequited loves are too continual to make it worth while to cite texts on the point.

²³⁹ The fear inseparable from courtly love (because it is never sure of return) is a commonplace traceable to Ovid, *Heroïdes*, I, 12:

> Res est solliciti plena timoris amor.

See on this point R. BOSSUAT, *Drouart la Vache, traducteur d'André-le-Chapelain* (1290), Paris, H. Champion, 1926, p. 75; and also, by the same author: *Le Livre d'Amours de Drouart la Vache*, H. Champion, 1926, p. 7, verses 213-218.

²⁴⁰ See the excellent analysis of the courtly doctrine by E. FARAL, *La Chanson Courtoise*, in J. BEDIER and P. HAZARD, *Histoire de la litterature francaise*, Paris, Larousse, 1923, t. I, pp. 44–46. Love as the source of virtue, the fruitfulness of suffering, and many other traits attest the influence of Christianity on this mode of feeling; but I do not touch this question which is much larger than that of the possible influence of Cistercian *mysticism*.

²⁴¹ On the part played by the *Sehnsucht*, see Ed. WECHSSLER, *Das Kulturproblem des Minnesangs*, pp. 252–253. The author is here inspired by E. Boutroux, a good philosopher, but clearly a mystic of secondary importance. For the rest there is something both good and bad about the description of mysticism given by E. Boutroux and Ed. Wechssler. This is not the place to discuss it, but we must at least remark that the very essence of Christian mysticism is missed by those who maintain with Ed. Wechssler that "The God of the mystic is not transcendent, but immanent" (*op. cit.*, p. 263). If God is immanent without being transcendent no mystical problem arises in the sense in which the Christians understand it. What they had to experience and to account for was, on the contrary, the immanence of a God Who is and remains transcendent. The passage from Christian mysticism to courtly love is very much simplified if you suppress the notion of divine transcendence; as soon as we recognize it, on the contrary, we see at once how inconceivable that passage is.

For the Augustinian definition of the *desiderium* see ST. AUGUSTINE, *Enarr. in Ps.* 118, VIII, 4; P.L., XXXVII, 1522. Cf. *Enarr. in Ps.* 62, 5; P.L., XXXVI, 750-751.

²⁴² Ed. WECHSSLER, *op. cit.*, pp. 253–256.

²⁴³ Ed. WECHSSLER, *op. cit.*, pp. 259–264.

²⁴⁴ *Ibid.*, p. 243.

²⁴⁵ I speak of the lyrical poets only, not of the authors of didactic works in

prose such as André-le-Chapelain, or of a poet like Dante who is the heir of all the theology of the thirteenth century. It may be pointed out that the testimonies accumulated by M. Wechssler are a very mixed collection. It is not difficult to prove the influence of mystical theology on Dante, but undeniable texts from Dante prove nothing as to the influence of theology on Jaufré Rudel, Bernard de Ventadour, or Chrétien de Troyes. These texts are not to be cited one after the other as if they all proved the same thing. The love Dante spoke of is no longer that of which the poets of courtly love had spoken; in him the spiritualization of love is an accomplished fact, and it is just because it is not so in the Troubadours or Trouvères that comparison of their works with those of St. Bernard is so full of pitfalls. Some people are in too much of a hurry; the questions involved should be properly classified and distinguished.

²⁴⁶ Ed. WECHSSLER, *op. cit.*, p. 313. These words open Chapter XIV, *Minne und Charitas.*

²⁴⁷ *Op. cit.*, pp. 315–316.

²⁴⁸ *Op. cit.*, p. 331.

²⁴⁹ On the incompatibility of love and marriage in the courtly poetry, see J. ANGLADE, *Les Troubadours*, pp. 95–96.—G. COHEN, *Chrétien de Troyes*, Paris, Boivin, 1931, pp. 224–225 and p. 562.
The problem is discussed, for and against, by Jehan Bretel: *Recueil général . . .*, LXVII, t. I, pp. 248–250.

²⁵⁰ Ed WECHSSLER, *op. cit.*, p. 269.

²⁵¹ *Op. cit.*, p. 317.

²⁵² *Op. cit.*, p. 321.

²⁵³ A. JEANROY, *Les origines de la poésie lyrique en France au moyen âge*, 3rd ed., Paris, Champion, 1925. On the meaning of the expression "poésie populaire", see *Introduction*, pp. XVI–XVII.

²⁵⁴ Ed. WECHSSLER, *op. cit.*, p. 321.

²⁵⁵ G. COHEN, *Chrétien de Troyes et son œuvre*, Paris, Boivin, 1931, pp. 223–225. M. G. Cohen notes, p. 223, although with some reserves, the moral tendencies of Chrétien's doctrine and his rehabilitation of marriage (p. 224). It will be observed that the poetry of this love ceases along with its "bourgeoisification by marriage", whereas on the contrary, for the Cistercian mystic, it is precisely in the marriage of the soul to the Word that poetry attains its fullest and most durable exaltation. Thus this moralization of courtly love brings it no nearer to Cistercian mysticism, where the spiritual nuptials know nothing of "bourgeoisification". It is precisely to avoid it that they would be spiritual.

²⁵⁶ The expression is M. Wechssler's, *op. cit.*, p. 328.

²⁵⁷ *Op. cit.*, p. 335. On the limited chastity of courtly love, see pp. 345–346.

²⁵⁸ *Op. cit.*, p. 376.

²⁵⁹ On the idea of grace, *op. cit.*, pp. 395–396.—On patience, p. 394.

²⁶⁰ See above, Chap. II, *Schola caritatis.*

²⁶¹ On the twelfth century as *aetas Ovidiana* see the very suggestive pages of Ch. H. HASKINS, *The Renaissance of the Twelfth Century*, Harvard Univ. Press, 1927, pp. 107–110.—The position then occupied by Ovid is very well marked by JOHN OF SALISBURY, *Metalogicon*, lib. III, cap. 8; edit. Cl. C. J. Webb, Oxford, 1929, p. 147: "Naso carmina, Cicero causas feliciter agit." Ovid himself gave himself out at least twice as the master *par excellence* of the art of loving: *Ars amatoria*, lib. II, v. 741–744; lib. III, v. 809–812; edit. H. Bornecque, p. 59 and p. 89. We may see on page VIII of this edition that the MS. authority is the Regius of Paris, of the tenth century, corrected in the eleventh and twelfth centuries.—Ovid is clearly indicated by William: "Nam et foedus amor carnalis foeditatis suae olim habuit magistros, ut ab ipsius foeditatis amatoribus et sociis, doctor artis amatoriae recantare cogeretur, quod intemperantius cantaverat; et de amoris scribere remedio, qui de amoris carnalis scripserat incendio" (*De nat. et dig. amoris*, I, 2; P.L., CLXXXIV, 381 A). The allusion to the *Ars amatoria* and to the *Remedia amoris* is transparent.—It was the *De natura et dignitate amoris* that was dubbed the *Anti-Nasonem* (P.L., CLXXXIV, 363–364.)

²⁶² *De nat. et dig. amoris*, I, 1; P.L., CLXXXIV, 379 C. Here is the formula: "Ars est artium ars amoris, cujus magisterium ipsa sibi retinuit natura, et Deus auctor naturae. Ipse enim amor a Creatore inditus, nisi naturalis ejus ingenuitas adulterinis aliquibus affectibus praepedita fuerit, ipse, inquam, se docet, sed docibiles sui, docibiles Dei (*Joan*, VI, 45)."

²⁶³ See E. GILSON, *Introduction a l'étude de saint Augustin*, Paris, J. Vrin, pp. 165-166.

²⁶⁴ "Ideosque amissa doctrina sua naturali, opus jam habet doctore homini, qui de beatitudine, quae naturaliter quaeritur amando, doceat admonendo, ubi, et quo, in qua regione, qua via quaeratur" (*De nat. et dig. amoris*, I, 1; P.L., CLXXXIV, 380-381).

²⁶⁵ "Amor ergo, ut dictum est, ab auctore naturae naturaliter est animae humanae inditus; sed postquam legem Dei amisit, ab homine est docendus. Non est autem docendus, ut sit tanquam qui non sit; sed ut purgetur, et quomodo purgetur; et ut proficiat, et quomodo proficiat; ut solidetur, et quomodo solidetur, docendus est" (*De nat. et dig. amoris*, I, 2; P.L., CLXXXIV, 381). The allusion to Ovid immediately follows: we need professors of divine love just as carnal love had its own.

²⁶⁶ On the vanity of philosophy see *De nat. et dig. amoris*, XIV, 41; P.L., CLXXXIV, 404.—That men who live the life of charity are the truly wise, *op. cit.*, XIV, 42; 405 BC.—On the spiritual society which they form among themselves, *op. cit.*, XIV, 43; 405-406.

²⁶⁷ "Visus ergo ad videndum Deum naturale lumen animae, ab auctore naturae creatus, caritas est. Sunt autem duo oculi in hoc visu, ad lumen quod Deus est videndum naturali quadam intentione semper palpitantes, amor et ratio" (*De nat. et dig. amoris*, VIII, 21; P.L., CLXXXIV, 393 A).

²⁶⁸ See above, note 265.

²⁶⁹ Remember that this method was suggested to the commentators by the text of *Cant. Cant.*, I, 7: "Nisi cognoveris te, O pulchra inter mulieres, egredere, et abi post vestigia gregum, et pasce haedos tuos." Gregory the Great there at once read an invitation addressed by God to the soul to know itself as made to His image (*Moral.*, lib. XVI, cap. 21). William enshrined this text in his commentary extracted from Gregory (*Comment. in Cant. Cant. ex libris Gregorii*, cap. I, v. 7; P.L., CLXXX, 444-445).—For the texts extracted from St. Ambrose, see above, Ch. III, p. 70, note 90.—Cf. ST. AUGUSTINE, *De Trinitate*, X, 9, 12; P.L., XLII, 980.

²⁷⁰ "Si", inquit, "ignoras te, egredere", hoc est ideo a temetipsa egrederis, quia ignoras te. Sed cognosce te, quia imago mea es, et sic poteris nosse me, cujus imago es, et penes te invenies me. In mente tua, si fueris mecum, ibi cubabo tecum, et inde pascam te" (WILLIAM OF SAINT-THIERRY, *In Cant. Cant.*, cap. I; P.L., CLXXX, 494 A).—"O imago Dei, recognosce dignitatem tuam; refulgeat in te auctoris effigies. Tu tibi vilis es, sed pretiosa res es. Quantum ab eo deficisti cujus imago es, tantum alienis imaginibus infecta es. . . . Adesto ergo tota tibi, et tota te utere ad cognoscendum te, et cujus imago sis, ad discernendum et intelligendum quid sis, quid possis in eo cujus imago es" (*ibid.*, 494 CD).

William himself linked up the Christian *Nosce teipsum* with its ancient fore-runner at the opening of one of his most important writings: "Fertur celebre apud Graecos Delphici Apollinis responsum: 'Homo, scito teipsum.' Hoc et Salomon, imo Christus in Canticis: 'Si non, inquit, cognoveris te, egredere' (*Cant.*, I, 7). Qui enim non immoratur in eis quae sua sunt, per sapientiae contemplationem, ingreditur necessario in aliena per curiositati vanitatem" (*De natura corporis et animae*, Prolog., P.L., CLXXX, 695- 696). On the *Scito teipsum* as the contrary of *curiositas*, see above, Appendix I, *Curiositas*, p. 155.

²⁷¹ "Et haec est imago et similitudo Dei in homine; talis vel tanta, qualis vel quanta esse potest in tam dissimili materia. Similitudo quippe ista ratio est, qua distat homo a pecore. Dei enim non reminisci, pecoris est; reminisci, non ad intelligendum, plus aliquid pecore, sed minus homine est; reminisci ad intelligendum, hominis est; intelligere usque ad amandum, vel amando fruendum, jam hominis perfectae rationis est, siquidem pia memoria cito

clarescit in quemdam intellectum de Deo, vel rationalem cogitationem: purus intellectus, seu cogitatio rationabilis, statim calescit in amorem, amor vero per affectum boni continuo summi boni induit imaginem, talem vel tantam, qualis vel quantus ipse est" (WILLIAM OF SAINT-THIERRY, *In Cant. Cant.*, cap. I; P.L., CLXXX, 503 CD).

[272] "Etenim cum in faciem novi hominis spiraculum vitae, spiritualem vim, id est intellectualem, quod sonat spiratio et spiraculum; et vitalem, id est animalem, quod sonat nomen vitae, infundit, et infundendo creavit; in ejus quasi quadam arce vim memorialem collocavit, ut Creatoris semper potentiam et bonitatem memoraret: statimque et sine aliquo morae interstitio, memoria de se genuit rationem, et memoria et ratio de se protulerunt voluntatem. Memoria quippe habet et continet quo tendendum sit; ratio, quod tendendum sit; voluntas tendit: et haec tria unum quiddam sunt, sed tres efficaciae, sicut in illa summa Trinitate una est substantia, tres personae" (WILLIAM OF SAINT-THIERRY, *De nat. et dig. amoris*, II, 3; P.L., CLXXXIV, 382 CD).

[273] *De nat. et dig. amoris*, XII, 35-37; P.L., CLXXXIV, 401-403.

[274] The most beautiful expression of this sentiment that I know in the work of William is to be found in the *De Contemplando Deo*, Prooemium; P.L., CLXXXIV, 365-367. These pages contain, in an admirably lyric form, an almost complete *résumé* of his doctrine. If no other page of William's be read these should be read. Nowhere has the mystical transvaluation of the most familiar Augustinian themes been more happily carried out.

[275] "... jam frequentes et improvisae theophaniae et sanctorum splendores animam continuo laborantem desiderio incipiunt refocillare, et illustrare" (*De nat. et dig. amoris*, IV, 10; P.L., CLXXXIV, 386 C). This expression is among those very rare ones which betray a direct influence of Dionysius on William. Also compare: *In Cant. Cant.*, cap II; P.L., CLXXX, 528 C, with the etymology of the word *Deus* proposed by JOHN SCOT ERIGENA, *De divisione naturae*, lib. I, 12; P.L., CXXII, 452 C.

It is true to say on the other hand that the text of the *Epistola aurea*, II, 3, 16; P.L., CLXXXIV, 348 CD, carries clearly Dionysian undertones; let us even say, with M. P. POURRAT (*La spiritualité chrétienne*, t. II, pp. 194-195), Eriginian. But I have not succeeded in finding the sources either in Dionysius or in Erigena. M. Pourrat seems to have been more fortunate, and we hope that in a new edition of his book he will take the opportunity to point them out.

[276] The most complete exposition of the apprenticeship of charity that William has left us is to be found in the *Epistola aurea*, the proper subject of which it is. A detailed *résumé* will be found in M.-M. DAVY, *art. cit.*

[277] *De nat. et dig. amoris*, II, 3; P.L., CLXXX, 382 B.

[278] *De contemplando Deo*, IV, 9; P.L., CLXXXIV, 372.

[279] *Op. cit.*, VII, 14; P.L., CLXXXIV, 375 A.

[280] Cf. p. 219, note 21.

[281] *In Cant. Cant.*, cap. I; P.L., CLXXX, 496 D, 498 C.—*In Romanos*, lib. V; 638 AB.—*Speculum fidei*, 392 BC.

[282] "Cumque efficitur ad similitudinem facientis, fit homo 'Deo affectus', hoc est cum Deo unus spiritus, pulcher in pulchro, bonus in bono; idque suo modo, secundum virtutem fidei, et lumen intellectus et mensuram amoris, existens in Deo per gratiam quod ille est per naturam. Nam et cum nonnunquam superabundat gratia usque ad certam de Deo, et manifestam experientiam rei, fit repente sensui illuminati amoris modo quodam novo sensibile, quod nulli sensui corporis sperabile, nulli ratione cogitabile, nulli intellectui extra intellectum illuminati amoris fit capabile; ubi, homini illi, non est aliud de Deo sentire quam per bonae experientiae affectum admire similitudinem ejus contrahere, secundum qualitatem et sensae speciei et sentientis amoris.

"Sicut enim, in rebus per corpus sensibilibus, sensus est sentiendo per quamdam mentis phantasiam in ipsam mentem contracta quaedam sensae rei similitudo, secundum qualitatem sensus sentientis et rei sensibilis, ut, verbi gratia, si ad sensum pertinet videndi quod sentitur, videri omnino non possit a vidente, si non prius visibile ejus per similitudinem cujusdam phantasmatis formetur in anima videntis, per quam transformetur sentiens in id quod sentitur, sic et multo magis idem opeiatur visio Dei in sensu amoris quo videtur Deus; siquidem et in illo corporearum sensu rerum, nisi cum sensu pariter etiam amor operetur, sensus ipse vix ad aliquem pervenit effectum, quia refugit continuo sentiens, si non aliquo amoris appetitu adhaereat rei quae sentitur. In visione vero Dei, ubi solus amor operatur, nullo alio sensu cooperante, incomparabiliter dignius ac subtilius omni sensuum imaginatione: idem agit puritas amoris ac divinus affectus, suavius affiçiens, fortiusque attrahens, et dulcius continens sentientem, totumque et mente et actu in Deum transfundens fideliter amantem, et confortans et conformans, et vivificans ad fruendum" (WILLIAM OF SAINT-THIERRY, *In Cant. Cant.*, cap. I; P.L., CLXXXIV, 505–506).

An exposé very like that of the commentary *In Cant. Cant.* may be read in the *Meditativae orationes*, med. III; P.L., CLXXXIV, 213. Cf. *Speculum fidei*, 390 D–391 A.

[283] *Loc. cit.*, 507 C.

[284] "Domine, Deus noster, qui ad imaginem et similitudinem tuam creasti nos, scilicet ad te contemplandum teque fruendum; quem nemo usque ad fruendum contemplatur, *nisi in quantum similis tibi efficitur;* summi boni species quae rapis omnem animam rationalem desiderio tui, tanto ad te ardentiorem quanto in se mundiorem, tanto autem mundiorem quanto a corporalibus ad spiritualia liberiorem, libera a servitute corruptionis id quod tibi soli deservire debet in nobis, amorem nostrum. Amor enim est qui, cum liber est, similes nos tibi efficit in tantum, in quantum nos tibi afficit sensus vitae, quo te sentit" (WILLIAM OF SAINT-THIERRY, *In Cant. Cant.*, Praef., P.L., CLXXX, 473). Cf. 479 D–480 A.—"Videre namque ibi seu cognoscere Deum, similem est esse Deo; et similem ei esse, videre seu cognoscere eum est. Haec cognitio perfecta, vita erit aeterna, gaudium quod nemo tollet habenti" (*Speculum fidei*, P.L., CLXXX, 393 C.)

[285] An abundant collection of such metaphors may be found in Père ROUSSELOT, *Pour l'histoire du problème de l'amour au moyen âge*, Appendix II, pp. 96–102.

[286] "In hoc siquidem fit conjunctio illa mirabilis, et mutua fruitio suavitatis, gaudiique incomprehensibilis, incogitabilis illis etiam in quibus fit, hominis ad Deum, creati spiritus ad increatum. Qui Sponsa dicuntur ac Sponsus, dum verba quaeruntur quibus lingua hominis utcumque exprimi possit dulcedo et suavitas conjunctionis illius, quae non est alia quam unitas Patri et Filii Dei, ipsum eorum osculum, ipse amplexus, ipse amor, ipsa bonitas, et quidquid in unitate illa simplicissima commune est amborum. Quod totum est Spiritus Sanctus, Deus, charitas, idem donans, idem et donum. Ibi enim comparat se sibi ille amplexus, et illud osculum, quo cognoscere incipit Sponsa sicut et cognita est" (*In Cant. Cant.*, cap. I; P.L., CLXXX, 506 BC).

[287] "Sed amoris dilatatus sinus, secundum magnitudinem tuam se extendens, dum amat te, vel amare affectat, quantus es, incapabilem capit, incomprehensibilem comprehendit. Quid vero dicimus: capit? Quin potius amor ipse, hoc est quod tu es; Spiritus Sanctus tuus, O Pater, qui a te procedit et Filio, cum quo tu et Filius unus es. Cui cum meretur affici spiritus hominis, spiritus spiritui, amor amori, amor humanus divinus quodam modo efficitur; et jam in amando Deum homo quidem est in opere, sed Deus est qui operatur. Non enim Paulus, 'sed gratia Dei' secum (I *Cor.*, XV, 10)" (*In Cant. Cant.*, cap. I; P.L., CLXXX, 508 B).

[288] "Amplexus iste circa hominem agitur, sed supra hominem est. Amplexus etenim hic Spiritus Sanctus est. Qui enim Patris et Filii Dei communio, qui charitas, qui amicitia, qui amplexus est, ipse in amore Sponsi ac Sponsae ipsa omnia est. Sed ibi majestas et consubstantialis naturae, hic autem donum gratiae; ibi dignitas hic autem dignatio; idem tamen, idem plane Spiritus" (*op. cit.*, cap. II; P.L., CLXXX, 520 B).

[289] "Qui autem scrutatur corda, scit quid desiderat Spiritus. . . . Estque in eo quaedam docta ignorantia, docta a Spiritu Dei, qui adjuvat infirmitatem nostram, excercendo humilians, et humiliando formans, et conformans hominem vultui quem requirit, donec renovatus ad imaginem ejus qui creavit

NOTES 251

eum, per unitatem similitudinis incipiat esse filius, qui semper sit cum patre, cujus sint omnia quae patris sunt. . . ." (*In Epist. ad Rom.*, lib. V; P.L., CLXXX 638 CD). Cf. *Speculum fidei*, P.L., CLXXX, 393 AB.

[290] *De contemplando Deo*, VIII, 16; CLXXXIV, 375 D. See Nos. 16-17, in their entirety.

[291] *Epistola aurea*, II, 3-16; P.L., CLXXXIV, 348 C.

[292] *Epistola aurea*, II, 3, 16, as a whole; P.L., CLXXXIV, 348-349. The texts cited above (p. 250, note 289) are sufficient authorization to interpret the divinization of man as a *unitas similitudinis;* but the *Epistola aurea itself* says as much in very clear terms: "Unde bene dicitur, quod tunc plene *videbimus eum sicuti est, cum similes ei erimus* (I *Joan.* III, 2); hoc est erimus quod ipse est" (*op. cit.*, II, 15; 348 B).

The analogous expressions of St. Bernard's continuator, GILBERT OF HOLLAND, *In Cant. Cant.*, III, 4; P.L., CLXXXIV, 19 D) may be interpreted in the same way. The expression: "ipsa (*anima*) . . . non est nisi ipse" must be explained in the light of the "in similem absorbetur qualitatem" which precedes it; here again we have an identity of likeness. And this expression in its turn carries us back to ST. BERNARD, *De diligendo Deo*, IX, 28; P.L., CLXXXII, 991 B. I mention Gilbert's text because M. l'Abbé A. Combes informs me that it has a history: difficulties, that is to say, have been made about it. As a mere reflection of St. Bernard's and William's it deserves neither the honour nor the indignity.

[293] P. POURRAT, *La spiritualité chrétienne*, t. II, p. 194. Cf. "This explanation of the perfect unity of man and God has a pantheistic flavour, and our uncertainty about the text of the Letter, undoubtedly edited, does not wholly remove it." I know of nothing that justifies this hypothesis of editing. Further, if a pantheistic flavour is felt in the formula: "what God is by *nature*, man is by *grace*" it will be rather difficult to find any satisfactory mystical texts at all. Is there not a confusion here between "what God is" and "to be God"? William carefully distinguishes them; to be what God is, is to be God by way of likeness.

[294] *Epistola aurea*, II, 3, 16; P.L., CLXXXIV, 349 B.

[295] *Op. cit.*, II, 3, 18; P.L., CLXXXIV, 350 B.

[296] *Op. cit.*, II, 3-15; P.L., CLXXXIV, 348 B.

BIBLIOGRAPHY

Of the principal texts and works relating to the mysticism of St. Bernard.

I

WRITINGS OF ST. BERNARD

A. *Collected edition*

S. BERNARDI, abbatis primi Clarae-Vallensis, *Oprea omnia* . . . post Horstium denuo recognita . . . curis D. Johannis Mabillon Migne, Pat. Lat., Vols. 182–185.

All citations are taken from this edition except where otherwise expressly noted.

B. *Partial editions cited in this work.*

1. *Lettres inédites*, published in Georg HÜFFER, *Der heilige Bernard von Clairvaux* . . ., pp. 184–246.

2. *Sermons inédits*, published by D. P. SÉJOURNÉ, *Les inédits bernardins du manuscrit d'Anchin*, in the collection: *Saint Bernard et son temps*, t. II, pp. 248–282.

3. W. W. WILLIAMS, *De diligendo Deo* and Barton R. V. MILLS, *De gradibus humilitatis et superbiae* (Cambridge patristic texts), Cambridge University Press, 1926—This edition, freely annotated, is based on the MSS. of Troyes 426 and 799 which represent a manuscript tradition other than that followed by Mabillon's text.—On the value of Mabillon's text see D. A. WILMART, *Auteurs spirituels* . . ., p. 90, note 2; and W. W. WILLIAMS, *The Anchin manuscript* (*Douai* 372), in *Speculum*, April 1933, pp. 242–254.

C. *Partial editions not cited in this work.*

B.GSELL and L. JANAUSCHEK, *Sancti Bernardi* . . ., *Sermones de Tempore, de Sanctis, de Diversis*, in *Xenia Bernadina*, Pars I, Wien, 1891—D. G. MORIN, *Trois manuscrits d'Engelberg à l'Ambrosiana*, in *Revue bénédictine*, Oct. 1927 (contains an unpublished sermon attributed to St. Bernard).—Another unpublished sermon is mentioned in *Analecta sacra Tarraconiensia*, 1932, I, pp. 135–139.—As regards the letters, G. HÜFFER (*op cit.*, p. 187, note 2) and VACANDARD (*Vie de saint Bernard*, I, p. XIV, note 1), point out that several have been published by Kervyn de Lettenhove, in the *Bulletin de l'Académie royale de Belgique*, 2nd series, t. XI., No. 2, and t. XII, No. 12—A letter, finally, of capital importance for the establishment of the true nature of the relations between Bernard and Aelred of Rievaulx, has lately, in a masterly way, been restored to St. Bernard by D. A. WILMART, *L'instigateur du Speculum caritatis d'Aelred, abbé de Rievaulx*, in *Revue d'ascétique et de mystique*, t. XIV (1933), pp. 369–395.

II

THE VITAE BERNARDI

The ancient *Lives* of St. Bernard are rich with information on his character and person. The most important of these documents is the one we owe to William of Saint-Thierry, it is a witness that none other could replace. These works are commonly distinguished by the following titles:

A. VITA PRIMA

This is a compilation made up of the following works:

1. WILLIAM OF SAINT-THIERRY, Liber I; P.L., CLXXXV, 225–226.

2. ERNAULD DE BONNEVAL, Liber II; P. L., CLXXXV, 267–302.

3. GEOFFROY D'AUXERRE, Libri III–VI; P. L., CLXXXV, 301–410 (on the two first parts of Lib. VI, see G. HÜFFER, *op. cit.*, p. 30).

4. Lib. VII: extracts from the *Exordium magnum* (P.L., CLXXXV, 415-454) and of HERBERT, *Liber miraculorum* (cf. G. HÜFFER, *op. cit.*, pp. 160–161).

To this group may be added the *Fragmenta Gaufridi*; P. L., CLXXXV, 523–530 sometimes entitled the *Vita Quarta*.

B. VITA SECUNDA

ALAIN D'AUXERRE, *Vita sancti Bernardi abbatis ;* P.L., CLXXXV, 469–524.

An abridgment, very much sugared and weakened, of the foregoing lives; the few additions in the *Vita secunda* leave it clearly inferior to its forerunners.

C. VITA QUARTA

JEAN L'HERMITE. *Vita sancti Bernardi abbatis ;* P.L., CLXXXV, 531–550 (cf. G. HÜFFER, *op. cit.*, pp. 153–157).

For introduction to the Cistercian surroundings and spirit, it is indispensable to become familiar with a document of the first importance, the *Exodrium magnum Ordinis Cisterciensis ;* P.L., CLXXXV, 995–1198.

On the history and value of these documents, see E. VACANDARD, *Vie de saint Bernard,* ed. cit., Introduction, t. I, p. XIII–LIV, but above all consult G. HÜFFER, *Der heiliage Bernard von Clairvaux, Eine Darstellung seines Lebens und Wirkens,* I Bd., Vorstudien, Münster, Aschendorff, 1886.

III

BIOGRAPHICAL STUDIES ON ST. BERNARD

VACANDARD (E.), *Abélard, sa lutte avec saint Bernard, sa doctrine, sa méthode,* Paris and Chernovitz, 1881.

—— *Vie de saint Bernard, abbé de Clairvaux,* 2 vol., Paris, J. Gabalda, 1927 (8ᶜ mille).

COULTON (G. G.), *Five Centuries of Religion.* I *S. Bernard, his predecessors, and successors : 1000–1200.* Cambridge, University Press, 1923.

LUDDY (A. J.), *Life and Teaching of S. Bernard,* Dublin, 1927 (deals more at length with the doctrine than does Vacandard).

GOYAU (G.), *Saint Bernard,* Paris, E. Flammarion, 1927.

Saint Bernard et son temps. Collection of memoirs and commentaries presented to the congress of the *Association bourguignonne des Sociétés savantes.* Congress of 1927. Dijon, *au siège de l'Academie, Palais des Etats*, 1928, 2 vol.

Contains several communications touching the life and thought of St. Bernard. We may mention: T. I. D. ALEXIS, *Un manuscrit des Fragmenta Gaufridi.*—D. CABROL, *Cluny et Cîteaux, saint Bernard et Pierre le Vénérable.*—D. CANIVEZ, *Les voyages et les fondations monastiques de saint Bernard en Belgique.*—Abbé CHAUME, *Les origines familiales de saint Bernard.*—F. CLAUDON, *A propos des archives de Cîteaux.*—A. FLICHE, *L'influence de Grégoire VII et des idées grégoriennes sur la pensée de saint Bernard.*—D. LE BAIL, *L'influence de saint Bernard sur les auteurs-spirituels de son temps.*—R. MARTIN, *La formation théologique de saint Bernard.*— P. VIARD, *Saint Bernard et les moines décimateurs.*—P. PIETRES-SON DE SAINT-AUBIN, *Notes sur les archives de l'abbaye de Clairvaux.*—M. VIGNES, *Les doctrines économiques et morales de saint Bernard sur la richesse et le travail.*—Tome II. D. ALEXIS, *La filiation de Clairvaux et l'influence de saint Bernard au XIIᵉ siècle.*— E. CHARTRAIRE, *Le séjour de saint Bernard à Sens en 1140.*— J. M. GAUTHERON, *Sur la continuité du rôle agraire des Cisterciens.* —J. LAURENT, *Un opusculé ascétique inédit attribué à saint Bernard : Meditatio secundum septem horas diei.*—D. P. SÉJOURNÉ, *Les inédits bernardins du manuscrit d'Anchin.*—W. W. WILLIAMS, *L'aspect éthique du mysticisme de saint Bernard.*

MITERRE (P.), *Saint Bernard de Clairvaux. Un moine arbitre de l'Europe au XIIᵉ siècle.* Librairie de Lannoy, Genual (Belgique) 1929.

IV

CHIEF WORKS RELATING TO THE MYSTICAL DOCTRINE OF ST. BERNARD

1. JANAUSCHEK (L.), *Bibliographia Bernardina*, in *Xenia Bernardina*, Pars IV., Vienna 1891.—(Refers to 129 manuscripts and 2761 editions of St. Bernard, or of works relating to his life and doctrine; stops at 1890).

2. RIES (J.), *Das geistliche Leben, in seinen Entwicklungsstufen nach der Lehre des hl. Bernard*, Freiburg, Herder, 1906 (very useful).

—— *Die Kontemplationsarten nach der Lehre des hl. Bernard*, in *Jahrbuch f. Philos, u. spekulative Theologie*, t. 23 (1909).—I have not been able to consult this work; nor that of JOSEPH A SPIRITU SANCTO, same title, same review, t. 22 (1908) to which that of Ries seems to be a reply.

3. ROUSSELOT (P.), *Pour l'histoire du problème de l'amour au moyen âge* (Beitr. z. Gesch. d. Phil, d. Mittelalt. Bd. VI, 6), Münster, Aschendorff, 1908.

4. WALTER (J. VON), *Die Sonderstellung Bernard von Clairvaux in der Geschichter der Mystik*, in Theologischer Festschrift für G. N. Bonwetsch, Leipzig, Deichert, 1918, pp. 64-71.

5. SCHUCK (J.), *Das religiöse Erlebnis beim hl. Bernard von Clairvaux, ein Beitrag zur Geschichte der christlichen Gotteserfahrung*, Würzburg, C. J. Becker, 1922. (By far the best book I know on the mysticism of St. Bernard; sets out, as its title indicates, to describe the mystical *experience* itself, and is therefore in no way replaced by the present work).

6. BUTLER (C.), *Western Mysticism, The teaching of SS. Augustine Gregory and Bernard on contemplation and the contemplative life*, London, 1922.

7. BERNHART (JOS.), *Die philosophische Mystik des Mittelalters von ihren Ursprüngen bis zur Renaissance*, Ernst Reinhardt, München, 1922 (St. Bernard, pp. 97–110).

8. BESSE (J.M.), *Les mystiques bénédictions des origines au XIIe siècle Essai historique*. Paris, Desclée, de Brouwer, 1927.

9. LINHARDT (R.), *Die Mystik des hl. Bernhard von Clairvaux*, München, 1928.

10. BUTLER (Dom C.), *Le monachisme bénédictin. Etudes sur la vie et la règle bénédictines*. trad. par Ch. Grolleau, Paris, J. de Gigord, 1924 (the English text is that dated 1909; very important even from the doctrinal standpoint, and particularly as regards St. Bernard's Benedictine sources).

11. GUILLOUX (P.), *L'amour de Dieu selon saint Bernard*, in *Revue des sciences religieuses*, Oct. 1926, pp. 499–512. Jan. 1927, pp. 52–68. Jan. 1928, pp. 69–90.

12. DAVISON (Ellen Scot), *The forerunners of Saint Francis*,

Houghton Mifflin, Boston and New York, 1927 (suggestive as regards the ideal of poverty prior to St. Francis).

13. MARÉCHAUX (B.), *L'œuvre doctrinale de saint Bernard*, in *La vie spirituelle*, July 1927, pp. 498–511. Sept. 1927, pp. 634–650. Oct., 1927, pp. 34–47. Nov. 1927, pp. 196–207.

14. BERLIÉRE (Dom U.), *L'acèse bénédictine des origines à la fin XII esiècle. Essai historique.* Paris, Desclée, de Brouwer, 1927.

15. BUONAIUTI (E.), Il *misticismo medioevale*, Pinerolo, 1928 (strongly emphasizes the connection between mediaeval mysticism and the monastic life, particularly in St. Bernard).

16. EGENTER (R.), *Gottesfreundschaft. Die Lehre von der Gottesfreundschaft in der Scholastik und Mystik des 12 und 13 Jahrhunderts.* Augsburg, B. Filser, 1928.

17. P. POURRAT, *La spiritualité chrétienne;* t. II, Le Moyen Age, Paris, J. Gabalda, 1928 (9th thousand), Ch. II, *Doctrine spirituelle de saint Bernard,* pp. 29–116.

18. GARRIGOU-LAGRANGE (R.), *Le problème de l'amour pur et la solution de saint Thomas,* in *Angelicum*, 1929, pp. 83–124 (the solution of St. Thomas is not opposed to that of St. Bernard but gives it precision and completes it).

19. DELSART (H. M.), *Traite de l'amour de Dieu par sain Bernard,* traduction nouvelle, Paris, Desclée et Lethielleux, 1929 (see Introduction pp. 1–11).

20. WECHSSLER (E.), *Deutsche und französische Mystik: Meister Eckhart und Bernard von Clairvaux,* in *Euphorion*, 1929, pp. 40–93. (Cf. *Recherches de théologie ancienne et médiévale,* 1930; Bulletin, p. 234).

21. DIDIER (J. Ch.), *La dévotion a l'humanité du Christ dans spiritualité de saint Bernard,* in *La vie spirituelle*, Aug.-Sept. 1930, pp. [1—19]—*L'imitation de l'humanité du Christ, selon saint Bernard,* ibid., 1930, pp. [79–94].—*L'ascension mystique et l'union mystique par l'humanité du Christ selon saint Bernard,* ibid., 1931. pp. [140–155]. (Cf. *Recherches du théologie ancienne et médiévale,* 1931 p. 4 28)

22. WILLIAMS (Watkin W.), *The mysticism of S. Bernard of Clairvaux,* London, Burns Oates, 1931.

23. DUMONTET (E.), *Les Docteurs au pied de la croix,* in *Revue apologétique*, Feb. 1932, pp. 129–148.

24. MITERRE (P.), *La doctrine de saint Bernard*, Bruxelles, éditions Halflants, 1932.

25. WILMART (Dom A.), *Auteurs spirituels et textes dévots du moyen âge. Etudes d'histoire littéraire*. Paris, Blood· et Gay, 1932 (An indispensable guide to the ascetic literature of the XIIth century).

26. LOT-BORODINE (M.), *La doctrine de la "déification" dans l'Eglise grecque jusqu'au XIe siécle*, in *Revue de l'histoire des religions*, t. 105 (1932), pp. 5-43; t. 106 (1932), pp. 525-574; t. 107 (1933), pp. 8-55 (on the method followed, see t. 106, p. 525, note I; in spite of certain technical deficiencies these suggestive pages may be usefully consulted for the whole Greek background of the Cistercian *deificatio*).

N.B.—While correcting this volume I hear of the appearance of a new review: *Collectanea Ordinis Cisterciensium reformatorum*, the first number of which appeared in April 1934, at the Cistercian Abbey of Forges-lez-Bourlers (Chimay) Belgium. Such a publication is absolutely indispensable and all who take an interest in the history of the Order will be grateful to its founders for undertaking it.

INDEX OF SUBJECTS

made all things for Himself, 131; assumes the soul in *raptus*, 106–108; loves Himself in us, 118.
GREATNESS, of the soul, 52, 53.

HELL, 84, 234.
HERESY, born of the *proprium consilium*, 57.
HIRELING, state of one who loves for the sake of reward, 95; who is moved by hope, 101; and follows his proper will, 95.
HOLY SPIRIT, law of the Divine life, 95, 235; love of God for God, 236; is charity, 98; unity of God, 94, 236; His law, 235; bond between soul and God, 98, 103, 210–211; admits the soul to mystical union, 150; teaching function, 101 (see SCHOOL); is the spirit of liberty, 96; His missions, 107; restores the lost likeness, 93; in the form of gift, 211; see CHARITY.
HONOUR, the affection of sons, 101; transcended in mystical marriage, 136, 139.
HUMANISM, of Cistercian authors, 7–8; of St. Bernard, 63, 229; of Aelred of Rievaulx, 63, 228; of William of Saint-Thierry, 63, 230; of Berenger the Scholastic, 167; influence of Cicero, 8–13, 136, 137, 159, 228. See CICERO.
HUMILITY, definition, 72; is the first heaven, 106–107; its twelve degrees, 29, 71, 156; leads to charity, 30, 71, 98, 100–101, 233; and self-knowledge, 71, 72; incarnate in Jesus Christ, 77, 98; in Gregory the Great, 19.
HYSSOP, symbol of humility, 101.

IGNORANCE OF SELF, breeds pride, 35, 100, 233; makes man kin to the beasts, 100.
IMAGE, *in mente*, 46, 203; lies in liberty, 46, 49, 236 (see DIGNITY); is natural, 135; predestines to mystical union, 118; makes it possible, 118, 127; and hoped for, 118; attests affinity of soul with the Word, 150; subsists after the fall, 65, 225, 236; and even in the damned, 234; although defaced, 135; pain of knowing itself so, 58; image essential and likeness accidental, 52, 54; see LIKENESS.
IMPUTATION, non-imputation of sin in St. Bernard, 241; different in Luther, 242.
INCARNATION, its motive, 77, 98, 106, 110.
INDUSTRIA (Zeal), 113, 134, 150.
INEBRIATION, in the mystical sense, 112, 113, 130.
INGRESSUS, by contemplation of God as Judge, 241.
INTENTION, 132; charity of intention, 59.
INTERNAL SENSE, see SENSE, INTERNAL.
INVITUS, opposed to *spontaneus*, state in which man is placed by proper will, 96.

JESUS CHRIST, sole Master, 62, 65; known by knowledge of self, 76; teaches humility, 77, 98, 102; has experienced our misery, 77; model of compassion, 77, 79, 98; necessity for devotion to His humanity, 80; reasons for sensible character of the Passion, 80; mystical fruits of meditation on Passion, 80, 81; Jesus Christ is the mystical *asculum*, 110; requires us to be one with Him, 208; way of access to divine union, 98; is a concrete ecstasy, 110; mediator between God and man, 205.
JOY (gaudium), one of the four *affectus*, 101; infused joy, 241.
JUDICIUM (see LIBERTY); meditation of divine judgment, 30; judgment of the soul by itself, 50, 100, 103.
JUSTICE, social, and charity, 76; born of love and of fear, 240.

KNOWLEDGE, and likeness, 92, 116, 148, 151, 208; and love, 115.
KNOWLEDGE OF SELF, 34, 70, 100, 202, 232; and Socratism, 103; required of all, 36; and ascesis, 69, 71; and humility, 71–73, 99–100; and fear of God, 73; and compassion, 73, 98; and wisdom, 155; and knowledge of God, 70, 133; sources of the doctrine, 70; to know as one is known, 73, 98, 129, 151, 250; see UNLIKENESS.

NARD, symbol of humility, 102.

NATURE, teaches love, 200, 236; is created, 42; is indestructible, 57; nature and natural in the sense of normal, 40, 41, 42, 201; we become by grace what God is by nature, 129, 213, 236.

NECESSITY, founded in nature, 39, 40, 67, 130, 231; aggravated by sin, 40; not to be eliminated in this life, 43, 222; *necessitas urget*, 41, 222; see CUPIDITY.

NIGHT, of knowledge, 105.

OBEDIENCE, state of the *discipulus*, 101, 111.

ORACLE OF DELPHI, 232, 248.

OSCULUM, in Origen, 216; Jesus Christ is the *osculum*, 110; desired by the Bride, 111; when drunken with love, 113; is love and experience of God, 115, 211; awaited in languor, 104.

PERSEVERANCE, analogue of eternity, 212.

PERSON, never destroyed in ecstasy, 121, 122; but rather confirmed in being, 27, 122; by elimination of unlikeness, 239; and information by likeness, 129.

PERVERSITY, of the will, 59; see PROPRIUM (*voluntas propria*).

PHANTASM, in knowledge, 208, 210.

POETRY, COURTLY, see COURTLY POETRY.

POVERTY, and Cistercian asceticism, 228, 233.

PRESENCE (praesentia), of God as Judge, Bridegroom or beatific vision, 81; of the soul to God by love, 68, 93, 231.

PRAYER, pure, 19.

PROPRIUM, condemned by St. Benedict, 29; or *suum*, 240; eliminated by purity, 98; and by charity, 116, 132; identical with unlikeness, 116; *voluntas propria*, 55, 59; *consilium proprium*, 56, 57, 59; rectified by ascesis, 76.

PRUDENCE, 59, 234; opposed to curiosity, 64; caused by fear and cause of joy, 240.

PURITY, of heart, as condition of sight of God, 97; or absence of *proprium*, 97; restores the likeness, 99; is the health of the heart, 41; in Gregory of Nyssa, 217.

PURGATION (*purgatus, purgare*), of the affections, 240.

PURITANISM, Cistercian, 233.

RAPTUS, of St. Benedict, 235; or mystical rapture, 106, 107.

RECTITUDO (uprightness), of soul, 53; lost by the *proprium*, 57–58; in St. Anselm, 226.

REDEMPTION, 78, 205.

RENAISSANCE, of the XIIth century, 1, 2, 195; *aetas ovidiana*, 247.

RULE (of St. Benedict), source of the Cistercian mystical movement, 14, 18, 60; and St. Bernard, 20, 31; and Cistercian ascesis, 28–31, 71, 98; *ante professionem voluntaria*, 63.

SADNESS, one of the four *affectus*, 101.

SANCTE, term applied to a love free from cupidity, 111.

SCHOOL, of charity, 9, 62, 67, 200; of the primitive Church, 61; opposed to the profane schools, 61–62; *schola spiritus*, 65; *schola Christi*, 230.

SCIENCE, of our dignity, 34; and zeal, 57; of the Cistercian, 69; and love, 80; of the world, 206.

SELF-KNOWLEDGE, see KNOWLEDGE OF SELF.

SENSATION, according to William of Saint-Thierry, 249.

SENSE, INTERNAL, its abduction in ecstasy, 105, 237.

SILENTIUM IN COELO, 104, 208, 219.

SLAVE (servus), state of fear, 95, 101, 111; and proper will, 96; subject to its own law, 95; see LOVE.

SOMNUS (sleep), 104.

SON, opposed to slave and hireling, 96; state inferior to that of bride, 111; for he thinks of his heritage, 138.

INDEX OF PROPER NAMES

266 INDEX TO PROPER NAMES

CISTERCIAN PUBLICATIONS, INC.
TITLES LISTING

—CISTERCIAN TEXTS—

BERNARD OF CLAIRVAUX

Apologia to Abbot William
Bernard of Clairvaux, Letters of
Five Books on Consideration: Advice to a Pope
Homilies in Praise of the Blessed Virgin Mary
Life and Death of Saint Malachy the Irishman
Love without Measure: Extracts from the
  Writings of St Bernard (Paul Dimier)
On Grace and Free Choice
On Loving God (Analysis by Emero Stiegman)
Parables and Sentences (Michael Casey)
Sermons for the Summer Season
Sermons on Conversion
Sermons on the Song of Songs I-IV
The Steps of Humility and Pride

WILLIAM OF SAINT THIERRY

The Enigma of Faith
Exposition on the Epistle to the Romans
Exposition on the Song of Songs
The Golden Epistle
The Mirror of Faith
The Nature and Dignity of Love
On Contemplating God: Prayer & Meditations

AELRED OF RIEVAULX

Dialogue on the Soul
Liturgical Sermons, I
Mirror of Charity
Spiritual Friendship
Treatises I: On Jesus at the Age of Twelve,
  Rule for a Recluse, The Pastoral Prayer
Walter Daniel: The Life of Aelred of Rievaulx

JOHN OF FORD

Sermons on the Final Verses of the
  Songs of Songs I-VII

GILBERT OF HOYLAND

Sermons on the Songs of Songs I-III
Treatises, Sermons and Epistles

OTHER EARLY
CISTERCIAN WRITERS

Adam of Perseigne, Letters of
Alan of Lille: The Art of Preaching
Amadeus of Lausanne: Homilies in Praise of
  Blessed Mary
Baldwin of Ford: Spiritual Tractates I-II
Gertrud the Great: Spiritual Exercises
Gertrud the Great: The Herald of God's
  Loving-Kindness
Guerric of Igny: Liturgical Sermons I-[II]
Helinand of Froidmont: Verses on Death

Idung of Prüfening: Cistercians and Cluniacs:
  The Case for Cîteaux
Isaac of Stella: Sermons on the Christian Year,
  I-[II]
The Life of Beatrice of Nazareth
Serlo of Wilton & Serlo of Savigny: Seven
  Unpublished Works
Stephen of Lexington: Letters from Ireland
Stephen of Sawley: Treatises

—MONASTIC TEXTS—

EASTERN CHRISTIAN TRADITION

Besa: The Life of Shenoute
Cyril of Scythopolis: Lives of the Monks of
  Palestine
Dorotheos of Gaza: Discourses and Sayings
Evagrius Ponticus: Praktikos and Chapters on
  Prayer
Handmaids of the Lord: Lives of Holy Women
  in Late Antiquity & Early Middle Ages
  (Joan Petersen)
Harlots of the Desert (Benedicta Ward)
John Moschos: The Spiritual Meadow
Lives of the Desert Fathers
Lives of Simeon Stylites (Robert Doran)
Luminous Eye (Sebastian Brock)
Mena of Nikiou: Isaac of Alexandra & St
  Macrobius
Pachomian Koinonia I-III (Armand Veilleux)
Paphnutius: Histories/Monks of Upper Egypt
Sayings of the Desert Fathers
  (Benedicta Ward)
Spiritual Direction in the Early Christian East
  (Irénée Hausherr)
Spiritually Beneficial Tales of Paul, Bishop of
  Monembasia (John Wortley)
Symeon the New Theologian: The Theological
  and Practical Treatises & The Three
  Theological Discourses (Paul McGuckin)
Theodoret of Cyrrhus: A History of the
  Monks of Syria
The Syriac Fathers on Prayer and the Spiritual
  Life (Sebastian Brock)

WESTERN CHRISTIAN
TRADITION

Anselm of Canterbury: Letters I-III
  (Walter Fröhlich)
Bede: Commentary...Acts of the Apostles
Bede: Commentary...Seven Catholic Epistles
Bede: Homilies on the Gospels III
The Celtic Monk (U. Ó Maidín)
Gregory the Great: Forty Gospel Homilies
Life of the Jura Fathers
Maxims of Stephen of Muret

CISTERCIAN PUBLICATIONS, INC.
TITLES LISTING

Meditations of Guigo I, Prior of the
   Charterhouse (A. Gordon Mursall)
Peter of Celle: Selected Works
Letters of Rancé I-II
Rule of the Master
Rule of Saint Augustine
Wound of Love: A Carthusian Miscellany

CHRISTIAN SPIRITUALITY

Cloud of Witnesses: The Development of
   Christian Doctrine (David N. Bell)
Call of Wild Geese (Matthew Kelty)
Cistercian Way (André Louf)
The Contemplative Path
Drinking From the Hidden Fountain
   (Thomas Špidlík)
Eros and Allegory: Medieval Exegesis of the
   Song of Songs (Denys Turner)
Fathers Talking (Aelred Squire)
Friendship and Community (Brian McGuire)
From Cloister to Classroom
Life of St Mary Magdalene and of Her Sister
   St Martha (David Mycoff)
Many Mansions (David N. Bell)
Mercy in Weakness (André Louf)
Name of Jesus (Irénée Hausherr)
No Moment Too Small (Norvene Vest)
Penthos: The Doctrine of Compunction in the
   Christian East (Irénée Hausherr)
Rancé and the Trappist Legacy
   (A.J. Krailsheimer)
Russian Mystics (Sergius Bolshakoff)
Sermons in a Monastery (Matthew Kelty)
Silent Herald of Unity: The Life of
   Maria Gabrielle Sagheddu (Martha
   Driscoll)
Spirituality of the Christian East
   (Thomas Špidlík)
Spirituality of the Medieval West
   (André Vauchez)
Tuning In To Grace (André Louf)
Wholly Animals: A Book of Beastly Tales
   (David N. Bell)

—MONASTIC STUDIES—

Community and Abbot in the Rule of
   St Benedict I-II (Adalbert de Vogüé)
Finances of the Cistercian Order in the
   Fourteenth Century (Peter King)
Fountains Abbey and Its Benefactors
   (Joan Wardrop)
The Hermit Monks of Grandmont
   (Carole A. Hutchison)
In the Unity of the Holy Spirit
   (Sighard Kleiner)
Joy of Learning & the Love of God:
   Essays in Honor of Jean Leclercq
Monastic Odyssey (Marie Kervingant)

Monastic Practices (Charles Cummings)
Occupation of Celtic Sites in Ireland
   (Geraldine Carville)
Reading St Benedict (Adalbert de Vogüé)
Rule of St Benedict: A Doctrinal and Spiritual
   Commentary (Adalbert de Vogüé)
Rule of St Benedict (Br. Pinocchio)
St Hugh of Lincoln (David H. Farmer)
Stones Laid Before the Lord (Anselme Dimier)
Venerable Bede (Benedicta Ward)
What Nuns Read (David N. Bell)
With Greater Liberty: A Short History of
   Christian Monasticism & Religious
   Orders (Karl Frank)

—CISTERCIAN STUDIES—

Aelred of Rievaulx: A Study (Aelred Squire)
Athirst for God: Spiritual Desire in Bernard of
   Clairvaux's Sermons on the Song of
   Songs (Michael Casey)
Beatrice of Nazareth in Her Context
   (Roger De Ganck)
Bernard of Clairvaux: Man, Monk, Mystic
   (Michael Casey) [tapes and readings]
Bernardus Magister (Nonacentenary)
Catalogue of Manuscripts in the Obrecht
   Collection of the Institute of Cistercian
   Studies (Anna Kirkwood)
Christ the Way: The Christology of Guerric of
   Igny (John Morson)
Cistercian Abbeys of Britain
Cistercians in Denmark (Brian McGuire)
Cistercians in Medieval Art (James France)
Cistercians in Scandinavia (James France)
A Difficult Saint (Brian McGuire)
Dore Abbey (Shoesmith & Richardson)
A Gathering of Friends: Learning & Spirituality
   in John of Forde (Costello and
   Holdsworth)
Image and Likeness: The Augustinian
   Spirituality of William of St Thierry
   (David Bell)
Index of Authors & Works in Cistercian
   Libraries in Great Britain I (David Bell)
Index of Cistercian Authors and Works in
   Medieval Library Catalogues in Great
   Britian (David Bell)
Mystical Theology of St Bernard
   (Étienne Gilson)
The New Monastery: Texts & Studies on the
   Earliest Cistercians
Nicolas Cotheret's Annals of Cîteaux
   (Louis J. Lekai)
Pater Bernhardus (Franz Posset)
A Second Look at Saint Bernard
   (Jean Leclercq)
The Spiritual Teachings of St Bernard of
   Clairvaux (John R. Sommerfeldt)

CISTERCIAN PUBLICATIONS, INC.
TITLES LISTING

Studies in Medieval Cistercian History (various)
Studiosorum Speculum (Louis J. Lekai)
Three Founders of Cîteaux
  (Jean-Baptiste Van Damme)
Towards Unification with God (Beatrice of
  Nazareth in Her Context, 2)
William, Abbot of St Thierry
Women and St Bernard of Clairvaux
  (Jean Leclercq)

MEDIEVAL RELIGIOUS
—WOMEN—

Lillian Thomas Shank and John A. Nichols, editors
Distant Echoes
Hidden Springs: Cistercian Monastic Women
  (2 volumes)
Peace Weavers

—CARTHUSIAN—
TRADITION

Call of Silent Love (A Carthusian)
Freedom of Obedience (A Carthusian)
Guigo II: The Ladder of Monks & Twelve
  Meditations (Colledge & Walsh)
Interior Prayer (A Carthusian)
Meditations of Guigo II (A. Gordon Mursall)
Prayer of Love and Silence (A Carthusian)
Way of Silent Love (A Carthusian Miscellany)
Wound of Love (A Carthusian Miscellany)
They Speak by Silences (A Carthusian)
Where Silence is Praise (A Carthusian)

—STUDIES IN CISTERCIAN—
ART & ARCHITECTURE

Meredith Parsons Lillich, editor
Volumes II–V are now available

—THOMAS MERTON—

Climate of Monastic Prayer (T. Merton)
Legacy of Thomas Merton (P. Hart)
Message of Thomas Merton (P. Hart)
Monastic Journey of Thomas Merton (P. Hart)
Thomas Merton/Monk (P. Hart)
Thomas Merton on St Bernard
Toward an Integrated Humanity
  (M. Basil Pennington, ed.)

CISTERCIAN LITURGICAL
—DOCUMENTS SERIES—

Chrysogonus Waddell, ocso, editor
Hymn Collection of the...Paraclete
Institutiones nostrae: The Paraclete Statutes
Molesme Summer-Season Breviary (4 volumes)
Old French Ordinary & Breviary of the Abbey
  of the Paraclete (2 volumes)

Twelfth-century Cistercian Hymnal
  (2 volumes)
The Twelfth-century Cistercian Psalter
Two Early Cistercian *Libelli Missarum*

–STUDIA PATRISTICA XVIII–
Volumes 1, 2 and 3

Editorial queries & advance book
information should be directed to the
Editorial Offices:

Cistercian Publications
1201 Oliver Street
Western Michigan University
Kalamazoo, Michigan 49008
Tel: (616) 387-8920 • Fax: (616) 387-8921

• • •

Customers may order
these books through booksellers
or directly by contacting the warehouse
at the address below:

Cistercian Publications
Saint Joseph's Abbey
167 North Spencer Road
Spencer, Massachusetts 01562-1233
Tel: (508) 885-8730 • Fax: (508) 885-4687
email: cistpub@spencerabbey.org

• • •

Canadian Orders:
Novalis
49 Front Street East, Second Floor
Toronto, Ontario M5E 1B3
Telephone: 416-363-3303 1-800-387-7164
Fax: 416-363-9409

• • •

British & European Orders:
Cistercian Publications
Mount Saint Bernard Abbey
Coalville, Leicester LE67 5UL
Fax: [44] (1530) 81.46.08

• • •

Cistercian Publications is a non-profit
corporation. Its publishing program is
restricted to monastic texts in translation
and books on the monastic tradition.

A complete catalogue of texts in
translation and studies on early,
medieval, and modern monasticism is
available, free of charge, by contacting
any of the addresses above.